JENNY LIND.

SWAIN

Express Steam
Locomotive Development
in Great Britain & France

André Chapelon, standing beside his great 4-8-4 express locomotive, No.242.A.1.
(Autographed and presented to the author by Chapelon.)

Express Steam
Locomotive Development
in Great Britain & France

Colonel H.C.B. Rogers OBE

Oxford Publishing Co.

Nord Railway of France No.3.628 built to the design of du Bousquet, incorporating the compound expansion principles of de Glehn. Later to become SNCF No. 230D116, this 4-6-0 was brought to Great Britain for preservation in 1972, and was acquired by the National Collection in 1980 because of its technical importance in the development of the steam locomotive. It is depicted at Didcot Railway Centre during the GWR 150 celebrations of 1985.
(Peter Nicholson)

A FOULIS-OPC Railway Book

© 1990 Colonel H. C. B. Rogers & Haynes Publishing
Group

British Library Cataloguing in Publication Data
Rogers, H. C. B. (Hugh Cuthbert Basset), *1905-*
Express steam locomotive development in Great Britain
and   France.
1. Great Britain. Steam locomotives, history 2. France.
Steam locomotives, history
I. Title
625.2'61'0941
ISBN 0-86093-469-1

Library of Congress catalog card number
89-81502

Published by:
Haynes Publishing Group
Sparkford, Near Yeovil, Somerset. BA22 7JJ

Haynes Publications Inc.
861 Lawrence Drive, Newbury Park, California 91320,
USA.

Printed by J.H. Haynes & Co. Ltd.

Endpapers: Engravings reproduced courtesy *The Engineer/*
P.D. Nicholson collection.

Contents

Great Western 'King' class 4-6-0s posed at Swindon shed, left to right Nos 6005, 6008, 6017, 6020, 6022, 6023 and 6024.

Introduction and Acknowledgements

In the writing of this book I am indebted to several eminent locomotive engineers who have rewarded my inquisitiveness over the past decades; some of whom, alas, are no longer alive. I must first mention R. A. Riddles, whose friendship I was fortunate enough to enjoy for over forty years – ever since I first encountered him (physically!) when we both rushed for the exit from an LMS lunch to see if the engine (he) and the guard of honour (me) had arrived for the naming ceremony of, "Baby Scot" No. 5504 *Royal Signals.* A Crewe and London & North Western man, 'Robin' Riddles, as he was known to his close friends, taught me much concerning the development of LNWR and LMS locomotives and the reasons underlying the choice of types and design aspects of his locomotives for the Ministry of Supply in wartime and for British Railways. Ever since the General Strike of 1926, when he had driven both four-coupled ('Georges') and six-coupled ('Princess') express locomotives, he had been impressed by the advantages in adhesion conferred by extra coupled wheels. This was confirmed by the great success of his 2-10-0s for Army service, in the Second World War, and the reason why he insisted on a 2-10-0 for British Railways, overruling the preference of R. C. Bond and of E. S. Cox, with his team of chief draughtsmen, for a 2-8-2. The outstanding success of the 9F 2-10-0 is well known, and Bond admitted to me that Riddles had been right.

Roland Bond was as typically a Derby and Midland man in his pre-Grouping allegiance, as Riddles was LNWR, and he was an enthusiast for the Midland Compounds, which Riddles conceded were good engines, but not in the same power category as a 'George'! But they were great friends and Bond, an intensely loyal man, would never argue with Riddles who had been his chief. Both regarded the shaping of fireboxes as much more important than whether they were of the Belpaire or the round top type. All the BR engines had the Belpaire (presumably against the wishes of the Doncaster Chief Draughtsman) but Riddles' wartime engines had been very successful with the round top variety, adopted to save cost in construction. For the same reason these 2-8-0s and 2-10-0s had parallel boilers. Bond in fact told me that he had never really accepted the theory behind the tapered boiler.

I suppose that Roland Bond was the greatest enthusiast for the steam locomotive that I ever met. It was his tragedy that when he became CME of British Railways he had to introduce the diesel locomotive which was to supplant the steam engine that he loved.

André Chapelon was a delightful character – a kindly, chivalrous, and humble little man. During our numerous meetings I never heard him say an unkind word about another engineer or criticise his work. I found it hard to keep pace with his brilliant brain and to follow the reasoning which lay behind various aspects of his designs. Several engineers were jealous of his achievements, and he encountered much hostility as a result. During the First World War he was an officer in the French Heavy Artillery and was mentioned in despatches for gallantry. During the Second World War he had to carry out his development work under the difficulties and frustration of the German occupation. He never married and his whole life was centred on the steam locomotive. His theories on the steam circuit, of course, had a strong influence on design practice under Gresley, Stanier, Bulleid and Peppercorn.

J. F. Harrison started his career on the Great Northern Railway when the Ivatt Atlantics were still the pride of the line. He related to me an account of his ride on the footplate of one of them which surpassed any other recorded trip. My description of the run in another book was criticised as being beyond the power of an Atlantic. I am reminded of a comment by E. L. Ahrons in his articles on 'Locomotive and Train Working in the Latter Part of the Nineteenth Century' (which appeared in the Railway Magazine). Discussing the haulage of trains weighing 250 to 270 tons by Stirling's 'singles', he writes, "The way the singles, unaided by any pilot except the initial pusher out of King's Cross, dealt with the trains up to Potters Bar was wonderful. One could prove mathematically that they could never do it, but there must have been some flaw in the premises, for they nearly always did do it."

Freddie Harrison went on to be Assistant Mechanical Engineer to Peppercorn, and finished his career as CME British Railways.

R. F. Hanks received his training at Swindon, and was there when *The Great Bear* was experiencing its troubles. Every day he would go to a vantage point where he could see the engine go through on a Bristol to Swindon express. At his house, where I visited him at Oxford, he had Great Western locomotive whistles mounted on the gate posts, and there were Great Western copper-capped chimneys and nameplates in the garden. There was also a garden railway with beautiful model steam engines. Reggie Hanks finished his active life as Chairman of the Western Area Board of British Railways, and, while he was there, it was at his suggestion (so he told me) that the 2-10-0 No. 92220 *Evening Star,* the last steam locomotive to be built for British Railways, was made an honorary Great Western engine by being turned out in Great Western livery with a copper cap to its chimney. Years later, Robert Riddles grumbled to me about that copper cap. I told him the story. He was amazed, because although Hanks was a great friend of his, he had never told him!

Another great engineer, who always regarded himself as a Great Western man and who was a devoted admirer of Churchward, was H. Holcroft. He worked on the cylinders for *The Great Bear* in the Swindon drawing office. Near the end of his long life he showed me a drawing he had made of a novel design connected with the front end of a locomotive (I cannot remember the details) and asked me to send it to Chapelon for his comments.

I did so, and Chapelon wrote back asking for more details. But Holcroft died before he could reply.

Others to whom I am indebted include T. C. B. Miller (who told me how I should fire an Ivatt Atlantic – though alas, I shall never have the opportunity to try), W. N. Pellew (former Locomotive Running Superintendent of the Great Western and friend of Churchward), K. J. Cook (who proclaimed beauty of line in Great Western locomotives and found celebrity in decorating at Doncaster a V2 with a copper capped chimney), P. N. Townend (writer of so much on LNER Pacifics and an enthusiastic supporter of the Chapelon exhaust). S. C. Townroe (with all his intimate knowledge of Bulleid Pacific tribulations), and G. W. Carpenter (who has such an encyclopaedic knowledge of French locomotives).

Bibliography

E.L. Ahrons, *Locomotive and Train Working in the Latter Part of the Nineteenth Century*, 6 vols, Reprinted from the *Railway Magazine*, ed. L.L. Asher (Cambridge, W. Heffer & Sons, 1952-54)

G.F. Bird, *The Locomotives of the Great Northern Railway 1847-1910* (London, The Locomotive Publishing Co., 1910)

D.L. Bradley, *The Locomotives of the L.B. & S.C.R.*, Part 3 (London, Railway Correspondence & Travel Society, 1973)

H.A.V. Bulleid, *Master Builders of Steam* (London, Ian Allan, 1963)

André Chapelon, *La Locomotive à Vapeur*, (Paris, J.B. Bailliere et Fils, 1952)

A. Gilbert, *Les Mountain Francaises*, (Editions du Cabri, 1978)

Charles H. Grinling, *The History of the Great Northern Railway 1845-1895*

N. Groves, *Great Northern Locomotive History, Vol. 1, 1847-66* (London, Railway Correspondence & Travel Society, 1986)

Locomotives of the LNER, Part 2A (London, Railway Correspondence & Travel Society, 1973)

H.C.B. Rogers, *The Last Steam Locomotive Engineer: R.A. Riddles, CBE*, (London, George Allen & Unwin, 1970)

H.C.B. Rogers, *Chapelon: Genius of French Steam*, (London, Ian Allan, 1972)

H.C.B. Rogers, *G.J. Churchward: A Locomotive Biography* (London, George Allen & Unwin, 1975)

H.C.B. Rogers, *Thompson & Peppercorn, Locomotive Engineers* (London, Ian Allan, 1979)

H.C.B. Rogers, *Bulleid Pacifics at Work* (London, Ian Allan, 1980)

Lucien Maurice Vilain, *Dix Décennies de Locomotives sur le Réseau du Nord (1845-1948)* (Levallois-Perret, Picador, 1977)

Lucien Maurice Vilain, *L'Evolution du Materiel Moteur et Roulant de La Cie Paris-Lyon-Mediterranée (PLM)*, 2nd Edn. (Paris, Dominique Vincent, 1973)

Lucien Maurice Vilain, *Un Siecle de Matériel et Traction sur le Réseau d'Orleans (1840-1938)*, (Paris, A. Gozlan, 1962)

Lucien Maurice Vilain, *L'Evolution du Matériel Moteur et Roulant de la Compagnie des Chemins de Fer du Midi*, (Paris, Les Presses Moderne, 1965)

I am grateful to Messrs George Allen & Unwin for their kind permission to quote any passages I wished from my books published by them.

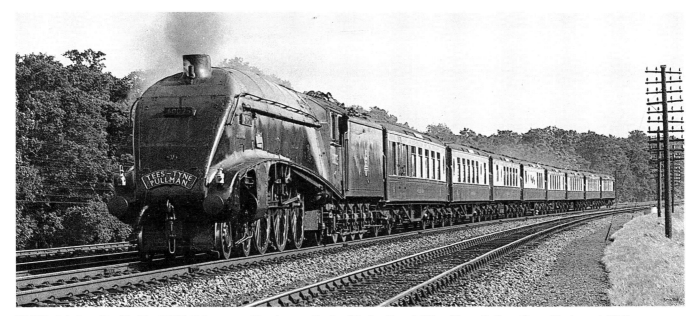

LNER A4 class Pacific No.60025 *Falcon* near Brookmans Park with the 'down' "Tees-Tyne Pullman" on 4th August 1953.
(Philip J. Kelley)

R.A. Riddles, standing by No.71000 *Duke of Gloucester* at Euston before the journey in which he drove the engine from Rugby to Crewe.
(Autographed and presented to the author by Riddles.)

Chapter 1

Sturrock and the Great Northern

It may seem unusual to begin a book on express locomotives with an account of track. But comparatively few writers have taken the influence of track on the development of locomotives into consideration; yet that influence was very important. To demonstrate that influence, two fairly extreme examples may be taken –the permanent way of the London & North Western Railway and that of the Great Northern Railway.

The London & North Western Railway claimed for many years that it had "the finest permanent way in the world"; and this was probably true, due to the care taken over its formation, its excellent ballast and the very high standard of inspection and maintenance. Of these factors, the ballast was perhaps the most important. For a long time its main lines were ballasted with broken blast furnace slag, screened to two inches. It was only after 1900 that, owing to the difficulty of obtaining supplies, broken granite gradually replaced it. The rails, it is true, were rather light during most of the nineteenth century, which did not interfere with the running but did limit the axle load of the locomotives, so that they were smaller than those of some other railways.

The main lines of the Great Northern Railway were in complete contrast. The Company came late on the railway scene and its lines were built in a hurry to establish an east coast route from London to the north as quickly as possible. Charles H. Grinling, in his classic work *The History of the Great Northern Railway* (Methuen & Co. 1898), says that at the London end of the system, "In the hurry to get the traffic running, burnt clay had been used for ballasting, and for this good clean gravel had now, in 1853-4, to be substituted; nor had this operation been thoroughly completed before it became necessary to commence reballasting generally. It was necessary also to renew at places the rails themselves, for it was found that, especially on the falling gradient between Potters Bar and the terminus, the traffic – and particularly the heavy coal traffic – had already, in 1854, inflicted serious injury upon the 'up' road. The switches and crossings had also to be renewed at most of the principal stations." That the permanent way remained in poor condition, despite the efforts to bring it up to an adequate standard, is shown by H.A. Ivatt's opinion of it when he succeeded Patrick Stirling as Locomotive Superintendent of the Great Northern Railway. Following rides on the footplate, and after walking the whole track from King's Cross to Doncaster, he remarked to W.L. Jackson, Chairman of the GNR, "Had I known the condition of the track I would not have come". To this, Jackson replied, "I will have the track made second to none. You just design the engines". (*Master Builders of Steam*, by H.A.V. Bulleid).

Over the good track of the LNWR, the 2-4-0 engines of Ramsbottom and Webb were working the Company's fastest trains, in the latter part of the nineteenth century, whereas Stirling's 2-4-0s could not run the Great Northern expresses; though his similar sized 'singles' had no difficulty. The coupled engines often buckled or even 'threw' their coupling rods. The same troubles beset the 2-4-0s built by his predecessor, Sturrock. Of these it was said that, "They could not keep their side–rods on" (*The Locomotives of the Great Northern Railway* by G.F. Bird, 1910). At that period the Great Northern was operating some of the fastest trains in the country, and it is apparent that the track would not stand up to the rigid wheelbase of a coupled engine at those speeds. It has been said that the GNR 2-4-0s were sluggish at speed because of inadequate port openings, but it is inconceivable that a competent engineer like Stirling would have designed a good steam circuit for his 'singles' and a poor one for his coupled engines. Stirling was obviously well satisfied with his 2-4-0s, for he built 139 to virtually the same design from 1867 to 1898; whilst the 2-2-2s and 4-2-2s that he produced over the same period numbered only 89. There was nothing the matter with the steam circuit of Sturrock's last class of 2-4-0s, for Stirling rebuilt them as 2-2-2s, without altering the front end, and they became very fast and successful engines, working express traffic for many years.

That Ivatt was still not sure that the track was up to the standard he wanted when he built his first Atlantic type engine in 1898 is suggested by the very close spacing of the coupled wheels, as if he wanted to make it as much like a 'single' as possible.

Archibald Sturrock, like so many great locomotive engineers after him, was a Great Western man who left that railway when the opportunity arose to seek a higher appointment with another company. In his youth he had formed a friendship with Daniel Gooch, in about 1834, and in 1840, when his friend was appointed Locomotive Engineer of the Great Western Railway, Sturrock had joined him as Principal Assistant. The Swindon Works opened in 1843 and Sturrock became Works Manager. In 1850, at the age of 34, he was selected to be Locomotive Superintendent of the new Great Northern Railway.

At the time of Sturrock's appointment, the passenger locomotives available for working the main line passenger trains consisted of:

1.   50 small 2-2-2s with 5ft 6in driving wheels and 15in by 20in cylinders, built by the well–known firm of Sharp Bros & Co., of their own design. Like all Sharp products, they were good little engines.

2.   20 2-2-2 engines built R. & W. Hawthorn to their standard design, with 6ft driving wheels and 15in by 21in cylinders. When larger engines were ordered from the same firm they became known as the "Small Hawthorns" (perhaps about the same time, the Sharp 2-2-2s were referred to as the "Little Sharps"). The last eight of these were received after Sturrock's arrival, and he directed various modifications, including domeless boilers.

3.   Two 2-2-2s from E.B. Wilson & Co. of their famous 'Jenny Lind' design, so- called after the first one to be built which was named after the famous singer, popularly known as the "Swedish Nightingale". Several

railways bought them, for they were fast and reliable engines, with 6ft diameter driving wheels and 16in by 20in cylinders. Initially they were on loan, but Sturrock liked them and they were accordingly bought by the GNR.

A Hawthorn feature which appealed to Sturrock was the compensating lever which allowed wheels to adjust themselves to unevenness in the track, and which connected the spring hangers of neighbouring wheels. He had doubtless by this time appreciated the deficiences of a track which would probably have horrified Brunel! Sturrock fitted them to all the "Little Sharps", connecting the springs of the driving wheels to those of either the front or rear carrying wheels. He later adopted them as a permanent feature of most of his engines, and on coupled engines they connected the spring hangers of the coupled wheels. Stirling subsequently abolished them as being too expensive and requiring too much maintenance. Perhaps the track was too bad for the levers to provide the required compensation!

In addition to the above engines, ten others of T.R. Crampton's design had been ordered from the firm of Longridge & Co. before Sturrock arrived. A principal feature of Crampton's engines was, as described by himself, "a boiler resting upon three points; one on the centre of a cross-spring, which bears upon the axleboxes of the driving wheels at the back on the firebox, and one on each side at the front on compensating springs, each of which springs bears upon the two axleboxes of the small supporting wheels". The engine, having the single pair of driving wheels behind the firebox and four small carrying wheels in front, could therefore be described as a 4-2-0.

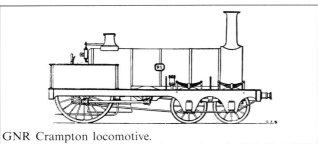

GNR Crampton locomotive.
(*Locomotives of the Great Northern Railway by G.F. Bird, 1910*)

In the vast majority of the engines the small carrying wheel axles were well separated with outside cylinders mounted between them. Crampton's aim was a large heating surface with a low centre of gravity by putting the big wheels at the back, so that the boiler could be mounted low. Most of his driving wheels were of 7ft diameter. The Crampton engines were very popular on the Continent, for they were fast and very steady, though rather hard riding. Nearly 300 were built for French and German railways up until 1864, but they were not popular in Great Britain. There were two disadvantages: they lacked adhesion because of the position of the driving wheels, and they had a rather long rigid wheelbase. In fact, one extra big Crampton built for the London & North Western Railway with six carrying wheels (a 6-2-0) had

such a long wheelbase that, when running at speed, it spread even the excellent LNWR track, rather as Gresley's 2-8-2 locomotives were later to spread the track between Edinburgh and Aberdeen.

But what made the Cramptons such fast runners (and even some of the engineers who used them did not seem to know it) was their excellent steam circuit. In his book, *La Locomotive à Vapeur,* that great locomotive engineer, André Chapelon, says that for many years locomotives had an average ratio of valve port areas to cylinder cross sections of about 1:10, and he gives the ratio on Stirling's eight-foot 'singles' as 1:12.1. However, Crampton had designed his engines with the remarkable figure of 1:8.4 – hence their great success. Of the Cramptons, Chapelon writes (author's translation), "From this point of view the Crampton engines of 1849, besides being renowned for the good results which they gave in service, constituted nearly a model".

The later Crampton design with inside cylinders, which had been ordered by the GNR, were apparently not quite so successful. The boiler had to be mounted rather higher and the cylinders drove on an intermediate crankshaft from which the drive was transmitted by outside connecting rods to the driving wheels.

Thomas Russell Crampton had been one of Daniel Gooch's technical assistants and a colleague of Sturrock's, who had been impressed with his ideas. Sturrock therefore advised the Great Northern Board to take the engines. However, he wanted to see Crampton engines in action and in March 1851 he travelled to France to watch their performance on the Nord Railway. He was cordially received by the Nord's Locomotive Superintendent, J. Petiet, who had twelve outside cylinder Cramptons running and who gave Sturrock every facility to study them. They had been in constant service for some two years, working all the express trains. They were exceedingly popular with the drivers, though it is fair to say that the Nord track was far better than that of the Great Northern.

The GNR's Cramptons were delivered during 1851-52, and in 1852 one of them drew the first train out of King's Cross on its way to York. However, the lack of adhesion soon proved a problem, and their fixed wheelbase was probably too much for the Great Northern's track. Sturrock accordingly modified them by

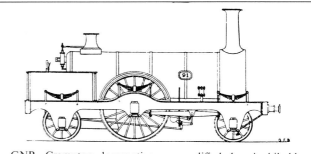

GNR Crampton locomotive as modified by Archibald Sturrock. (*Locomotives of the Great Northern Railway by G.F. Bird, 1910*).

moving the second pair of carrying wheels from their position under the boiler and using them to replace the rear driving wheels, which he transferred to the conventional place in front of the firebox, previously occupied by the dummy crank axle. They were now, in appearance, ordinary 2-2-2s, but they retained Crampton's excellent boiler and steam circuit, and were for a long time some of the best express engines on the line. During the 1850s and 1860s they took a prominent share in working the light Manchester expresses. Later on Stirling rebuilt them by fitting his own boilers; but it seems unlikely that this would have improved their performance.

When Sturrock came to the GNR, the rapidly growing railway was in need of more locomotives quickly. The Great Northern had as yet no works of its own to build locomotives and Sturrock stated his requirements to various locomotive building firms. He was determined to have engines that would demonstrate the ability of the standard gauge to equal in power and speed the broad gauge motive power. There is no doubt that the locomotives he ordered were built to his own designs, even though boiler mountings and other features conformed to the practice of the firms that produced them. It was not indeed until the time of his successor Patrick Stirling, that Great Northern engines exhibited the features that were to be characteristic of the Great Northern Railway and, later, the London & North Eastern Railway until Nationalisation.

Sturrock's first passenger engines were some 2-4-0s which had been ordered before his arrival, but which he was able to have modified before delivery. They were built by the firms of R. & W. Hawthorn and E.B. Wilson, five by the former and 15 by the latter; all with 16in by 22in cylinders and 6ft driving wheels. They were delivered in 1851, and in accordance with Sturrock's intention of building locomotives comparable with those running on the broad gauge they had the high pressure for the time of 150psi and an unusually large heating surface, particularly in the firebox.

It is likely that, as Crampton had been a colleague, Sturrock would have discussed the designs with him, particularly that of the steam circuit. It may be, indeed, that Sturrock reproduced Crampton's front end completely, with the result that his engines were able to work the Great Northern expresses which, in spite of the poor track, became the fastest in the country. If so it would appear, from the high valve port to piston area ratio of his eight-foot 'singles', that its significance had not been appreciated by Stirling.

Sturrock's next express engines, the so-called "Large Hawthorns", were twelve very fine 2-2-2s built by R. & W. Hawthorn, numbered 203-214, and delivered in 1852-53. They had 16in by 22in cylinders, a grate area of 13.64 sq ft, and 6ft 6in driving wheels. No. 210 of this class achieved fame because of an astounding feat. G.F. Bird, in his *The Locomotives of the Great Northern Railway* relates the incident as follows: "The 'down' Scotch express was going down Retford bank, signals all clear, when Oliver Hindley saw a goods train going east from Sheffield to Lincoln which would meet him on the level crossing (ie where the Manchester, Sheffield & Lincolnshire Railway line crossed that of the Great Northern on the level). He could not stop, and with that clear mind, which is so marked in Englishmen in time of danger, he put on full steam, and sent Mr Sturrock's beautiful express engine clean through the goods train, scattering the trucks like splinters, and carrying all safe. When asked about the matter Hindley said that he could not keep clear, so he would clear away his obstruction. There is no doubt that had he hesitated or feared, many lives would have been sacrificed. No. 210 engine carried the dents and scars like an old warrior and looked more handsome than ever for this brush with the enemy of express trains". Even having regard to the light construction of goods trucks at this time, the occurrence is a tribute to the sturdy workmanship of the Hawthorn products.

At that time the best Great Northern express trains were timed to cover the 188 miles from London to York in five hours, an average speed (including stops) of just under 38mph and the North Eastern and North British Railways continued the East Coast express service to reach Edinburgh in 11 hours from London – an hour less than that taken by the West Coast trains.

In 1853 Hawthorns delivered to the Great Northern a

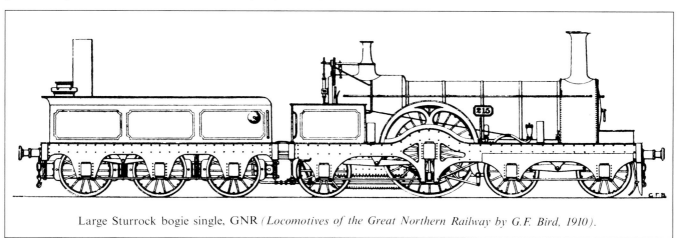

Large Sturrock bogie single, GNR *(Locomotives of the Great Northern Railway by G.F. Bird, 1910)*.

4-2-2 express locomotive of Sturrock's design. It was intended to prove to the directors of the Great Northern Railway that it was practicable to reach Edinburgh from King's Cross in eight hours stopping only at Grantham, York, Newcastle and Berwick. This engine, a prototype for a possible class, was almost a standard gauge equivalent of Gooch's 'Iron Duke' class for the broad gauge Great Western Railway. Common to both were flangeless single driving wheels, four fixed carrying wheels in front and two carrying wheels at the rear. The boilers of both were domeless; that of Sturrock's No. 215 was pressed at 120psi and the 'Iron Dukes' at 115. Both had big driving wheels – Sturrock's 7ft 6in and Gooch's 8ft. Whilst engines with such a long fixed wheelbase rode easily on Brunel's magnificent permanent way, the Great Northern's wretched track would not take them, and Sturrock had to replace his four fixed leading wheels by a bogie.

With such a revolutionary design, 'teething' troubles were almost inevitable, and a tolerant GNR Board were soon asking why No. 215 was costing about £1,000 more than the estimated £2,500. Sturrock explained that much had been altered during its progress through the shops of R. & W. Hawthorn, from whom the engine had been ordered. He regretted the increase in cost but believed that it was worth it.

During trials there were steaming troubles that were corrected by enlarging the blastpipe orifice, and there were derailments that were cured by modifying the bogie. The bogie had been built with sandwich frames, and the wooden inserts of the sandwich, swelling in wet, caused the main and bogie frames to foul and stick. Plate frames were therefore substituted for the sandwich type, and once these problems had been solved the engine was put into regular service.

On 26th November 1853 Sturrock reported to the Directors that No. 215 had been running on ordinary services between London and Peterborough during the previous ten days. He said that on an 'up' express it had run the 16 miles from Hatfield to the Holloway ticket platform in 17 minutes pass to stop. The trials he considered had been perfectly successful. It was not, however, the type of engine he would build for the ordinary traffic of the Great Northern, but he reminded the Board of the object for which the engine had been built and he believed that that objective could be met, if required, by a class of such engines.

Many years later, in 1907, Sturrock said that his 4-2-2 was designed "to show that, if permitted, I could horse the East Coast through trains all the way from London to Edinburgh in eight hours". (Sturrock was a keen hunting man, hence, doubtless, the equine equivalent.) It is a curious coincidence that Ivatt's first large boiler Atlantic, No. 251, had a number with the same digits as Sturrock's bogie 'single', No. 215.

The Great Northern 'Plant Works' at Doncaster came into full operation in 1853. One of Sturrock's assistants at Doncaster was F. Cortazzi, who suggested the use of inclined sliding surfaces in radial axle boxes to give greater control over side movements. This was to become a permanent feature of GNR and LNER designed locomotives with trailing carrying axles until the end of steam on the railways of Great Britain.

Sturrock was luckier than many locomotive superintendents in that he had the enthusiastic backing of the Great Northern Board, and in particular its Chairman, the great Edmund Denison. The instructions by the Directors to Sturrock had been: "Expend such a sum as will ensure efficiency without reference to cost per mile". (Grinling's *History of the Great Northern Railway*, p135); and this was amplified by Denison who said, "When the Manager applies to the Board for 25 or 30 engines, which cost £3,000 each, or for 1,000 wagons, which cost £75 each, it makes one stare; but then the question is whether it is prudent to say, "No, we will not have these engines and wagons", for that would at once stop the increase in traffic". Because the Great Northern was 'fed from its extremities,' it had to have not only more locomotives, but those of better quality than were possessed generally by the other companies.

In 1854 the working of trains over the Leeds, Bradford & Halifax Railway (which the Great Northern eventually acquired) was presenting problems because of its heavy 1 in 50 gradients. Sturrock asked for authority to have constructed six 2-4-0 engines; and this being granted, his designs were put out to tender. That of R. & W. Hawthorn was selected, and the engines, numbered 223 to 228, were delivered the following year. They had 6ft 6in coupled wheels and 16½in by 22 in cylinders.

In 1855 the heaviest main line express trains were being worked by the twelve "Large Hawthorns", the two 'Jenny Linds' and the ten "Converted Cramptons". But train weights were getting heavier and Sturrock reported to the Board that twelve larger engines would be needed if all express passenger services were to continue at existing schedules. Permission for their construction was granted immediately. For the period, Sturrock's design was brilliant. It was a 2-2-2 engine with driving wheels of 7ft diameter, cylinders 17in by 22in, a boiler barrel of 4ft diameter, and a very long firebox with a longitudinal mid-feather. Sturrock copied the layout of the Crampton engines by putting the leading wheels under the centre line of the smokebox, and this position was maintained on all subsequent Great Northern 2-2-2s and 2-4-0s. Presumably, in order to speed delivery, the order was distributed between three firms: Kitson, Sharp Stewart, and R. Stephenson; and all had been delivered by 1861. They were numbered 229 to 240, and proved to be excellent engines. They were still working the King's Cross and Cambridge expresses in 1893, and an account in September of that year said that No. 235, on the 'up' Cambridge 4.35pm express, its "only stop en route being Finsbury Park, arrived at King's Cross 'on time'. I have a note to the effect that speed was very high near Welwyn and down from Potters Bar". One might guess that these engines had the Crampton steam circuit. Under Stirling they eventually received new boilers, and some had their cylinders enlarged to 17in by 24in.

At the end of 1864 that grand old man, Edmund

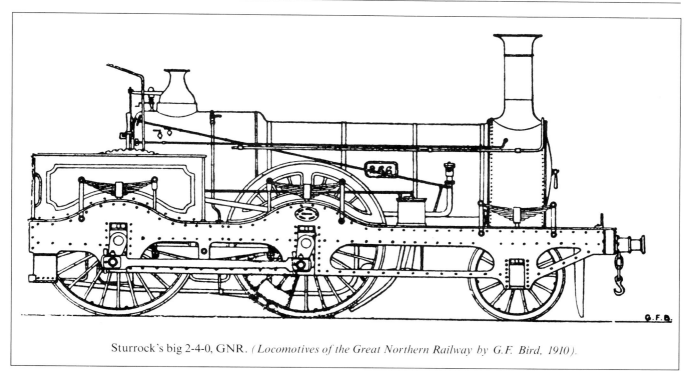

Sturrock's big 2-4-0, GNR. *(Locomotives of the Great Northern Railway by G.F. Bird, 1910)*.

Denison aged 77 and crippled with gout, retired from his Chairmanship of the Great Northern. He had been the 'father' of the railway from its inception, and with his departure there appears to have been some change in the direction of affairs. It could be that the Locomotive and Carriage Department was was no longer to have its previous freedom. At any rate, F. Parker, the Works Manager at Doncaster, resigned in September 1865, and Archibald Sturrock submitted his own resignation shortly afterwards, it being agreed that this should take effect from 31st December 1866.

Before he left the GNR Sturrock designed two more classes of passenger engines, both 2-4-0s. The first consisted of ten engines built by Sharp Stewart, Nos 251-260. They had 5ft diameter driving wheels and 16½in by 22in cylinders. They were followed in 1866-67 by six very much larger engines with 7ft coupled wheels, 17in by 24in cylinders, and a grate area of 19.7 sq ft. Three of them, Nos 264-266, were ordered from John Fowler and

the other three, Nos 267-269, from the Yorkshire Engine Co. They were originally intended to be 'singles' and to run additional expresses, so that the overloaded 10am and 5pm Scotch express trains could be relieved of the Nottingham and West Riding carriages which had been attached to the rear of these trains. However, at Sturrock's suggestion they were altered to 2-4-0s to give them extra adhesion over the heavy banks on the Nottingham and West Riding lines, but the Great Northern track could not take those big coupled wheels, and so Stirling converted them to 'singles' in 1873-78.

Like Stanier when he went to the LMS, Sturrock remained a 'Great Western' man, and his affection for his old railway was shown in his adoption of the Great Western Brunswick green livery, with chocolate frames, for his engines. (They were not the only ones, Holcroft, when he transferred to the South Eastern & Chatham – as he told the author – brought his affection and enthusiasm for his old company with him.)

Chapter 2
The Nord: From Cramptons to Compounds

Meanwhile in France, J. Petiet on the Nord, owing to the increasing weight of the trains, was suffering from the lack of adhesion of his otherwise excellent Cramptons. From 1862 he had tried tank engines with independent driving axles, but they proved unstable and unreliable and were soon abandoned. Next, trials were carried out with a 2-4-0 of the PLM Railway, of a type which had been adapted from Forquenot's famous brass-covered engines of the Paris-Orleans Railway, but it was too unstable at the greater speeds run on the Nord.

Sturrock (who kept in touch with locomotive affairs after retirement) probably approved. These 4-4-0 engines were the first in France with this wheel arrangement.

In 1884-85 another batch of engines was produced, practically identical with the above, but with a rather surprising reversion to the single leading axle. However, all these modified Sturrocks built from 1873 onwards were subsequently given a bogie, and this time with lateral displacement instead of the fixed pivot of the previous

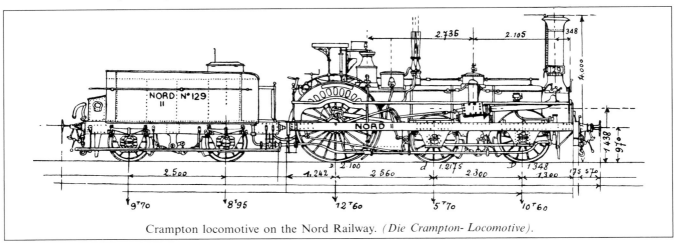

Crampton locomotive on the Nord Railway. *(Die Crampton- Locomotive)*.

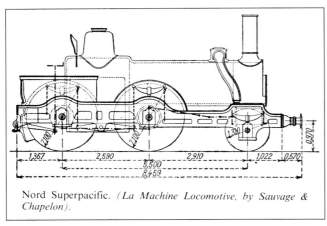

Nord Superpacific. *(La Machine Locomotive, by Sauvage & Chapelon)*.

Finally Petiet approached his friend Sturrock, who sent him drawings of his Great Northern 2-4-0 of 1866. Petiet had twelve engines built to this design, with some detail modifications, in 1870-71. They had a round top firebox with a large dome on top of it, inside cylinders, Stephenson valve gear, and double outside frames. In 1873 the type was modified by Petiet's successor, E. Delebecque, who substituted a Belpaire firebox and moved the dome forward. His engine built in 1875-77 retained the same general scheme, but with some minor alterations. So far, then, Sturrock's design was still largely adhered to; but in 1877-79 the leading carrying axle was replaced by a bogie. Having done the same thing himself some 25 years earlier,

4-4-0s. This modification was carried out in 1890-92.

All the above engines produced by Petiet and Delebecque were known as the *'Outrance'* (ie 'Ultimate') because of the great power they were able to produce. It is strange that the 'ultimate' development of Sturrock's last express engines should have taken place on the Nord Railway of France rather than on the Great Northern Railway of England.

In normal service the 'Outrance' class worked express trains of 150 to 160 tons, climbing gradients of 1 in 200 at 40mph and running down them at 60mph, or, if they were running late, up to 70mph. At these speeds they ran very steadily.

With its inside cylinders, outside plate frames, curves of the running plate, wheel splashers, and position of the leading carrying axle, an 'Outrance', in its 2-4-0 form, looked surprisingly similar to the engine as Sturrock built it, apart from the French engine's outside pipes and boiler mountings.

In their heyday the 'Outrances' worked express trains from Paris to Calais, Lille and Hirson. After 1900 they were on stopping trains over both main and secondary lines, and in 1914 they were at sheds all over the Nord system. After the First World War they were still widely used, but by 1931 only seven were left. A total of 103 were built, and three of those withdrawn in the 1920s had each run of 1½ million miles. This modified Sturrock design was a tribute to the genius of a great locomotive engineer, and it must have pleased him that so many were still running when he died, still an active old man, in his nineties.

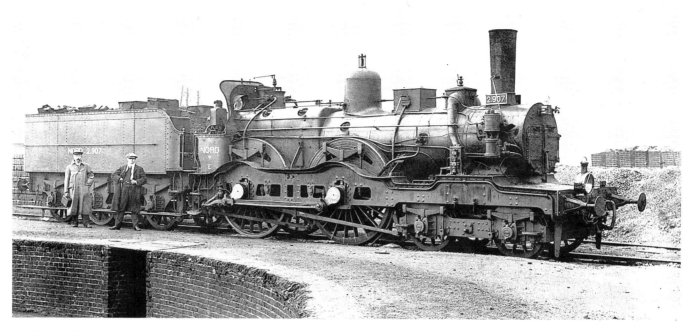

Delebecque 'Outrance' class 4-4-0 of the Nord Railway, No.2.907.
(F. Burtt Collection, Courtesy National Railway Museum, York).

Right: Delebecque 'Outrance' 4-4-0, No.2.210.
(F. Burtt Collection, Courtesy National Railway Museum, York).

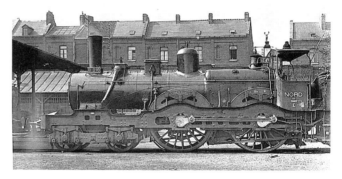

The influence of Archibald Sturrock on the Nord continued in a rather interesting fashion. In 1886 Alfred de Glehn (a Frenchman of English descent), Chief Engineer and Manager of the Société Alsacienne de Constructions Mećaniques, suggested to Gaston du Bousquet, Engineer-in-Chief of Rolling Stock and Motive Power on the Nord, his idea of a 2-4-0 compound locomotive of the same principal dimensions as the 'Outrance' class, but with four cylinders, of which two would be high pressure inside the frames and the other two, low pressure outside. The engine duly appeared as No. 701. The HP cylinders drove the leading driving axle and the LP cylinders the second driving axle. The driving wheels were not coupled, which made the engine a 2-2-2-0 and rather prone to slipping. The inside HP cylinders were actuated by Stephenson's gear and the outside LP by Walschaerts. A single reversing gear allowed the adjustment of cut-offs for the two groups of cylinders. The regulator could admit live steam to the intermediate receiver for starting, with a valve to limit the maximum pressure. The boiler was almost identical with that of the 'Outrance' class. No. 701 was shown at the Exhibition of 1899. In 1892 its leading carrying axle was replaced by a bogie.

On ordinary express services between Paris and Lille

No. 701 burnt 7.81kg of coal per kilometre as compared with an average of 9.60kg burnt by six simple expansion 'Outrance' locomotives. The engine went into regular service and worked express trains until the arrival of the Atlantics, when it was transferred to secondary services and withdrawn in 1928. In 1970 the author was shown No. 701 being restored in the Dunkirk Locomotive Works in preparation for its display in the Mulhouse railway museum.

After the good results obtained with No. 701, the Nord company built in 1891 two express compound locomotives with a leading bogie, Nos 2121 and 2122; the first engines to be designed jointly by Gaston du Bousquet and de Glehn. This time the HP cylinders were outside and the LP cylinders inside; the HP cylinders driving on the second driving axle and the LP on the leading driving axle. As an experiment the driving wheels of No. 2122 were initially uncoupled, but, in comparison with the coupled No. 2121, it slipped badly and vibrated, so the wheels were soon coupled. Both engines had Belpaire fireboxes and Adams safety valves.

The steam to the rather small steam chests was supplied through vertical steam pipes running down each side of the boiler and having a large cross-section to prevent undue fluctuation during transmission. To provide extra power at starting, a bypass arrangement allowed the high pressure cylinders to exhaust directly into the atmosphere, so that the engine could be operated as a four-cylinder simple; live steam being admitted to the intermediate receiver which supplied the low pressure cylinders. If necessary the engine could work as a two-cylinder simple, using either the high pressure or the low pressure cylinders, thereby enabling it to move even if partially disabled. Each set of cylinders had its own independently controlled valve gear, so that when working compound the driver could control the admission of steam into the two sets of cylinders by separate adjustment.

These two engines were so satisfactory that in 1893 another 15 were built, nearly identical but with some minor differences. After them there were 20 more, and these were fitted with the Westinghouse brake. The per-

formance of the class allowed a considerable improvement in the timing of the express trains. The average speed between Paris and Amiens was now 54.5mph with 140 tons behind the tender, and between Paris and St Quentin it was 48mph with 200 tons.

At this time the Midi Railway had excellent relations with the Nord and in 1893 it ordered 14 4-4-0 compound express locomotives which, except for some standard Midi fittings, were identical with the Nord engines. However, these Midi engines never equalled the performance of their Nord sisters because the fuel used on the Midi was of such poor quality. The Midi therefore asked Société Alsacienne to build for them some more powerful engines of the same type. This new 1751 class of 34 engines was built in 1895-1901. The first came into service in 1896 and did so well that in 1897 one was tried on the Est Railway and then on the Belgian Etat. The Est liked the trial engine so much that they built 24 of the same type, though slightly more powerful than those of the Midi. The Ouest Railway, in its turn, ordered 60

"Les Grands Chocolats" - No.2.160 of the Chemin de Fer du Nord 2.158 class 4-4-0s, as introduced in 1896.

Nord "Grand Chocolat" compound 4-4-0 No.2.166. *(F. Burtt Collection, Courtesy National Railway Museum, York).*

(Engraving reproduced courtesy *The Engineer*/P.D. Nicholson collection)

engines of the Midi design.

In 1896 the Nord purchased three larger 4-4-0s, Nos 2.158-2.160, from the Société Alsacienne which were very similar to the Midi 1751 class. They had the same principal dispositions as their predecessors on the Nord, but with a grate area some 20% larger. They proved very successful in service and in the following year the Nord ordered 20 more, calling the whole lot the 2.158 class. They did excellent work on the Paris-Calais expresses and become a familiar sight to British travellers. In reference to their size and the striking brown livery of the Nord, they were nicknamed by the enginemen "Les Grands Chocolats". Lord Monkswell recorded a run behind one of the "Grands Chocolats" in 1899, the year before they were superseded on the best trains by the Atlantics. The train was the "Nord Express", which was allowed 102 minutes for the 95 miles from Paris to St Quentin, and on this occasion it weighed 140 tons. After a slow start, due to work on the line, a distance of $11\frac{1}{4}$ miles was covered in 11 minutes 2 seconds, almost all of it up a gradient of 1 in 200. The train was then stopped by a signal, and then stopped again just beyond Creil. Starting again, 36 minutes 21 seconds after leaving Paris, the engine brought its train into St Quentin only 17 seconds late. It had covered the last $63\frac{1}{2}$ miles in 65 minutes 56 seconds, in spite of at least two minutes lost through having to cross to the 'up' line for a mile or two on a stretch where the 'down' line was being relaid. During the latter part of the run the engine hauled its train over a practically level stretch of 8.1 miles in 6 minutes 59 seconds – a speed of 69.3mph. This was a fine performance, even though the load was light.

However, du Bousquet was not altogether satisfied with the steam circuit and ordered a study to be made of the steam path to find out where the suspected trouble lay. Experiments were carried out by Barbier of the Nord on "Grand Chocolat" No. 2.158 in 1897, with the result that steam circuit proportions were determined which included large steam chests to regulate the flow of steam between boiler and cylinders, and so lessen losses from fluctuations in the pressure caused by throttling.

Following this study, du Bousquet, in 1898, enlarged the 4-4-0 design into an Atlantic which had much wider steam passages. The port/cylinder area ratio was now 1:8.64 in the high pressure cylinders and 1:12.21 in the low pressure; which compared with 1:10.2 high pressure and 1:14.33 low pressure in the 4-4-0. The first engine of this very famous Atlantic class, No. 2641, was shown at the Paris Exhibition of 1900. The Atlantic had 13.4in by 25.2in high pressure cylinders, 22in by 25.2in low pressure cylinders, 6ft $8\frac{1}{2}$in diameter coupled wheels, 29.7sq ft grate area, 228 psi boiler pressure, an adhesive weight of 37 tons

and a total weight of 70.6 tons. The success of the Atlantics seems to have been largely due to du Bousquet, and it is a pity therefore that they are almost universally referred to in Great Britain as the "de Glehn Atlantics". In fact, du Bousquet and de Glehn collaborated so closely that it is now impossible to say how much credit for the design should be allocated to each. The compound system was undoubtedly de Glehn's. From the evidence of his later work, du Bousquet probably designed the boiler and the improved steam passages. The bogie, commonly called in France *le bogie alsacien*, was designed at the works of the Société Alsacienne and was widely used on the PO, Nord, Est, and Midi Railways, and, with slight differences, in Germany. It is probably attributable to de Glehn and its description in the United Kingdom as the 'de Glehn bogie' is seemingly justified.

These remarkable Atlantics soon set standards of running that were unequalled anywhere else in the world. In 1902, for instance, No. 2645, with 250 tons behind the tender, covered the 184.4 miles from Paris to Calais, start to stop, at an overall average speed of 64.4mph, gaining 27 minutes on scheduled time. Returning on the "Calais-Mediterraneé Express" of 160-200 tons, the engine gained about 40 minutes on schedule! On this run the average speed, including the Amiens stop, was 65.6mph, and the average running speed 67.5mph. In the same year No. 2656, with 161 tons, gained 25 minutes between Boulogne Ville and Paris; the 50.1 miles from Creil to Paris being covered in 40 minutes, at an average speed of 75mph. Also in 1902 No. 2660 ran the 68 miles from Soissons to Paris with 200 tons in 58 minutes – an average speed of 70mph. In assessing the merits of these runs, it is important to remember that drivers on French railways were not allowed to exceed a speed of $75\frac{1}{2}$mph.

Such performances startled the railway world, and several companies promptly ordered Atlantic locomotives of similar design. In 1901 the Midi obtained some of the Nord pattern and they were soon working its expresses in brilliant fashion. The PO also acquired similar Atlantics, though rather larger than those of the Nord, with 14.3in by 25.2in high pressure cylinders and 23.6in by 25.2in low pressure cylinders, and a bigger grate area of 33.4sq ft. In 1905 the Etat bought Atlantics which were practically the same as the larger PO variety for their difficult main line from Paris to Bordeaux via Chartres, Saumur, Niort, and Saintes. But there was another potential buyer; in England George Jackson Churchward of the Great Western Railway was taking a keen interest.

It is now time to retrace our footsteps and see what was happening in England after Sturrock's departure from the Great Northern.

Chapter 3
Stirling and Webb

The Great Northern Railway and the London & North Western Railway both acquired new Locomotive Superintendents at about the same time, and the two are perhaps the best remembered amongst locomotive engineers of the latter nineteenth century – Patrick Stirling and Francis Webb.

Stirling, appointed in 1866, sent in a report in that year, recommending the construction of 20 coupled express passenger engines (2-4-0) to work the main line "so as to make sure of better time-keeping under the varying circumstances of load and weather". He added that the existing engines working main line passenger trains were "completely overweighted" so could not attain the requisite speed and lost much time in ascending gradients. He thought Sturrock's engines "fit for a train of 12 or 14 coaches (say about 150 tons) at express speed", but he did not think they could do it in all circumstances. The Board accepted this and other recommendations he made. Alas, in recommending coupled engines for Great Northern express trains, Stirling had not yet become acquainted with the deficiences of the Great Northern track!

The 20 2-4-0s were delivered in 1868. With them Stirling introduced his own characteristic outline, which was to be the distinctive 'trade mark' of a Great Northern or London & North Eastern steam locomotive until steam vanished from the railways of the British Isles.

The 2-4-0s had a round-top firebox and flush topped boiler, the only mountings on which were a built-up chimney and a shapely brass cover to the safety valves. Plate frames were used with outside bearings on the leading wheels. In place of Sturrock's spectacle plate, the enginemen's comfort was catered for by the provision of a cab. The inside cylinders were 17in by 24in, the coupled wheels were 6ft 7in in diameter, and the boiler had a diameter of 3ft 10½in. In working order the engine weighed 35 tons.

The performance of these engines on express service was disappointing. Nevertheless, Stirling obviously appreciated that if he needed engines for quick acceleration from stations with stopping trains, or with the necessary adhesion for the Great Northern's more difficult routes, they would have to be coupled. In fact he built no less than 139 2-4-0s, all of practically the same design as this first class, during his time as Locomotive Superintendent. This compares with 36 2-2-2s and 53 of his 'eight-foot' bogie singles.

Following the indifferent performance of the coupled engines on fast trains, Stirling designed in 1867 a 2-2-2 for the most important main line expresses, and twelve had appeared in traffic by 1869. The driving wheels were 7ft 1in in diameter and there were inside bearings for the leading and trailing axles. The cylinders were inside and of the same dimensions as those of the previous coupled engines, and the boiler was practically the same.

Whilst the 2-4-0s worked semi-fast trains and most of the express traffic between Doncaster and Leeds, they were not allowed on the Scotch expresses, which were reserved exclusively for 'singles' during the whole of Stirling's time as Locomotive Superintendent.

In 1870 there was a further 2-2-2, for Sturrock's fine bogie single had been withdrawn, and its big 7ft 7in driving wheels, too good to be destroyed, were used for a new single, the only one of its class. Most of its dimensions, however, were the same as those of the other singles. Both in his 2-2-2s and 2-4-0s, Stirling continued Sturrock's later practice of putting the leading carrying axle below the centre line of the smokebox.

Whilst returning to Doncaster, from his frequent visits to London to see the Directors, Stirling would log the performance of the engine drawing his train, which would always be either one of his single or one of his coupled engines. With trains of the same weight the single would invariably beat the coupled engine, even up the climb from King's Cross to Potters Bar. As the single and coupled engines were virtually identical, except for their wheel arrangement, this shows the retarding effect of the Great Northern track. During the same period, the London & North Western track did not hamper the progress of Francis Webb's coupled express engines.

The rapid increase in the weight of Great Northern trains, and the speeds demanded of them, soon posed a problem, for Stirling's new engines were already being tested nearly to their limit. The obvious answer would have been a big coupled engine, but the state of the track prohibited not only a coupled engine for the speeds required, but also a heavy one; so a big boiler was ruled out. Stirling's solution was a 'single' with very big driving wheels, big cylinders, and a small boiler. At 38½ tons this was presumably just about what the track would stand. He chose 8ft diameter driving wheels because, as he maintained, the bigger the wheels the greater the adhesion. He wanted big cylinders to produce the power to work trains at speed up the gradients of the Great Northern main line, and he mortgaged the boiler's capacity to supply these large cylinders by restoring the boiler pressure through early cut-offs during the subsequent descents. The system worked; and it says much for Stirling's ingenuity in tailoring his engines to the track over which they had to work.

At this period in locomotive history broken crank shafts were all too frequent, and it is conceivable that Stirling was bothered about the possibility of crankshaft failure from the thrust of inside cylinders on such big wheels at speed; for he decided on outside cylinders. But outside cylinders would prevent him placing a leading carrying axle in his favoured position under the smokebox. Moving the axle back would create a short wheelbase, and he was doubtless well aware of the 'nosing' at speed of the LNWR's 'Lady of the Lake' class, with their outside cylinders and overhanging front end. So for stability he chose a leading bogie. The result was an outstanding success and one of the most beautiful classes of engine ever to run on a British railway. The cylinders of the 'eight-foot singles' were 18in by 28in, the boiler diameter was

3ft 10½in, and the grate area was 17.6 sq ft.

Sturrock's big 2-4-0s of 1866-67, which had proved so successful on the Nord, were rebuilt by Stirling in 1873-78 into 2-2-2s, because of the usual GNR trouble with coupled engines. Except for this modification, they probably remained as Sturrock had built them, and proved such good engines that in 1885-89 they were all given new Stirling boilers. Some of them, after their alteration to singles, took their turn on the fastest expresses between King's Cross, Peterborough and Leeds.

In 1885 there was a curious alteration in express locomotive policy. Stirling brought out the first two of a new class of 'single' express locomotives, followed by ten more the following year and another eleven in 1892. But these had smaller driving wheels of 7ft 7½in diameter

extra power and adhesion up the long climbs. In practice, both types seem to have been used indiscriminately, the smaller wheeled engines exhibiting the same speed and ability as their eight-foot sisters. During the races to Edinburgh and Aberdeen they shared the running of the East Coast trains from King's Cross to York with the bogie engines. In fact the record run of 1888 was performed by 2-2-2 No. 233, which on 25th August ran

Right: Stirling 'Eight-Foot Single' No.53, built 1875.
(Courtesy National Railway Museum, York, G. Tod Collection).

Below: Stirling 7ft 7in 2-2-2 No.236, built 1887.
(Courtesy National Railway Museum, York)

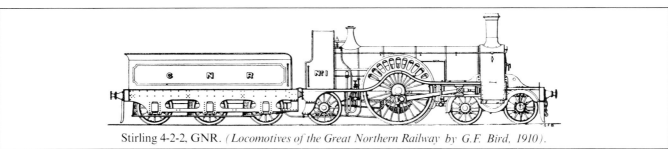

Stirling 4-2-2, GNR. *(Locomotives of the Great Northern Railway by G.F. Bird, 1910).*

and, since Stirling was apparently satisfied to have crank axles with such wheels, there was a single leading carrying axle rather than a bogie. It is even more curious that there had been ten more bogie singles in 1884 and a final six in 1894, so that the two types were being built at the same time. In their final dimensions the boilers of the two types were virtually the same, but the 4-2-2s had 170psi pressure as compared with the 160 of the 2-2-2s, and the former had a grate area of 20 sq ft, whilst that of the latter was 18.4 sq ft. The 4-2-2's cylinders were considerably the larger at 19½in by 28in, for those of the 2-2-2 were 18½in by 26in. At 49½ tons, the latest of Stirling's 'eight-foot singles' were some 11 tons heavier than the first and 9 tons heavier than his final 2-2-2s. The bogie singles had a considerably greater tractive effort and were therefore presumably intended for the heavy trains, needing the

the 105¼ miles from London to Grantham in 105 minutes at an average speed of 60.2mph.

E. L. Ahrons, in his *Locomotives and Train Working in the Latter Part of the Nineteenth Century* (contributed to the *Railway Magazine*), has some interesting observations on Stirling's engines. There were three sets of main line expresses: to Edinburgh (as far as York), to Leeds and Bradford, and to Manchester via Retford and the Manchester Sheffield & Lincolnshire Railway. The 10am from King's Cross, becoming known as the "Flying Scotchman" (spelling at this period which modern Scots strangely reserve for their whisky) was popularly supposed to be the fastest, but its speed was actually below that of the "Manchesters". (The GNR section to Retford had to be covered in fast time to make up for the slower running over the more difficult MSL section to Man-

chester.) In addition, one or two of the crack Leeds expresses were also faster than the "Scotchmen". During the early 1880s the 10am from King's Cross was timed to cover the 105¼ miles to Grantham in 2 hours 8 minutes. Ahrons' only record was with the eight-foot single No. 666, with ten coaches weighing about 150 tons. The 59 miles from post 16 to post 75 (1¼ miles south of Peterborough) was run in 60 minutes 17 seconds, a sustained speed of 58.7mph, the maximum being 70.6mph. From Grantham he took the 10.10am train from King's Cross behind one of Stirling's 7ft singles, No. 55, with a load of 180 tons. This made a good run, taking 13 minutes 18 seconds from the 110th post to the 124th, at 61.8mph. On an 'up' Leeds express, with a 6ft 7in 2-4-0, No. 207, the Retford bank was climbed at a slow speed with a load of 180 tons. Retford to Newark took 23 minutes 58 seconds for the 18½ miles, and Newark to Grantham 21 minutes 20 seconds for the 14¾ miles. In an effort to make up time, No. 207 ran seven miles in 6 minutes 44 seconds, with a maximum of 66.7mph. Ahrons noted that the Stirling coupled engines never gave a good account of themselves on fast trains.

With the exception of three trains, the whole of the express and stopping passenger services between Leeds and Doncaster was worked by the 2-4-0s stationed in Leeds. Two morning expresses to King's Cross were haul-ed by eight-foot singles that had come down on early morning stopping trains. An evening London express had either a 7ft single, or No. 92, the 7ft 6in single built round the driving wheels of Sturrock's 4-2-2.

In the summer months of 1896-98, Ahrons had runs behind the 229 class 7ft 6in 2-2-2s built during the period 1885-92. All of these runs were on the 5.45pm Leeds 'Diner' from King's Cross. This, probably the heaviest train of the day, was always worked by a single as far as Grantham, either an 'eight-footer' or a 229 class 2-2-2, the load generally being 16 or 17 coaches - say 250 to 270 tons. As related in the introduction the performance was wonderful, although in theory they could not do it unaided, but nearly always they did!

A tribute to the Great Northern Railway, as it was in 1889, appears in W. M. Ackworth's *The Railways of England.* He wrote: "The Great Northern has for years been unrivalled in speed . . . and the speed on the Great

Right: Stirling 2-4-0 Great Northern Railway No.995, built 1894.
(Courtesy National Railway Museum, York).

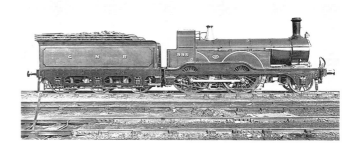

Northern is simply phenomenal, not merely on the through trains to the great towns of the North, to Manchester and to Scotland, but to second rate provincial towns, such as Lincoln and Cambridge. Take Cambridge, for example, which is 58 miles from London and on a branch line. The Great Northern supplies it with seven expresses each way daily, twelve of which vary between 77 and 85 minutes, while only two are as slow as 90.

"Lincoln also is on a branch line 130 miles from London. It has nine 'down' trains every day, the fastest accomplishing its journey in 2 hours 47 minutes, while the slowest only takes 3 hours 43 minutes. Three of these trains are timed well over 40 miles an hour. Two others are yet more remarkable. The 5.15am stops ten times *en route* and runs at the rate of 39 3/5 miles an hour; the 2pm (Saturdays only) stops nine times, and is timed at the rate of 40 miles an hour throughout.

". . . Though the best train each way between Cambridge and London is timed at over 45 miles an hour . . . their really fast services are three–the East Coast, the West Riding, and the Manchester expresses . . . The famous "Flying Scotchman" goes to York (188 miles) in 3 hours 45 minutes, or at the rate of a fraction over 50 miles an hour, and is timed to pass Doncaster (156 miles) 3 hours 6 minutes after leaving King's Cross. But the 1.30pm Leeds train draws up at the Doncaster platform in 3 hours 3 minutes, and the 9.45am takes only one minute longer . . .

"From Euston to Manchester is only 189 miles (by the road some of the trains take through the Potteries it is six miles shorter still); from St Pancras it is only 191¼; while from King's Cross it is no less than 203 . . . For the Great Northern, therefore, to hold it own against . . . its two rivals, means simply that it must run 3 miles an hour faster than what are almost, if not quite, the fastest series of trains in the world. And it does it . . . To say that it reaches Manchester in the same time that the "Dutchman" and the "Zulu" take to Exeter, nine miles nearer, is only to give a faint idea of the speed; for while the Great Western runs along an almost dead flat, the road from Sheffield to Manchester is 20 miles up one side of the roof of a house, immediately followed by a second 20 miles down the other, and in this part of the road very high speed is, of course, impossible. Accordingly, while the "Flying Scotchman" takes 2 hours and 4 minutes over the 105¼ miles between Grantham and London, and the fastest of the Leeds trains takes the same, the 2pm *ex* Manchester does this distance in 3 minutes under the 2 hours, or at the rate of a fraction over 54 miles an hour. The "Dutchman", which long held the palm as the fastest train in the world, only averages 53 ⅓ even as far as Swindon."

It is worthwhile citing these opinions of a writer who later, as Sir William Ackworth, became a world-wide acknowledged expert on railways and who served on railway commissions in England, Ireland, Canada, Southern Rhodesia, India, Austria, and Germany. The summary of Great Northern train services is also a tribute to the genius of Patrick Stirling, who tailored his engines

to suit the track over which they had to operate.

The story of London & North Western Railway locomotives under Francis Webb is more complicated. Webb is probably remembered particularly for, on the one hand, his 2-4-0 simple expansion engines of the 'Precedent' class, which performed so brilliantly in the 1895 races to Aberdeen, and on the other hand for his controversial 'double single' compounds of which one, *Jeanie Deans,* became paradoxically almost a household name.

When Webb took over from his predecessor, John Ramsbottom, there was a stock of passenger engines which were quite adequate for the existing services, but without much reserve for increased demands. Before Ramsbottom became Locomotive Superintendent for the whole of the LNWR, responsibility for locomotive production and operating had been split between the Northern and Southern Divisions, with headquarters at Crewe and Wolverton respectively. As regards motive power, the two divisions were run almost as two separate railways; but in 1861 J. E. McConnell retired as Locomotive Superintendent of the Southern Division and the direction of locomotive affairs was centralised under Ramsbottom until his own retirement in 1871.

On the Southern Division, during McConnell's time, passenger services were operated by three classes of engine. The principal class consisted of the so-called "Large Bloomers", which worked most of the heavy express trains. Built from 1851 to 1862, they were 2-2-2s with 7ft diameter driving wheels, 16in by 22in cylinders, a grate area of 23½sq ft and a boiler pressure of 150psi. They were designated 'large', to differentiate them from the "Small Bloomers", somewhat similar 2-2-2s, but of

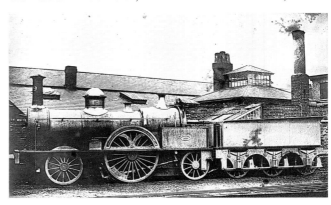

McConnell "Large Bloomer" 2-2-2 No.249, LNWR, built 1851.
(F. Burtt Collection, Courtesy National Railway Museum, York).

lesser proportions, which worked the secondary services. Then there were McConnell's masterpiece, the "Extra Large Bloomers", of which three were built in 1861, with driving wheels of the large diameter of 7ft 6in, 18in by 24in cylinders, a grate area of 25sq ft, and a boiler pressure of 150psi. (The term "Bloomers" was derived from a Mrs Bloomer who invented a knickerbocker-like garment for

Ramsbottom 2-2-2 No.531 *Lady of the Lake* **LNWR.**
(Courtesy National Railway Museum, York).

ladies to wear when riding a bicycle. McConnell's "Bloomers" showed much more of their wheels than was customary, and hence they were likened to this apparel which revealed more of female legs than usual at this period.)

On the Northern Division the 'Problem', or 'Lady of the Lake', class outside cylinder 2-2-2s had been designed by Ramsbottom, and 60 of these beautiful little engines were built in 1859-65. They had 16in by 24in cylinders, driving wheels of 7ft 7½in diameter, 14.9sq ft of grate area, and 120psi boiler pressure. In 1879 they

were rebuilt with new boilers, and *Marmion* and *Waverley* took part in the 1888 races to Edinburgh between the East and West Coast routes. On one occasion *Waverley* hauled the 80 ton racing train from Euston to Crewe at an average speed of 53¼mph. Webb was very fond of these little engines and in 1895-97 he rebuilt them again with new boilers, larger fireboxes, and thicker tyres, and increased the pressure to 150psi.

In 1866 Ramsbottom introduced coupled ex-

Webb 'Precedent' class 2-4-0 No.260 *Duke of Connaught* **LNWR, built 1882.**
(Chisholm Collection, Courtesy National Railway Museum, York).

press engines on the LNWR. The 'Newton' class appeared in 1866, and Webb built 20 more of them in 1872-73. They were intended for the Crewe-Carlisle section with the long steep climbs to Shap summit, and these very successful little engines practically monopolised the passenger services on this part of the West Coast main line, until Webb's bigger 'Precursors' were turned out from Crewe in 1874. The 'Newtons' were 2-4-0s with 17in by 24in cylinders, 6ft 7½in diameter coupled wheels, 17.1sq ft grate area, a boiler pressure of 140psi, and a weight of 32.75 tons.

In 1874 Webb produced two classes of 2-4-0 engines, the 'Precedents', with coupled wheels of 6ft 7½in for the more easily graded main lines, and the 'Precursors' with 5ft 6in wheels for the heavy gradients between Crewe and Carlisle. Both classes had 17in by 24in cylinders, a grate area of 17.1sq ft, and 140psi pressure. Most of the other dimensions were identical except that the 'Precedents' had a larger firebox. Of the 'Precursors', 20 were built in 1874 and another 20 in 1878-79. They worked the Scotch expresses from 1874 to 1877 over the Crewe-Carlisle section, but their wheels were too small for the speeds required and the 'Precedents' soon showed that, in spite of their big wheels, they could easily master the ascent to Shap with the trains of the period.

Between 1874 and 1882 70 'Precedents' were built; and then during 1887-1894 all 96 of Ramsbottom's 'Newtons' were scrapped and replaced by 'Precedents' of an improved type, bearing the same names and numbers. Of this batch, it was No. 790 *Hardwicke*, hauling a light train of 70 tons in the 1895 races to Aberdeen between the East and West Coast routes, which ran from Crewe to Carlisle, start to stop, at the remarkable average speed of 67.2mph– the finest locomotive performance on either route, and a record over this section that was destined to stand for very many years. *Hardwicke*, incidentally, demonstrated that on a good track coupled wheels were no impediment to fast running! In 1893 to 1901 the 70 earlier 'Precedents' were rebuilt in the same fashion.

Another Webb replacement was that of Ramsbottom's little 'Samson' class 2-4-0s, of which 90 had been built between 1863 and 1879 for secondary services. In the same way as the 'Newtons' had been replaced by 'Precedents', so the 'Samsons' were replaced in 1889-96 by 'Whitworths', again taking the same names and numbers. These were virtually 'Precedents' with 6ft coupled wheels, and were very capable engines.

E. L. Ahrons, in his *Locomotive and Train Working in the Latter Part of the Nineteenth Century,* dealt with the LNWR classes described above. In 1876 the "Large Bloomers" were still doing by far the largest share of the express work between London and Rugby. Nevertheless, the 'Lady of the Lake' class worked several London expresses. Two famous trains were always worked by a 'Lady': the 7.45am from Manchester, due Euston at 12.30pm and the 4pm from Euston to Manchester, with an arrival time of 8.45pm. In 1878 one of the Birmingham expresses was being worked by a 'Newton', but the heaviest trains of the day between London and Birmingham were all 'Precedent' worked.

Although the 'Precedents' were only small engines, they were the largest and heaviest on the LNWR at this period. They hauled all the 'up' and 'down' Scotch expresses except the 8.50pm "Limited Mail" and the early morning 'up' "Scotchman", which were still drawn by the "Large Bloomers" between Rugby and London. North of Rugby, however, they were headed by 'Precedents'.

By 1881 the 'Precedents' were taking 16 of the best trains daily out of Euston, and in 1882 the 'Ladies' ceased working the London expresses. Their two Manchester trains became the exclusive property of the famous 'Precedent', *Charles Dickens*. (Whether Dickens would have appreciated the honour of his name being carried by an engine is probably doubtful, for he was injured in the accident to the South Eastern Railway's 'up' "Tidal" boat train from Folkestone in 1865, and ever afterwards feared travel by train.)

The fastest LNWR trains around 1880 were the 4.10pm Euston to Birmingham, which averaged 51mph from Willesden to Northampton, and the corresponding 'up' train at 7.30am from New Street, Birmingham, which ran from Rugby to Willesden at 50.4mph. By comparison, the 'down' 10am Scotch express had a rather more leisurely progress from Willesden to Rugby at 47mph; whilst the 8.50pm "Scotch Limited Mail" could manage no more than 45mph between stops. The fastest train in 1882 was the 9.30am from Northampton to Willesden at 51.6mph.

The changing of engines on these trains is of some interest. In 1876-1880 Manchester and Liverpool expresses normally changed engines at Rugby; the Scotch expresses changed at Crewe, and the Irish Mails at Stafford. Stafford was the home of the 'Lady of the Lake' class. There were about 15 there, divided into two links, one of which ran the Irish Mails both north and south of Stafford, and the other link worked some of the trains to Birmingham, Rugby, and Crewe.

At this period the Stafford 'Ladies' hauled all the Irish Mails between Euston and Holyhead. They were light enough to be well within the capacity of these attractive little engines, because the running average was only 42mph (even though they were sometimes referred to as the "Wild Irishmen"!). At the end of 1881 or the beginning of 1882 'Precedents' replaced the 'Ladies' on the Irish Mails between Euston and Crewe.

That enthusiastic railway recorder, Charler Rous-Marten, was a great admirer of the 'Precedents'. He wrote an article on them in the *Railway Magazine* entitled 'Some Wonderful Little Engines', in which he referred to, "The 'Precedent' or 'Jumbo' class of express locomotives which, in my experience, has done heavier work than that of any other engine, present or past, of similar weight". He continued: "I have styled these North Western locomotives of the 'Precedent' class "wonderful little engines" and I have done so advisedly in no spirit of partisan enthusiasm, but in calm view of their actual performance. When a cheaply built little engine, weighing only 32¾ tons, can and does perform satisfactorily the same work as is allotted on some other lines to large and costly locomotives, weighing 47 to 52 tons, it is surely warrantable to attribute to the smaller engines exceptional merit in design and construction . . .

"I now come to three cases, which in some respects stand alone. They comprise one of the best start-to-stop runs I have ever had on a British line, and two instances of the highest speeds I have ever recorded, with the single exception of my 90 miles an hour record for three quarters of a mile with a Midland single wheeler.

"Starting from Penrith 50 minutes late, a 6ft 6in coupled and a "rebuilt" 6ft coupled actually made up $16\frac{1}{2}$ minutes on the run to Preston . . . with a load of 194 tons . . . One length of 35 miles was done in 29 min 53 sec, or at an average speed of 70.3 miles an hour, and maxima of 81.8 and 85.7 miles an hour were attained at two different points . . . In the other two cases still greater speeds were reached, although, owing to checks, the total journey did not show such high averages. The 11.50pm from Euston, which weighed 304 tons, had been delayed by signal stops, and making up time subsequently, was run by two 6ft 6in coupled engines of the 'Precedent' class, from Shap summit (passing at 15 miles an hour) to the stop at Carlisle, $31\frac{1}{2}$ miles, in 28 min 12 sec with slacks past Eamont Junction and Penrith curve. From the last named station the run of nearly 18 miles to the Carlisle stop was done in 15 min 10 sec, two miles being run in 41 seconds each, or at the rate of 87.9 miles an hour, an absolute record in all my experiences up to that date.

"Strangely enough the record was broken on the very next day and by one of the same pair of engines going in the opposite direction. The load was 211 tons, and a pilot (of the 'Samson' class) was taken from Carlisle to the Shap summit, the $31\frac{1}{2}$ miles, mostly up – 1 in 125 and 1 in 132 – being climbed in 37 min 36 sec from start to stop. Dropping the pilot the train engine then ran the next $31\frac{1}{2}$ miles to a signal slack at Carnforth in 28 min 26 sec, and attained a maximum speed of 88.2 miles an hour, several successive miles being done in 40.2 seconds each. That, with the one exception noted above, is the highest speed of which I have any authentic record. It may interest those, who regard such velocities as the peculiar prerogative of single-wheelers and large wheeled engines, to note that these rates of 88.2 and 87.9 respectively were attained by coupled engines with wheels of 6ft 6in in diameter."

So why did Webb build compound engines when he had such fast and capable coupled ones? Compound locomotives were of very recent introduction, for it was only in 1878 that Anatole Mallet had shown, at the Paris Exhibition of that year, one of the three little two-cylinder compound 0-4-2 tank engines that he had built two years earlier for the Bayonne & Biarritz Railway. In 1880 von Borries took Mallet's idea to the Prussian State Railways, designing his own version of a two-cylinder compound which was immediately successful. So Webb, in building the first of his 'Experiment' class three-cylinder compounds for the London & North Western in 1882, was one of the pioneers of railway compounding. But the question still remains as to why he did so instead of building a bigger 'Precedent' for the increasing weight of the trains.

In 1883, in a paper presented to the Institute of Mechanical Engineers, Webb said that he had two main objects in designing his first compound, the *Experiment:* firstly to obtain economy in fuel consumption, and secondly to do away with coupling rods whilst obtaining a greater weight for adhesion. There would be less grinding action in passing round curves and it would not even be necessary that one pair of driving wheels should be the same diameter as the other. All this is true, but, as a recent sophistry has it, one must suspect Webb of being "economical with the truth"! There was no reason to suppose that the speed of Webb's coupled engines was being hampered by the grinding round curves making their driving wheels of unequal diameter, and because coal was so cheap there was only a marginal benefit to be derived from the saving in fuel consumption.

One might now return to the Great Northern Railway where, as we have seen, poor ballast and light rails hindered coupled engines from running at high speed; but there was no such hindrance on the excellent permanent way of the London & North Western, over which 2-4-0s could run every bit as fast as Stirling's 'singles'. Nevertheless, there was undoubtedly a widespread opinion among locomotive men that engines with single driving wheels ran more freely. It is conceivable, therefore, that Webb fancied the idea of a 'double single' that is, an engine with four uncoupled driving wheels, so that he could get the adhesion of the coupled engine and the freedom of running of the single. Such an engine would need a divided drive, which could be obtained by three, or perhaps four, simple expansion cylinders. But Webb may have been fascinated by the idea of compounds and have been impressed by the success of von Borries with his two-cylinder variety. Two cylinders would not of course be satisfactory for a divided drive. Webb chose three, and became the first locomotive engineer to build three-cylinder compounds. He thought first of having one inside high pressure cylinder and two inside low pressure ones, but finally opted for the reverse – one big inside low pressure cylinder and two small outside high pressure cylinders. He may have been influenced in this decision by marine practice. Obtaining authority to build these new engines may have been helped by his forecast, to the economy-conscious LNWR directors, of savings in running costs.

The advantages claimed for the LNWR compounds were that they were considerably more powerful than simple engines of the same weight and that they could take loads up steep inclines that had never hitherto been attempted without a pilot engine. These claims are rather surprising because they do not appear ever to have been stated by Webb amongst his reasons for building them; but arose from practical experience in traffic. The average economy in fuel was said to have been six pounds a mile. Most comments on the Webb compounds have been hostile, but such comments seem to have been made by persons hostile to compound engines as such and repeated by later writers without a fair examination of the facts.

Webb built 30 of his first, or 'Experiment' class of

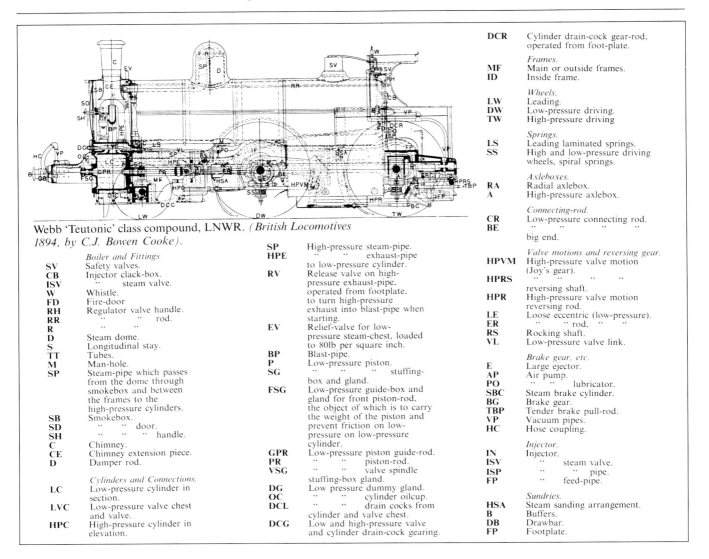

Webb 'Teutonic' class compound, LNWR. (*British Locomotives 1894, by C.J. Bowen Cooke*).

Boiler and Fittings
SV	Safety valves.
CB	Injector clack-box.
ISV	" steam valve.
W	Whistle.
FD	Fire-door.
RH	Regulator valve handle.
RR	" " rod.
R	" "
D	Steam dome.
S	Longitudinal stay.
TT	Tubes.
M	Man-hole.
SP	Steam-pipe which passes from the dome through smokebox and between the frames to the high-pressure cylinders.
SB	Smokebox.
SD	" " door.
SH	" " handle.
C	Chimney.
CE	Chimney extension piece.
D	Damper rod.

Cylinders and Connections.
LC	Low-pressure cylinder in section.
LVC	Low-pressure valve chest and valve.
HPC	High-pressure cylinder in elevation.

SP	High-pressure steam-pipe.
HPE	" " exhaust-pipe to low-pressure cylinder.
RV	Release valve on high-pressure exhaust-pipe, operated from footplate, to turn high-pressure exhaust into blast-pipe when starting.
EV	Relief-valve for low-pressure steam-chest, loaded to 80lb per square inch.
BP	Blast-pipe.
P	Low-pressure piston.
SG	" " " stuffing-box and gland.
FSG	Low-pressure guide-box and gland for front piston-rod, the object of which is to carry the weight of the piston and prevent friction on low-pressure on low-pressure cylinder.
GPR	Low-pressure piston guide-rod.
PR	" " piston-rod.
VSG	" " valve spindle stuffing-box gland.
DG	Low-pressure dummy gland.
OC	" " cylinder oilcup.
DCL	" " drain cocks from cylinder and valve chest.
DCG	Low and high-pressure valve and cylinder drain-cock gearing.

DCR	Cylinder drain-cock gear-rod, operated from foot-plate.
	Frames.
MF	Main or outside frames.
ID	Inside frame.
	Wheels.
LW	Leading.
DW	Low-pressure driving.
TW	High-pressure driving
	Springs.
LS	Leading laminated springs.
SS	High and low-pressure driving wheels, spiral springs.
	Axleboxes.
RA	Radial axlebox.
A	High-pressure axlebox.
	Connecting-rod.
CR	Low-pressure connecting rod.
BE	" " " " big end.
	Valve motions and reversing gear.
HPVM	High-pressure valve motion (Joy's gear).
HPRS	" " " " reversing shaft.
HPR	High-pressure valve motion reversing rod.
LE	Loose eccentric (low-pressure).
ER	" " rod, " "
RS	Rocking shaft.
VL	Low-pressure valve link.
	Brake gear, etc.
E	Large ejector.
AP	Air pump.
PO	" " lubricator.
SBC	Steam brake cylinder.
BG	Brake gear.
TBP	Tender brake pull-rod.
VP	Vacuum pipes.
HC	Hose coupling.
	Injector.
IN	Injector.
ISV	" steam valve.
ISP	" pipe.
FP	" feed-pipe.
	Sundries.
HSA	Steam sanding arrangement.
B	Buffers.
DB	Drawbar.
FP	Footplate.

compounds from 1882 to 1884. They were very nearly, in their dimensions, compound versions of the 'Precedents'. The two outside high pressure cylinders were 13in by 24in and the inside low pressure cylinder 20in by 24in. Driving wheels were 6ft 7½in diameter, the grate area was 17.1sq ft, and the boiler pressure 150psi. Weight in working order was 37.75 tons; rather heavier than the 'Precedents'. On the whole they were successful engines, in spite of being of such a revolutionary design. Their successors, the 'Dreadnoughts', of which 40 were built from 1884 to 1888, were bigger and were the most powerful express engines that the LNWR had yet possessed.

The 'Teutonics', of which ten were built in 1884-90, were a development of the 'Dreadnoughts'. Both had 14in by 24in high pressure cylinders, a 30in by 24in low pressure cylinder, and 175psi boiler pressure; but the 'Teutonics' had driving wheels of 7ft 1in as compared with the 6ft 7in of the 'Dreadnoughts' and, more important, there was a difference in the valve gear. Instead of the separate reversers for high pressure and low pressure cylinders, as the 'Experiments' and 'Dreadnoughts', the

'Teutonics' (though initially the same) had the reversing gear for the inside low pressure cylinder replaced by a slip eccentric which ensured that the low pressure cylinder was always in full gear. This was so successful in improving performance that all the 'Dreadnoughts' and some of the 'Experiments' were similarly modified.

Webb followed the 'Teutonics' with two classes of larger three-cylinder compounds, the ten 'Greater Britain' class of 1891-94 and ten 'John Hick' class of 1894-98. They were both 2-2-2-2s with a long boiler, including a combustion chamber in the barrel, and the slip eccentric. The two classes only differed in the size of their driving wheels, those of the 'Greater Britains' being 6ft 7in in diameter, whilst those of the 'John Hicks' were 6ft 3in. Some commentators have stated that the 'John Hicks' were the worst of Webb's compounds, though they do not explain why a difference of four inches in driving wheel diameter should make them so.

As previously stated, the Nord Railway, in 1891, tested two compound engines with leading bogies and four driving wheels which were identical, with the exception

Above: Webb 'Teutonic' class 3-cylinder 2-2-2-0 compound No.1309 *Adriatic*, LNWR, built 1890.
(*P.W. Pilcher Collection, Courtesy National Railway Museum, York*).

Below: Webb 'Alfred the Great' class compound 4-4-0 No.1949 *King Arthur*, LNWR, built 1901.
(*Chisholm Collection, Courtesy National Railway Museum, York*).

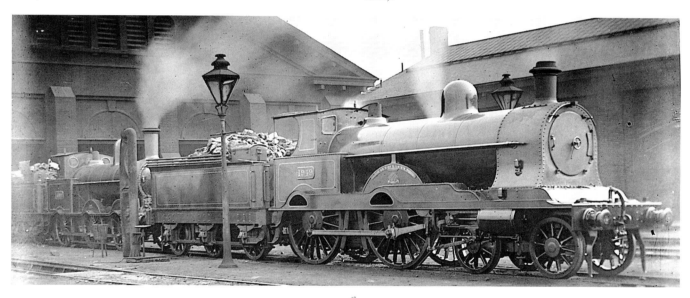

that one of them had the driving wheels coupled and the other did not. The tests favoured the coupled engine and all Nord engines thenceforward had their wheels coupled.

It is not known whether Webb was influenced by these tests, but his next compound express engines, the four-cylinder 'Jubilees' of 1897, were coupled (4-4-0). Mistakenly, however, instead of the slip eccentric, the valve gear of all four cylinders was notched up simultaneously – the valve gear for the inside low pressure cylinders operating the valves of the outside high pressure cylinders by means of rocking levers. The result was the

engines were sluggish compared to those with slip eccentrics. There were 40 'Jubilees' and they were followed in 1901-03 by 40 of the 'Alfred the Great' class, similar but with larger boilers. But Webb's last work in design was, in September 1903, to authorise a modification to 'Alfred the Great', No. 1952 *Benbow*, by which it was fitted with 'duplex' reversing gear. The outside high pressure cylinders had separate sets of Joy valve gear and the original gear operated the inside low pressure cylinders only – the HP and LP gears being adjusted separately. This was so successful that all the engines of this class had been converted to 'Benbows' by the end of 1907. The engines were generally driven with the low pressure cylinders in full gear (as with the slip eccentric) and the high pressure ones adjusted as required. Although the 'Alfreds' were so modified, the 'Jubilees', for some reason, were not. The 'Benbows' were equal in performance to the much praised 'Precursor' simple 4-4-0s of Webb's successor, Whale. Whale, however, was a running man and not a designer. The 'Precursors' were produced by the Crewe drawing office and were typical Webb engines, being the natural development of the 'Precedents'.

The effect of the ratio between the high pressure and low pressure cylinders of compound engines has been much exaggerated by several writers on the subject. André Chapelon, the great French locomotive engineer, told the author that the importance of cylinder ratios had been greatly overrated. In his book, *La Locomotive à Vapeur* of 1952, he produces, on p61, a table giving the cylinder ratios of twelve large modern compound locomotives (nine of them Pacifics) belonging to various French and German railways. These ratios vary between 1:2.55 and 1:2.1. It is interesting that these two extreme figures relate to Paris-Orleans Pacifics rebuilt by Chapelon himself; the first being the 3500 class with coupled wheels of 6ft $4\frac{3}{4}$in and the other the 4500 class with wheels of 6ft $0\frac{3}{4}$in, the latter being rebuilt as a 4-8-0. (These engines are discussed later on in this book.) As Chapelon wrote: "In fact, the great importance which at one period was attached to the ratio between the volumes of the low pressure and high pressure cylinders was very far from being justified". Criticisms of Webb's compounds on this count can therefore be disregarded.

The 'Dreadnoughts', when they appeared, had a boiler that was the best as regards steaming qualities that Crewe had so far produced. Some of their performances were noteworthy. Rous-Marten recorded a run with No. 643 *Raven* from Willesden to Rugby in 85 min 20 sec (including one signal check) with a load of 180 tons, and then on over the $75\frac{1}{2}$ miles from Rugby to Crewe in 78 min 56 sec, an average speed of 57.4mph. With No. 571 *Achilles* the 90 miles from Preston to Carlisle over Shap took 100 min 3 sec, the load behind the tender being 190 tons. Rous-Marten was also on the tender of *Dreadnought* itself when it was on a test run to see if the engine could handle a load of '=25', that is (by the method of calculating loads then in force) about 300 tons, unaided. *Dreadnought* accomplished this with ease, and Rous-Marten wrote later that it was the first time he had ever experienced a locomotive so completely master of its load.

As that very knowledgeable LNWR enthusiast Rodney Weaver pointed out in a letter to the Friends of the National Railway Museum *Newsletter,* there has been much misunderstanding of this method of calculating loads and of its revision. The original figures were based on a six-wheeled carriage, weighing about 12 tons and reckoned as '=1' and a short eight-wheeled carriage of some 18 tons rated as '=$1\frac{1}{2}$'. The maximum unaided load for a 'Dreadnought' or a 'Teutonic' to haul unaided up Camden Bank had originally been fixed at '=$20\frac{1}{2}$', that is about 250 tons, whilst 'Precedents' and 'Experiments' were allowed '=$12\frac{1}{2}$', or 150 tons. These were the maximum loads for all passenger trains worked by the large compounds and the smaller engines respectively. In October 1901 the weights for the larger engines were reclassified as '=17', and this was widely interpreted as a reduction due to the inability of Webb's compounds to cope with the prevous limits unassisted. In fact it was the reverse. By 1901, owing to the advent of larger bogie carriages, some of the vehicles still rated at '=$1\frac{1}{2}$' weighed considerably more than 18 tons. The '=17' rule was introduced to restore the maximum load of 250 tons. It is quite extraordinary how eagerly arguments have been seized upon to denigrate Webb's compounds!

Charles Rous-Marten wrote another article in the *Railway Magazine* of 1901 entitled 'What Mr Webb's Compounds have Done', in which he cited with enthusiasm the performances of the 'Teutonics'. He wrote: "Over and over again I have travelled behind No. 1304 *Jeanie Deans* in the Scottish corridor diner, and in no case did she ever lose a minute of time either way between Euston and Crewe when I was on the train; although the absolutely smallest loads I noted were 256 and 264 tons respectively, each on one occasion only, while in all the other cases the loads equalled or exceeded 300 tons. Yet in all of these cases the speed from start to stop for the $91\frac{1}{2}$ miles from Nuneaton to Willesden averaged over 53mph". Rous-Marten also quotes experience of very capable performances by the 'Greater Britain' class, including speeds of 78, 80 and 80.3mph.

C. J. Bowen Cooke (later, of course, CME of the LNWR) was a great advocate of the LNWR engines. In his book *British Locomotives 1894* (written when he was Outdoor Assistant to Webb) he paid particular attention to the work of the 'Teutonics' and included details of a remarkable run by No. 1309 *Adriatic*. With a light load of 170 tons behind the tender, the train left Crewe seven minutes late and arrived Rugby right time. A maximum speed of 87.5mph was recorded at Norton Bridge and the average speed start to stop was 56.2mph. The vehicles in the train and their weights are of interest in the light of the above comments on 'equal to': Brake van 12 tons 14cwt, Caledonian vehicle 18 tons, Third class carriage 21 tons 9cwt, Composite carriage 21 tons 15cwt, Composite brake 18 tons 13cwt, Composite carriage 21 tons 15cwt, Composite carriage 21 tons 15cwt, Brake van 12 tons 14cwt. It will be noted that the weight of the LNWR main line carriage had already climbed well above the 18 tons. On the old calculations this train would have been assessed as 140 tons.

Chapter 4
Churchward and du Bousquet

George Jackson Churchward, after spending about three years with the South Devon Railway as a pupil of John Wright the Locomotive Superintendent, moved to Swindon in 1877 – the year that the SDR was amalgamated with the Great Western Railway. Here he completed the last year of his pupillage, after which he worked on various tasks in the drawing office until 1880. He was then put on to vacuum brake design, until 1882 when, at the age of 25 he became Assistant Carriage Works Manager. In 1885 he was appointed Carriage Works Manager, and ten years later, now 38, he was transferred to the Locomotive Works as Assistant Works Manager, with the intention that he should succeed Samuel Carlton, the Works Manager, who was due to retire at the end of the year.

At this time William Dean had been Locomotive, Carriage and Wagon Superintendent since 1877 and was aged 55. The leading express engines were his beautiful bogie singles (4-2-2s). The first 30 of these were built in 1891-92 as 2-2-2s, of which eight were originally constructed as 'convertibles' to run on the broad gauge until it disappeared in the latter year. Being too heavy at the front end and therefore unsteady at speed, the frames of all 30 were lengthened and the leading axle was replaced by a bogie. In 1894-99 50 more were built. Most of these 80 engines worked the West of England expresses between Paddington and Newton Abbot. They were comparatively large by contemporary standards. Cylinders (inside) were

19in by 24in, the boiler barrel was 11ft long and 4ft 3in in diameter, the grate 20.8sq ft in area, boiler pressure 160psi, driving wheel diameter 7ft 8½in, and the weight in working order was 49 tons. In the opinion of many observers they were the most attractive steam locomotives ever built. Their lines can be admired now, for a full sized model stands at the head of the train in the Madam Tussaud Royalty & Empire Exhibition at the Great Western station in Windsor.

These Dean singles were extremely successful and, with the provision of water troughs, ran non-stop between Paddington and Exeter. A few were employed on the South Wales expresses via the Severn Tunnel, running non-stop between Paddington and Newport.

At the time of Churchward's move to the Locomotive Works, the new 'Duke of Cornwall' class 4-4-0s were under construction. They were intended to work the West of England expresses over the heavy gradients between Newton Abbot and Penzance. It was on the development of these engines that Churchward was first to show his genius. As originally built, they had a flush round top firebox, an extended smokebox (the unusual appearance of which inspired my father to make a

Dean 'Achilles' class 4-2-2 No.3060 *John G. Griffiths* (originally *Warlock*) built 1895, GWR.
(F. Burtt Collection, Courtesy National Railway Museum, York).

drawing of one of them), cylinders 18in by 26in, a boiler barrel 11ft long and 4ft 5in in diameter, grate area 19sq ft, boiler pressure 160psi, coupled wheels 5ft 7½in, and a weight of 46 tons. The frames, bogie and valve arrangements were of the same type as those of the bogie singles, but the boiler was based on that of Dean's excellent 2301 class of 0-6-0 goods engines.

In September 1891 Churchward was appointed Chief Assistant Locomotive Superintendent, in addition to remaining as Works Manager. He was now clearly designated as the eventual successor to Dean.

By this time the heaviest trains between London and Bristol were becoming a little beyond the capacity of the singles with their limited adhesion. Accordingly a large wheeled development of the 'Duke' class was designed. The 'Badminton' class of 20 4-4-0s with 6ft 8½in coupled wheels was turned out from Swindon between December 1897 and January 1899. Cylinders were 18in by 26in, boiler barrel 11ft long and 4ft 5in diameter, grate area 18.32sq ft, boiler pressure 180psi and weight 52 tons 3cwt. They were the first engines in which the influence of Churchward is apparent. Drawings incorporating a round top firebox had already been issued when Churchward had it changed to the Belpaire pattern. At this time, although the Belpaire firebox was quite common on the Continent, it had been little used in Great Britain. Churchward was attracted by the direct system of staying, as well as the increased steam and water surface. His own design had a space of 1ft 11⅝in between the crown of the firebox and the outer casing. This was almost immediately increased to 2ft, which was retained as the standard on all subsequent Swindon boilers.

It was in 1898 that the hand of Churchward became really apparent in the locomotives constructed at Swindon. Indeed, he was already taking over some of the functions of Locomotive Superintendent because, as H. Holcroft learned from Sir Felix Pole (General Manager of the GWR), Dean's mental powers were failing and the Directors established Churchward as 'Regent', with authority to take decisions (Holcroft in a letter to the author). Dean was never told this and was allowed to believe that he remained in full control. It says much for Churchward's character and delicacy of feeling that he was able to carry out this difficult task, whilst still treating his nominal chief with the deference to which he had been accustomed.

By this time most of Brunel's wooden trestle viaducts in Cornwall and Devon had been replaced by stone structures, which allowed heavier locomotives to be used on these difficult routes.

In 1898-99 20 more 'Dukes' were built with sundry improvements, including thicker tyres which increased the diameter of their coupled wheels to 5ft 8in, and four of them had raised Belpaire fireboxes and a boiler pressure increased from 160 to 180psi. One of the 20 engines, *Bulldog,* was very different from the remainder of the batch. It had a much larger boiler and a straight-sided and larger Belpaire firebox. This large boiler marked a turning point in Great Western locomotive design, for it

was the prototype of Churchward's Standard No. 2, though it still retained a dome.

Of the 20 'Badminton' class engines, *Waterford,* completed three months after *Bulldog,* had the same boiler but without a dome; the safety valves in their brass casing being mounted in the position previously occupied by the dome. The reason for the change was that Churchward had now verified by experiment his belief that steam collected from the top of a flat firebox casing resulted in less priming than when collected from a dome. In October 1899 there was another step forward when a new 4-4-0 engine *Camel* emerged from Swindon. It was in essence another 'Duke', but the boiler was similar to that of *Waterford,* except that it had a cylindrical smokebox carried on a saddle built up from the cylinders. On this engine the traditional steel plate chimney with a copper top was replaced by a plain one of cast iron. *Camel* was the first of a large class of 4-4-0s known as the 'Bulldogs', after the first engine with a Churchward boiler. (*Bulldog* itself later received a 'Camel' type boiler and a number of 'Dukes' were rebuilt as 'Bulldogs'.) Most of the 'Bulldogs' were sent to reinforce the 'Dukes' in the West Country and take over from them the most important express trains west of Newton Abbot.

In 1900 a 4-4-0 named *Atbara* with 6ft 8½in coupled wheels was built with the same boiler as *Camel,* and bearing the same relationship to the 'Badmintons' as the 'Bulldogs' did to the 'Dukes'. The 'Atbaras' also became a large class. They were at first put on the same duties as the 'Badmintons', but, as they grew in numbers, they replaced the singles on the West of England expresses east of Newton Abbot, and eventually took over the best South Wales, Wolverhampton, and Shrewsbury via Bristol trains. A noteworthy feature of these engines was the large area of the steam and exhaust ports, with a new ratio of port area to piston area increased to 1:9, which was getting near the 1:8.4 of the Cramptons, whilst on the railways of the United Kingdom at that time, 1:10 was considered good. The 'Atbaras', in consequence, were free steaming and fast-running engines. The importance of the steam circuit was, it will be noticed, engaging Churchward's attention. Of course, excellent goods and tank engines were also being built, but we are concerned here only with express locomotives, for which the efficiency of the steam circuit is supremely important.

Churchward had taken particular care in the design of the boiler. When Patrick Stirling fitted domeless boilers to his engines, he avoided the risk of priming by lowering the top of the inner firebox. This reduced the circulation of the water in the boiler, a reduction that was not acceptable in Great Western engines because they had to work so much harder. In order to avoid reducing the circulation, Churchward increased the distance between the tops of the inner and outer fireboxes by raising the latter (as Chapelon pointed out in a letter to the author). Churchward's Standard No. 2 boiler, as fitted to the 'Bulldogs' and 'Atbaras', was undoubtedly the best in Great Britain at the turn of the century, perhaps in the world.

In May 1902 Churchward officially succeeded Dean

as Superintendent of the Locomotive and Carriage Department. In September of that year one of the 'Atbara' class 4-4-40s, *Mauritius,* built in 1901, was given a larger boiler. This boiler resulted from trouble experienced in the 4-6-0 No. 100 (to be mentioned later) which had developed cracks at the junction of the boiler barrel and the firebox. Churchward instructed G. W. Pearson and J. W. Cross, in charge of experimental and development work, to investigate the trouble. They discovered that it lay with the boiler circulation and, as a result of their report, Churchward increased the size of the water legs of the firebox by curving the sideplates, and enlarged the diameter of the boiler at the firebox end by coning the upper part of the rear barrel plate (though leaving the lower part horizontal). The resulting sweep of the firebox ensured the success of the Churchward standard boiler. Churchward thus achieved his object of a free flow to and from the firebox and free circulation, both for the rising steam and for the incoming feed water that took its place. The boiler fitted to *Mauritius* (the first engine to receive one) was constructed to this new design and became the Standard No. 4 boiler. *Mauritius* was the prototype of the famous 'City' class, ten of which were built between March and May 1903. Except for the boilers they were similar to the 'Atbaras', and subsequently nine of these latter engines were provided with this boiler and thus converted to 'Cities', making a total of 20 in the class. The account by Charles Rous-Marten of the record run of *City of Truro,* in which it became the first British locomotive

Churchward 'City' class 4-4-0 No.3440 *City of Truro*, GWR, near Whitchurch on the Didcot, Newbury & Southampton line in 1957. *(J. Russell-Smith Collection, Courtesy National Railway Museum, York.).*

to exceed a speed of 100mph, is too well known to be repeated here.

So far all these express engines had been developments of Dean's practice: not that Churchward disapproved of this practice, for he went on building double-framed 4-4-0s until 1910. But a drawing of January 1901 shows that he regarded his production of these and other Dean derivatives as an interim measure whilst a range of vastly different standard engines was being designed to deal with the various types of traffic, with as many components as possible common to all: and all were to have 18in by 30in outside cylinders and $8\frac{1}{2}$in diameter piston valves. Six classes were envisaged and the passenger engine for express duties was to be a 4-6-0 with 6ft $8\frac{1}{2}$in diameter coupled wheels. The first of these was turned out from Swindon in February 1902, whilst Dean was still nominally Locomotive Superintendent. It was a prototype and many of its features were to be improved vastly in its successors. The piston valves, probably because of difficulties that were still being experienced with these types of valve, were only $6\frac{1}{2}$in in diameter; the motion being derived from Stephenson valve gear transmitted through rocking levers. The ratio of port area to piston area was about 1:10. The boiler had a Belpaire firebox with a grate area of 21.62sq ft. This was the prototype of Churchward's Standard No. 1 boiler, and it had the then high pressure of 200psi. It was an enlargement of the 'Camel' type, but the traditional steel chimney with a copper cap reappeared. The engine, No. 100, was later, in honour of Churchward's retiring chief, named *William Dean.* At a meeting of the Association of Railway Locomotive Engineers on 28th November 1902, H. A. Ivatt, Locomotive Superintendent of the Great Northern Railway, mentioned the excellent work that was being performed by the compound

Atlantics of the French Nord Railway. Churchward then announced that he had ordered one from the Société Alsacienne to compare with the Great Western engines.

The boiler fitted to *Mauritius* having proved successful, similar modifications were made to the Standard No. 1 boiler of No. 100. Churchward's next 4-6-0, No. 98 (later 2998 *Ernest Cunard*) was built in March 1903 with this modified No. 1. But No. 98 embodied many other improvements as well as some features that Churchward had taken from American practice. Pains had been taken to secure a very free exhaust, for Churchward insisted that this was of far greater importance than admission. The 18in by 30in cylinders had inside admission valves of diameter no less than 10 inches, with steam ports $1\frac{1}{2}$ inches wide and exhaust ports of $4\frac{1}{2}$ inches, driven by Stephenson link motion inside the frames through rocking shafts. The valves had a long travel and long steam lap. For economical running, maximum use must be made of the expansion of steam, and on a simple engine this entails running with a short cut-off. (This is not necessary with a compound engine because expansion is carried out in two stages in successive cylinders.) With the valve gear usual at this time, with a short travel, the port openings were gradually reduced as the motion was linked up, until the entry of steam into the cylinder and (more importantly) its exit to exhaust became so restricted as to throttle the steam and so cancel the advantages of running with regulator fully open.

On most railways, therefore, it was the practice to compromise by running with partially opened regulator and longer cut-offs, so losing part of the steam expansion and wasting energy. It was the design of his valve gear and the structure of his boilers that were responsible for the outstanding performance of Churchward's engines. As regards the former, Churchward increased the valve travel by over 50% of that normally used and nearly doubled the length of the laps. The result of this was to increase at all cut-offs the steam port opening and the expansion period, and extend the duration of a full exhaust port opening. The theoretical advantages of long travel valves were well known, but many engineers disliked it because of the increased wear entailed by the longer travel. To a certain extent this fear was justified with slide valves, but much less so with piston valves because of the decreased friction.

The coupled wheels of No. 98 were 6ft $8\frac{1}{2}$in in diameter, the grate area was 27sq ft and the boiler pressure was 200psi. The large piston valves, of 10in diameter, allowed a considerable steam chest volume and a ratio of port area to cylinder cross section of probably 1:7 – an excellent figure. No. 98 was, without doubt, the most outstanding engine in Great Britain at the time of its construction. E. C. Poultney, in his *British Express Locomotive Development,* calls it the 'keystone of the arch'; and indeed it was, because every subsequent outstanding British engine owed its success in some degree to the incorporation of principles and aspects of design that first appeared in No. 98.

On 31st March 1903 Churchward aired some of his thinking during the discussion of a paper on *American Locomotive Practice* read before the Institution of Civil Engineers. He pointed out that a sloping top to the firebox was practically a necessity with long boilers, because when the brake was applied the water ran to the front end to such an extent that the back of the roof sheet was uncovered, and by dropping the back of the box by three inches the benefit of three inches of water was obtained on application of the brake.

On 19th October 1903 thirteen large packing cases, containing the parts of the French Atlantic that was to become Great Western No. 102 *La France,* were landed at Poplar Docks. They were sent to Swindon, where the engine was erected and connected to a standard Great Western tender. After trials, it entered service on 2nd February 1904. Charles Rous-Marten travelled behind it to Exeter and back. The $193\frac{3}{4}$ miles from Paddington to Exeter via Bristol took 3 hours 23 minutes, which was $6\frac{3}{4}$ minutes under schedule; and this in spite of two dead stands at signals, totalling 3 minutes 45 seconds, and ten slacks, adding up to $20\frac{3}{4}$ minutes, so that the net time for the run was 3 hours $2\frac{1}{4}$ minutes. Rous-Marten reported that, "the maximum rate attained during the whole run was on the dead-level and after several miles of absolutely flat road, when *La France* by sheer force of steam, without the slightest aid from gravitation, reached 84.9mph, the fastest I have ever noted on the dead level unaided by gravitation".

On 18th March 1904 the eminent French locomotive engineer, Edouard Sauvage, read a paper to the Institution of Mechanical Engineers on the subject of compound locomotives. Sauvage outlined the

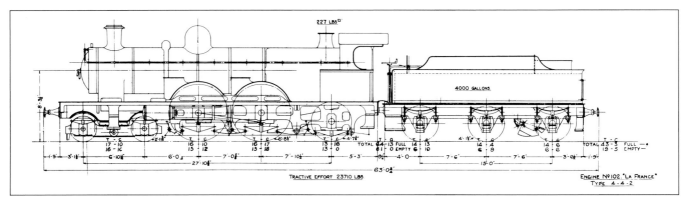

development of compound locomotives in France and said that they had enabled French railways to run faster and heavier trains without any large increase in the consumption of coal. He thought it would be difficult to build a simple expansion locomotive that was quite equal to the latest compounds because with the ordinary valve gear steam at such a high pressure could not be so well used as in a compound.

In the subsequent discussion, Churchward said that the compound locomotive had been brought to greater perfection in France than in any other country, which was why he had purchased *La France*. He believed, however, that "no really fair and square tests" had ever been made between the compound and simple systems. Trials had been carried out between compound locomotives with a pressure of 200psi and simples with 175psi, but he would no doubt be told that it was believed impossible with any known valve gear to use the higher pressure to advantage in a simple cylinder. He thought that this had yet to be proved, and he had fitted a simple engine with 18in by 30in cylinders and a boiler pressure of 225psi with the deliberate idea of finding out whether such improvements could be made in the valve gear and consequent steam distribution as to enable steam at that pressure to be used as efficiently in a simple engine as a compound. On trials he had made the powers of a simple engine (with 200psi pressure) and *La France* at high speed practically equal. In the latter he had used the recommended cut-offs of 55% in the high pressure and 65% in the lower pressure cylinders, whilst in the simple engine he had used 20 to 25%. He added that it would appear ambitious to expect with these respective cut-offs that the simple should develop the same power as the compound, "But", he added, "I am pleased to say that with the assistance of an efficient staff, a good deal of hard work, and a determination to see what could be done with valve gear, I believe such improvements have been made with the steam distribution that a satisfactory result can be

obtained from as high a cut-off as 15 to 20%".

When *La France* arrived, another 4-6-0 was being built for competitive running with the French engine. This was No. 171 *Albion* (later No. 2971) which was completed in December 1903, with the higher pressure of 225psi to afford a more exact comparison with the French compound's 228. Apart from the pressure, it was similar to No. 98. Comparative trials between the two engines were carried out for some months. However, being a 4-6-0, *Albion* had about 50% more adhesive weight than *La France;* so to make the comparison still closer, Churchward altered *Albion* into an Atlantic by replacing the trailing pair of coupled wheels by a two-wheel truck.

In the meantime the Paris-Orleans Railway had ordered some Atlantics similar to those of the Nord but rather larger and had been carrying out tests with them in 1903. The results were impressive and Churchward obtained authority to order two similar engines from the Société Alsacienne to compare them with *La France* and his own engines. The two new French engines became No. 103 *President* and No. 104 *Alliance* (in reference to the new *Entente Cordiale* between the United Kingdom and France). They were delivered to the Great Western in June 1905.

Churchward was not only trying simples against compounds but also 4-6-0s against 4-4-2s. Of his own express engines he built during 1905, 13 more Atlantics similar to *Albion* and six more 4-6-0s identical with the Atlantics except for the wheel arrangement. The Atlantics were so built that they could be converted later to 4-6-0s if desired. In 1906 another ten 4-6-0s were ordered to make the numbers of the two varieties more even.

Further trials between Churchward's engines and all three of the French ones confirmed his opinion that there

Du Bousquet/de Glehn compound Atlantic No.103 *President* GWR.
(Courtesy National Railway Museum, York).

was little to choose between compounds and his own development of simple engines, and that, having regard to the extra cost and complexity of the compounds, he would not be justified in building them. On the other hand, the compounds, with their four cylinders, divided drive, and balanced reciprocating masses, were much smoother riding than the Great Western engines with their two outside cylinders. Churchward decided that it would be worth building a similar type of four-cylinder engine, but as a simple instead of a compound, and with two sets of valve gear instead of the four which the French engines had, on account of the independent reversing gear to the high pressure and low pressure cylinders. Churchward admired the beautiful workmanship of the French compounds and their light Walschaerts valve gear, which he described as a "watchmaker's job". However, it was too light to drive two valves and he would need something heavier. He liked the French inside big ends and decided to adopt them. He also liked the bogie and two years later he took that into use as well.

Because he had not yet made up his mind between the relative advantages of 4-6-0s and Atlantics, Churchward came to the conclusion that it would be better to build his four-cylinder engine as an Atlantic, thus enabling him to make the most exact comparison yet between simple and compound. This historic locomotive was given the number 40 (which was later to be altered to 4000). It was completed in April 1906 and in the following September it was named *North Star* after its famous predecessor – the first successful engine the Great Western ever had – and which had been broken up a few months before.

No. 40 had a standard boiler, but the taper extended over the whole length of the barrel instead of being confined to the rear plate. The cylinder arrangement was similar to that of the French compounds, except that the inside cylinders were further forward to enable the connecting rods to be nearly the same length; for it was intended that the four valves should be operated by two sets of valve gear and rocking levers. Inside Stephenson's valve gear had been fitted to the two-cylinder engines, but this was not practicable with a four-cylinder locomotive because Churchward's large axleboxes and crankpins left insufficient room. Churchward did not like outside valve gear. He produced reasons that obviously did not convince his devoted disciple Stanier, because he used outside valve gear as soon as he got to the LMS. One suspects that he just did not like outside fitting because he thought they spoilt the appearance of his engines. He opted, therefore, for inside Walschaerts gear. That Churchward was proud of the appearance of his engines is confirmed by the following story told to the author by W. N. Pellow, one-time Locomotive Running Superintendent of the GWR: "I remember when W. A. Stanier was sent to the USA to study some of the ways of American engineers, and came back with scores of ideas and suggestions. A number of these the old man rejected out of hand. He did not wish, he said, to spoil the clean lines of his locomotives".

The boiler pressure of No. 40 was 225psi. The outside

cylinders drove the trailing coupled wheels and the inside cylinder the leading ones. The cylinders were 14⅛in by 26in and the piston valves 8in in diameter. The port area to cylinder cross section ratio was about 1:8.

Trials with *North Star* showed Churchward that he had at last got an engine that rode as well as the French Atlantics, in addition to being comparable with them in power and economy. He decided, therefore, to stick to simple expansion. There remained the question of the wheel and cylinder arrangement. Comparison in service showed the 4-4-2 to be rather freer running and more comfortable in its riding than the 4-6-0, but that the latter's extra adhesive weight was invaluable on the steep gradients in the West and in bad weather. Churchward's second decision, therefore, was that all future large express engines should be 4-6-0s.

As regards the relative advantages of two and four cylinders, Churchward thought that more experience was needed. Ten more 4-6-0s of each kind were therefore ordered. The two-cylinder engines had names starting with 'Saint' (conferring on all the two-cylinder variety the class name of 'Saint') and the four-cylinder engines had names that ended with 'Star', which similarly gave the class name to all the four-cylinder 4-6-0s.

Opposite top: Churchward 'Saint' class 2-cylinder 4-6-0 No.2913 *Saint Andrew*, GWR, on a Cardiff-Brighton train near Fox's Wood.
(G.H. Soole Collection, Courtesy National Railway Museum, York).

The final decision was made in 1907, as a result of experience in running. In the opinion of the locomotive inspectors, the 'Stars' were a coach better than the 'Saints' on fast trains of from 12 to 14 coaches, and they ascribed this to the smoother riding and the shorter cut-offs possible with the Walschaerts gear. On the other hand, the 'Saints' were better at getting away from stops, though the pull that they could exert was limited by the need to stop the explosive exhausts from pulling the fire about. Indeed, above a speed of 40mph the maximum cut-off had to be limited to 40%. (This trouble was eventually cured by fitting a 'jumper' top to the blast pipe, which lifted to give increased area for the exhaust at cut-offs over 40%.)

Opposite: Churchward 'Star' class 4-cylinder 4-6-0 No.4006 *Red Star*, GWR, at Bristol (Ashley Hill).
(Courtesy National Railway Museum, York).

In the light of these reports, Churchward decided that the 'Saints' were the normal express engines, but that a limited number of the more expensive 'Stars' should be built for heavy non-stop trains running at high speeds. They would run more smoothly, and he believed that under these conditions they would make up their higher first cost by a greater mileage than the 'Saints' between general repairs.

The various tests and comparisons discussed above

were probably the most important ever carried out in the history of the British steam locomotive; for as a result of them the 4-6-0 with two outside cylinders eventually became the most widely used of all passenger and mixed traffic locomotives on the mainline services in the British Isles; whilst the multi-cylinder simple expansion six-coupled engine was adopted by all the pre-Nationalisation companies for the heaviest express passenger duties.

Whilst Churchward was developing 4-6-0 express locomotives for the Great Western Railway, du Bousquet was doing the same thing for the Nord Railway of France, for in 1905 he found that he was needing more adhesion than he could get with his Atlantics, because of the extra weight of the trains with the advent of third class corridor coaches. This great man was the only locomotive engineer of the time who could compare with Churchward, so it is worth while describing how he tackled the problem. The strengthening of certain structures on some of the weaker Nord main lines was being undertaken to allow an axle load of 18 tons – the existing limit being 17 tons. The problem was to provide an engine with the requisite power and adhesion within that limitation. Du Bousquet insisted on the Atlantic boiler, but this would entail cutting weight elsewhere. He wanted a 4-6-0, to obtain the adhesion, but

the size of its coupled wheels would have to be reduced below that which he would have liked, in order to meet the permissible weight.

In 1896 the Midi Railway had put into service their 1301 class of mixed traffic four-cylinder 4-6-0s, with 5ft 8in coupled wheels and the de Glehn compound arrangement, which were limited to a maximum speed of 56mph. These engines had been derived from some similar locomotives designed by the Société Alsacienne for the Baden State Railways in 1893. The Midi engines had been so successful that they had been adopted by the Paris-Orléans, the Nord, and the Etat, and also by railways in Germany, China and Spain. The Nord batch of these useful locomotives, was known as the 3100 class. Du Bousquet decided to take them as a basis and modify them to run at the then authorised maximum speed in France of 75mph, and even more if later allowed. But the 5ft 8in diameter of the coupled wheels would have to be retained if the permissible weight was not to be exceeded. To

Du Bousquet 3413 class 4-6-0 Nord Railway (SNCF class 230.D) No.230.D.14 at Paris (La Chapelle) on 23rd March 1937. *(Philip J. Kelley).*

Above: Du Bousquet 4-6-0 SNCF No.230.D.22 at Abbeville 1965.
(P. Ransome-Wallis Collection, Courtesy National Railway Museum, York).

Below: Du Bousquet 4-6-0 SNCF No.230.D.143.
(P. Ransome-Wallis Collection, Courtesy National Railway Museum, York).

make up for their small size, therefore, he increased the ports by 30% in the high pressure cylinders and by 25% in the low pressure cylinders. Chapelon pointed out in a letter to the author that he could have done even better if he had multiplied the port areas of the Atlantic, first by the ratio of the smaller coupled wheels to the larger, which was 1.7, and then by the ratio of the new cylinder diameters to the old, which would have produced port areas of 20sq in high pressure and 36sq in low pressure, instead of 19sq in and 32sq in respectively. However, the differences were not very great and du Bousquet achieved remarkable results.

The improvement in the steam circuit was such that the rebuilt engines of class 3513 could easily sustain the permitted maximum speed of 75mph with the heaviest trains. Du Bousquet had, in fact, produced a locomotive that was, in its way, as much a landmark in locomotive development as was Churchward's *North Star*. For, just as all subsequent Great Western four-cylinder engines, as well as the Stanier Pacifics for the LMS, stemmed from the *North Star*, so did the famous 'Superpacifics' follow the design principles of No. 3513. Moreover it was du

Bousquet's success that inspired the Paris-Orleans to rebuild its own Pacifics, and it was this decision that enabled André Chapelon to go very much further along the same path in his brilliant rebuilding of P-O Pacific No. 3566.

The first batch of the 3513s, 25 in number, was put into service in 1908-09 with slide valves, though they were balanced for the high pressure cylinders. In 1911 piston valves were adopted, and another 60 of the class, built in 1913, were superheated. During 1929-34 the earlier engines were superheated and given piston valves. From 1935 onwards their development was completed with Lemaitre exhaust and wide chimneys, which, by lowering the back pressure, increased their power. They long outlasted the Atlantics and were working express trains in the 1960s. The author talked to one of their admiring drivers at the Gare du Nord in 1962. One of them has been preserved in England and, at time of writing, is running successfully on the Nene Valley Railway – a preservation tribute that would have delighted André Chapelon.

Du Bousquet 4-6-0 SNCF 230.D class on a Boulogne-Etaples freight train near Dammes, 1962.
(P. Ransome-Wallis Collection, Courtesy National Railway Museum, York).

Chapter 5
The Ivatt Atlantics

In March 1896 H.A. Ivatt started his examination of Great Northern train working, together with its problems and needs. At the time of his arrival both freight and passenger traffic were growing and new coaches, particularly, were making express trains heavier. With their limited adhesion, the famous Stirling 'eight-foot singles' were having difficulty in keeping time. Ivatt, of course, knew of the impediments to running fast experienced with coupled engines, and he must have suspected the track. At any rate, he walked every foot of it from King's Cross to Doncaster and found it deplorable. He reported that it was inadequate for the larger engines that were now needed, and he almost humiliated W.L. Jackson, the Great Northern Chairman by adding: "Had I known the condition of the track I would not have come". Such a statement from the former Locomotive Superintendent of the Irish Great Southern & Western Railway must have indeed been a shock to Great Northern pride! Jackson replied shortly: "I will have the track made second to none: you just design the engines". Ivatt's grandson, H.A.V. Bulleid, recounts the story in his excellent book, *Master Builders of Steam*.

6ft 10in apart, which meant that there were only $2\frac{1}{2}$ inches between the tyres of the neighbouring wheels. There was allowance for lateral play in the trailing wheel axle boxes, so that the rigid wheelbase was only the above mentioned 6ft 10in. The boiler diameter of 4ft 8in was large for those days, the grate area was a respectable 26.75sq in, the cylinders were $18\frac{3}{4}$in by 24in, and, with a weight of 58 tons, the engine was considerably heavier than any previous Great Northern passenger locomotive. It was also the first 'Atlantic' in Great Britain, beating the Lancashire & Yorkshire Railway Atlantic designed by Ivatt's friend, J.A.F. Aspinall, by a short head.

Trial results were very satisfactory, and whether due to the improved track or the close-set coupled wheels, there was no impediment to fast running. As compared with Stirling's singles, the adhesive weight went up from $19\frac{1}{2}$ tons to 32 tons, and the engine was very free steaming.

The new engine, No.990, having proved itself, it was decided to build another ten of the same class, and all were in traffic by 1900. In 1902 Ivatt built a four-cylinder version, No.271, to see if four cylinders offered any advantages over two. The cylinders were all in line and drove

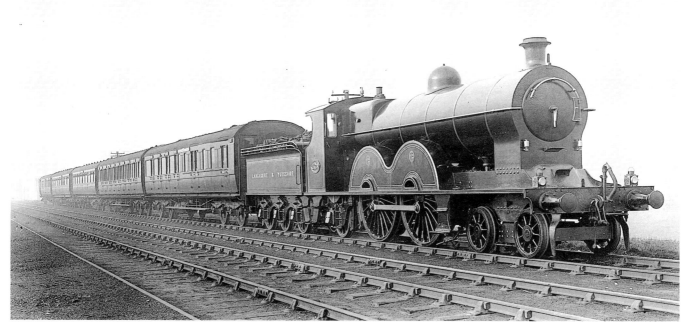

Aspinall Atlantic No.1424, Lancashire & Yorkshire Railway.
(Courtesy National Railway Museum, York).

In February 1897 Ivatt obtained authority to build for trial the type of express passenger engine which he felt would be suitable for Great Northern needs. It was a 4-4-2, or 'Atlantic', which followed the layout of Stirling's 'eight-footers' by having a leading bogie and trailing carrying axle, but differed in that two coupled driving axles replaced the single one of Stirling's engines. But perhaps Ivatt had doubts as to whether the whole of the Great Northern main line was yet ready for a coupled engine because he placed the driving axles as close together as he could. The diameter of these wheels was 6ft $7\frac{1}{2}$in, but their centres were only

on the leading coupled axle, as compared with No.990 which operated the trailing axle. There was, perhaps, a very slight advantage over the two-cylinder arrangement, but not nearly enough, in Ivatt's opinion, to justify the extra cost in construction and maintenance.

At the end of 1902 there appeared Ivatt's masterpiece and one of the greatest of all British locomotive designs – large boiler Atlantic No.251. It was a develop-

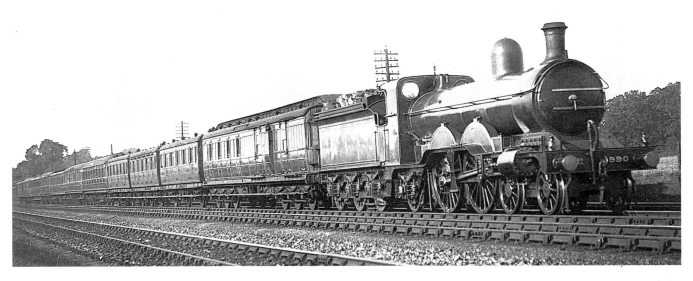

Ivatt small Atlantic No.990 *Henry Oakley* GNR, built 1898, with a train of mixed bogie and six-wheeled carriages.
(C. Laundy Collection, Courtesy National Railway Museum, York).

ment of No.990, with a very large boiler, a wide firebox, and a greatly enlarged grate. The thinking behind the design was expressed in the discussion on the paper presented by Sauvage on 18th March 1904, as mentioned in the previous chapter. Ivatt said: "The measure of the power of a locomotive is the boiler. Mr Sturrock, who left the position which I myself now occupy on the Great Northern Railway over thirty years ago (and who, I am glad to say, comes to see me at Doncaster and talk locomotives now and then), says that the measure of the

Ivatt large Atlantic No.278 GNR, built 1904.
(Courtesy National Railway Museum, York).

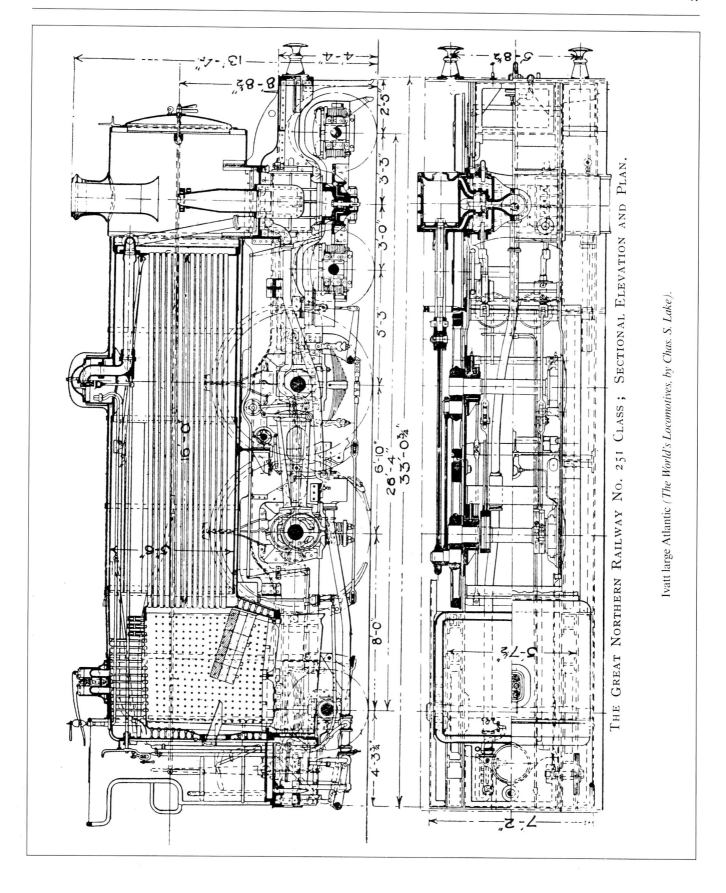

THE GREAT NORTHERN RAILWAY No. 251 CLASS; SECTIONAL ELEVATION AND PLAN.

Ivatt large Atlantic (*The World's Locomotives, by Chas. S. Lake*).

power of a locomotive is its capacity to boil water".

Certainly No.251 had the capacity to boil water! With a 5ft 6in diameter boiler, it had the biggest heating surface and largest grate area (30.0sq ft) of any locomotive in the country. Boiler pressure was 175psi, and in cylinders, wheels and length, it was practically identical with No.990. The weight of the engine was 68 tons 8 cwt. By 1911 no less than 91 of these large Atlantics had been built.

Except for a short valve travel, the design of the front end was good, with ample steam passages and large direct ones for exhaust. When notched up beyond some 30% however, these passages became too restricted, but with the engine's capacity to boil water, it could run with full regulator opening and 30% cut-off indefinitely.

The General Manager of the Great Northern Railway, Oliver Bury, was interested in compounding, and, perhaps at his suggestion, the Directors instructed him and Ivatt to discuss with five locomotive firms the possibility of their designing and building a compound Atlantic. However, none of the designs submitted was considered suitable, and Ivatt advised no further action. Bury disagreed with this and advised the board to approve the purchase of a compound Atlantic from the Vulcan Foundry Company. The Board accepted this recommendation.

Ivatt was not in favour of compounds. He had compounded two engines on the Great Southern & Western Railway, which had proved about equal in capacity to the simple engines on that line; but they had been more complicated to construct and more expensive to maintain. But since a compound was to be purchased, he decided to build a compound Atlantic himself.

The Vulcan Foundry's engine, No.1300, was a four-cylinder Atlantic with the de Glehn system of compounding, but without the du Bousquet boiler and steam circuit. The late R.C. Bond, who succeeded R.A. Riddles at the head of British Railways locomotive affairs, had himself spent some years at Vulcans and he told the author that No.1300 was not a very good design. (Roland Bond was largely responsible for writing the history of the Vulcan Works.)

Ivatt's compound, No.292, was ready in 1905, and was of the same general design and appearance as No.251, and with the same boiler and wheels. The high pressure cylinders, 13in by 20in, were outside whilst the 16in by 26in low pressure cylinders were inside the frames. (It will be noted that, rather unusually, the high and low pressure cylinders had strokes of different lengths.) The four cylinders were in line, the high pressure driving the trailing coupled wheels and the low pressure the leading coupled wheels. Another oddity was that whilst Walschaerts valve was used for the outside cylinders, the inside ones had Stephenson's. The low pressure cylinders could be supplied at will, for any length of time, with either live steam or exhaust steam. There were two reversing levers, which could be operated either independently or together. The boiler pressure was 200psi, and, to afford a direct comparison, a 251 class engine had its pressure raised to the same figure. The result of trials with all three engines confirmed Ivatt's results on the GS&WR.

Discussions with Worsdell, who was building two-cylinder compounds for the North Eastern Railway, persuaded Ivatt to build another compound Atlantic with the low pressure cylinders two inches greater in diameter than in his previous one. This engine, No. 1421, was turned out from Doncaster in 1909. Any improvement there might have been did not justify the extra cost of construction and maintenance. Indeed, it would have been surprising if there had been an improvement, for, as André Chapelon remarked (Chapter 3) the importance of the ratio between the dimensions of high and low pressure cylinders has been over estimated.

In 1909 there was an exchange of express locomotives between the Great Northern and the London & North Western Railways for a series of comparative trials between Ivatt's large Atlantics and Whale's 'Precursor' class 4-4-0 engines. Atlantic No. 1449 went to the LNWR to work traffic between Euston and Crewe, whilst 'Precursor' No. 412 Marquis came to the GNR for the express services between King's Cross and Doncaster, and King's Cross and Leeds. Atlantic No. 1451 shared the Great Northern trains with Marquis on alternate days.

It was when they were superheated that the Atlantics displayed their real brilliance; and here we are anticipating a little because superheating belongs to the next chapter. Ivatt superheated his last ten Atlantics in 1910-11. After he retired in the latter year, his successor, H.N. (later Sir Nigel) Gresley, carried on this development and increased the degree of superheat. The improvement in the engines was so great that when the Great Northern Railway became part of the London & North Eastern Railway in 1923, the Ivatt large Atlantics were, with the exception of the recently completed Pacifics, the finest express engines contributed by any of the recently amalgamated companies to the new system.

An astounding run by No. 4404 on 28th July 1936 was recorded by Cecil J. Allen who was travelling on the train, the 1.20pm "Mid-Day Scotsman" from King's Cross to Edinburgh, with 17 coaches weighing 585 tons. The A3 class Pacific hauling this train ran hot at Grantham, and Atlantic No. 4404 had to be substituted at a moment's notice. The Gateshead crew from the Pacific took over this, to them, unfamiliar Great Northern engine and had to set back twice to get the heavy train started. Driver Walker and Fireman Barrick lost two minutes in the 15 miles to Newark, but then gained one minute to Retford, and another three minutes on to Doncaster. The 68 miles were covered in 68 minutes. York was then reached 2½ minutes ahead of the normal Pacific schedule, the 82.7 miles from Grantham to York having been run in 87 minutes 40 seconds, or 87 minutes net. When Allen went along to congratulate the crew, Driver Walker merely remarked, "Grand engines these".

On the following 4th September, No. 4452 had to take over the 'up' "Silver Jubilee" at York, and ran from there to King's Cross at an average speed of 67.3mph.

Perhaps the most outstanding of all these Atlantic performances was related to the author by J.F. Harrison, former CME of British Railways (and vastly proud of having been brought up as a Great Northern man). The run has been disparaged as impossible, but Harrison was on the footplate and timed it himself. He says: "The day was a Saturday in 1925-26 when the "Scarborough Flyer" ran in two parts from King's Cross to York. On this particular day the first part weighed 510 tons and was hauled by GN Atlantic No. 3273, whereas the second part of 365 tons had a Pacific (A1 at the time), No. 2543 I think. No. 3273 took 17 minutes to pass Finsbury Park (usual time $6\frac{1}{2}$ to 7 minutes) and in that short initial period of the run the exhaust injector failed and we were left with one cold water injector for the rest of the journey. From Finsbury Park to Challoners Whin Junction (just short of York) the locomotive averaged 70.5 mph! The Pacific running behind us never saw us, much to the amusement of the King's Cross driver, as No. 3273 was driven by Molson of Doncaster shed. During this journey every ounce of coal was used, ie about $7\frac{1}{2}$ tons at 50lb per mile."

T.C.B. Miller, formerly Chief Engineer (Traffic and Rolling Stock) British Railways, had experience of firing these Atlantics, and told the author that they were comfortable engines – good riding, though very lively in an easy sort of way. He regarded them as excellent. There was a particular technique in their firing, he says: "as soon as the pressure dropped by 5lb, eight shovelfuls were put on, one in each corner and four down the middle'.

Ivatt small and large Atlantics Nos 990 and 251 on the 5pm train King's Cross to Peterborough passing Potters Bar on 16th September 1953.
(Philip J. Kelley).

The ultimate development of the large Atlantics was reached in 1934 when the fitting of the Robinson pattern 32-element superheaters to all the engines of the class was completed. Withdrawal began in 1943, and was hastened after the War by the rapid production of the new B1 class 4-6-0s. Seventeen Atlantics survived to enter British Railways stock, and the last, No. 3294 (though by now No. 62822) was withdrawn immediately after working the "Ivatt Atlantic Special" from King's Cross to Doncaster in November 1950. In 1953 the original large Atlantic, No. 251, which had been preserved, was put into running order in connection with the centenary of Doncaster Works, and has appeared subsequently on special trains.

I have early memories of the Great Northern Atlantics. Periodically, from about 1910, I travelled north from King's Cross to Newcastle, and thence to my mother's family home (and my birthplace) at Wylam-on-Tyne, The changing of engines at York was a thrill for a small boy – watching the Great Northern Atlantic coming off the train and a North Eastern Atlantic backing on. Many years later, in 1932, I would watch Atlantics in immaculate green livery racing through Baldock on the Cambridge buffet car expresses (the "Beer trains"). Then, early in 1942 when heavy snow had broken down many bays on the telegraph route of the LNER main line, I was asked to undertake its repair with linemen from my own Signal Regiment (which then formed part of the forces organised to resist any German attempt to invade East Anglia). When visiting my detachment engaged on this work, I saw my last Great Northern Atlantic – black and rather dirty, but still looking magnificent.

Chapter 6
Superheating

It is not easy to give a consecutive story of superheating, for it suggested different advantages to various locomotive engineers. To some it offered an alternative means of achieving the economy in consumption provided by compounding, but with simpler construction and cheaper maintenance. To others, primarily concerned with simple expansion locomotives, it appeared that, by superheating steam, the same power could be obtained by lowering boiler pressures and thus reducing maintenance costs. A third category of engineers visualised greater power being obtained with engines, basically of the same design. To yet others, the attraction lay in the abolition of condensation in the cylinders without going to the expense and complication of compounding. It was probably only a minority who believed that the future lay with a superheated compound locomotive.

The theory of superheated steam was well known, but its practical application was a different matter. Water in an open vessel at sea level boils, of course at 212°F (100°C). If the vessel is closed and heat still applied, the temperature needed to boil the water is increased. A boiler with a pressure of 175psi saturated steam would have a temperature of 370.8°F. If extra heat is added to it after it has left the boiler, by passing it through a superheater to add 200°F to its temperature, its volume will be increased by 32% and more work can be obtained from it. In addition, when superheated steam comes into contact with the cooler cylinder walls, it can lose heat without condensation taking place.

On the Lancashire & Yorkshire Railway, J.A.F. (later Sir John) Aspinall thought, in 1897, of slight superheating as a method of reducing both steam consumption and condensation.

Two years later he decided to try low degree superheating in one of his Atlantics, and charged Horwich drawing office with the task of producing a suitable design. As a result, Atlantic No. 737 was fitted with a low degree superheater in 1899 – the last engine of the first batch of 20, built in that year, and the first British superheated locomotive. To accommodate the equipment, the front tube plate of the boiler was recessed, so extending the smokebox, and into this space was installed a cylindrical drum, slightly smaller in diameter than the boiler barrel. The steam travelled vertically up and down through the drum five times before passing through the steam pipe to the steam chests. The degree of superheat achieved was so low that the apparatus was really little more than a steam drier. The last five engines of the 1902 batch were similarly fitted, but all were in due course altered to saturated working. The saving in coal had not been appreciable, but the engines were indeed stated to run more freely than their non-superheated sisters.

A much more successful smokebox superheater was designed by Wilhelm Schmidt of Kassel a year before that of Aspinall, and fitted to a two-cylinder simple 4-4-0 of the Prussian State Railways, built by the firm of Borsig. This showed an impressive economy in consumption, as compared with the simple engines of that line, of 20% in coal and 30% in water, in attaining an indicated horsepower of 1,100. A similar engine was shown at the Paris Exhibition of 1900.

In 1901 Schmidt produced his tube superheater, which was a greatly superior type and, indeed, the model from which practically all subsequent superheaters were developed. It was first fitted to a locomotive designed by Flamme of the Belgian State Railways, but was thereafter widely adopted by British, French, and many other railways. Its success was so pronounced that the question was soon asked as to whether compounding was still worthwhile when such economies could be produced by superheating or when condensation could be so avoided without the complication and expense of compounding.

Although it was not the first British railway to adopt tube superheaters, the London, Brighton & South Coast's superheated tank engines were probably the first to demonstrate, and forcibly, the advantages to be derived from this latest in steam technology.

In 1907 Douglas Earl Marsh, Locomotive Superintendent of the London, Brighton & South Coast Railway produced the first of his I3 class express 4-4-2 tank engines. This, No. 21, was tried out on the London expresses and was an immediate success; for it could run very fast and rode steadily at the highest speeds. Its only disadvantage was that its coal consumption with heavy trains was high, with an average of 43.2lb per mile. This was more than the B4 class 4-4-0s, which had the same boiler, and even more than the big Atlantics. This was a disappointment to Marsh who was keen on economy in coal consumption. Some months earlier, in search of greater savings in fuel and water, he had ordered five boilers equipped with the Schmidt superheater for some of his smaller tank engines, and he now decided to try a Schmidt superheater on the second of his I3s, No. 22.

Instead of No. 21's slide valves, No. 22 had 20in diameter piston valves with large ports, short steam passages, and a free exhaust; all with the object of providing a good steam circuit. The boiler pressure was lowered from the 180psi of No. 21 to 140psi, with the object (as mentioned above) of reducing maintenance costs – though it was soon raised to 160.

Teething troubles delayed the appearance of No. 22 until May 1908. On the LBSCR's principal express services, both Nos 21 and 22 ran well and, to have thorough trials before making a decision with regard to superheating, ten more I3s were ordered, four of them superheated and the other six saturated. A further five were projected, but their construction was delayed, pending the result of the trials.

Both types ran very well, though the superheated engines were the more lively; but there was a great difference between them in their consumption figures. Whilst the saturated I3s burnt an average of 34.2lb of coal per train mile, the superheated engines used only 30.5lb, and there was a similar difference in water consumption. As a result the Locomotive Committee decided that no

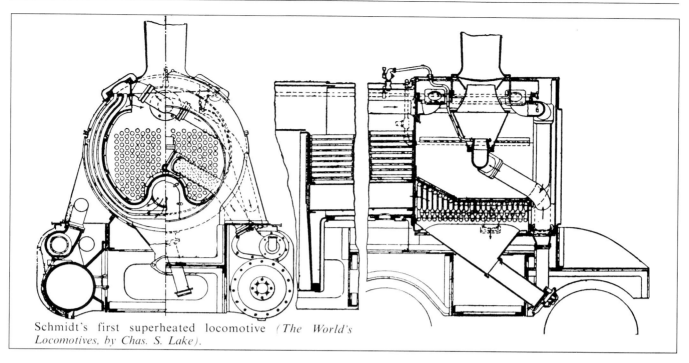

Schmidt's first superheated locomotive (*The World's Locomotives, by Chas. S. Lake*).

Right: Marsh I3 class superheated 4-4-2 tank engine No.30 LBSCR, built 1910, as Southern Railway No.2030 near Pulborough. (*Courtesy National Railway Museum, York*).

more saturated main line engines should be built.

On 1st March 1905 a train was inaugurated by the London & North Western and the London, Brighton & South Coast Railways to provide a through service for the inhabitants of Liverpool and Manchester to South Coast resorts, the train using the West London and West London Extension Railways to pass from the LNWR at Willesden Junction to the LBSCR at Clapham Junction. Though instituted as a summer service, it was so successful that in the following year it became an all the year round daily train and was called the "Sunny South Special" - later changed to "Sunny South Express".

The changeover between LNWR and LBSCR engines took place at Willesden Junction. Initially the LBSCR worked the train with their B4 class 4-4-0s (No. 68 *Marlborough* hauled the inaugural train from Willesden to Brighton). Then, in 1909, following their trials with the I3 4-4-2 tank engines, the LBSCR started using the superheated variety on the train. The LNWR took great interest in this use of a four-coupled tank engine, and, in order to compare this superheated locomotive with their own saturated 4-4-0s, they suggested comparative trials.

The train was normally composed of six LNWR corridor carriages and a dining car, with a tare weight of $233\frac{1}{2}$ tons. The LBSCR was to provide the locomotive power from Brighton to Rugby one day, working back the next; whilst alternate trips would be run by a LNWR engine.

The LNWR selected 'Precursor' class No. 7 *Titan* to work the train. The 'Precursors' were virtually a development of Webb's 'Precedents', with a leading bogie instead of the single carrying axle, and the cylinders and Joy valve gear of his mixed traffic "Cauliflower" 0-6-0s (so-called from the ornate surround of the LNWR Britannia badge displayed on the centre splashers). The LBSCR choice was No. 23, with No. 26 as a standby.

The round trip was 264 miles, and of these, the $90\frac{1}{2}$ miles between East Croydon and Rugby were to be run non-stop without taking water, and the $77\frac{1}{4}$ miles between Willesden and Rugby (also non-stop) had to be run at an average speed of about 53 mph. Marsh was not sure that No. 23 could run the East Croydon-Rugby stretch without taking water, and on the first few journeys he had milk churns full of water carried in the leading luggage compartment. Most LNWR men also shared these doubts; indeed, some of them did not believe that the engine could do it. But it did. No. 23 carried out eleven of the twelve round trips worked by the LBSCR, and No. 26 the other one; all being completed successfully. It was said that on some of its runs, *Titan* arrived at Brighton with its smokebox door red hot, and No. 23's driver was reprimanded for exceeding 75mph over part of the London & North Western track, and for failing to observe speed limits at junctions. For running was indeed

hard, but time was kept.

The results provided an astounding vindication of the value of superheating. No. 23 burnt 27.4lb of coal per mile and 22.4 gallons of water, compared with *Titan's* 41.2lb and 36.6 respectively. The I3 class engine's performance astonished much of the locomotive community, and No. 23 had probably a greater influence on the rapid spread of superheating in Great Britain than did any other engine.

The reaction of the LNWR to these trials was the production by its CME, C.J. Bowen Cooke, of superheated versions of the 'Precursor' 4-4-0s and 'Experiment' 4-6-0s – the 'George the Fifth' and 'Prince of Wales' classes respectively. The exploits of the former are famous, and the late R.A. Riddles told the author that the latter were the best express engines the London & North Western Railway ever had. (He drove one on express trains during the General Strike of 1926.)

Before embarking on superheating, however, Bowen Cooke carried out trials between otherwise similar superheated and saturated 4-4-0s, one of each being completed in June 1910 – No. 2663 superheated and No. 2664 saturated. On these two engines the maximum steam port area of the 'Precursors' was increased from 23.49sq in to 31.35sq in and the maximum valve travel to $5\frac{1}{2}$ in. The superheated engine was named *George the Fifth*

Bowen Cooke 'George the Fifth' class superheated 4-4-0 No.445 *P.H. Chambres* LNWR, built 1910.
(Courtesy National Railway Museum, York).

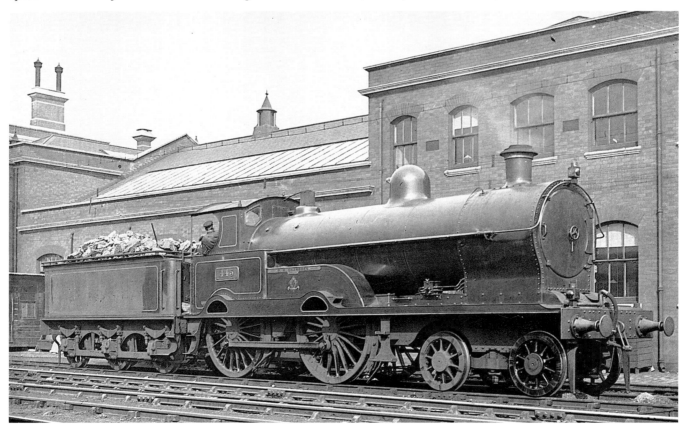

and the saturated one *Queen Mary*. Observations of their running were made during 1910. The superheated engine remained under test, but the running of the saturated engine was so much better than the 'Precursors' that nine more were built at Crewe in October and November 1910.

Meanwhile, comparative running between the *George the Fifth* and the *Queen Mary* continued; the two engines working in turn the heaviest and fastest expresses between Euston and Crewe for some months. The superheated engine proved 27.6% the more economical in coal consumption, and on one round trip from Crewe to Euston and back with a load of 357 tons, it set up new records in sustained high speeds and power output. A further ten superheated 4-4-0s were consequently built in November 1910 and January 1911.

On the Great Western Railway, G.J. Churchward had been early in the field with superheating, for the first of his engines to be so fitted was the two-cylinder 4-6-0 No. 2901 *Lady Superior* in 1906. In the following year a 'Star' class four-cylinder 4-6-0, *Western Star* was equipped with a Cole superheater. Subsequently, three designs of Swindon superheater were produced in 1907 and 1909. No. 4011 *Knight of the Garter* got the first one, No. 2922 *Saint Gabriel* the second, and No. 2913 *Saint Andrew* the third design, which thenceforward became the standard pattern.

Churchward did not favour high superheat, believing that a low degree of superheat, sufficient to ensure the absence of condensation in the cylinders sufficed for his requirements. Also he had doubts as to whether the oil available at the time would stand up to a high superheat. So the steam temperature of Great Western engines was about 550°F, whereas that of Bowen Cooke's London & North Western superheated engines was about 650°F.

Robert Riddles, when an apprentice at Crewe, noted the effects of high superheat on the 'Georges' and 'Princes'. In a letter to the author he wrote: "I remember the trouble we had with carbonisation in the early days, with valve rings being seized up, etc., and carbon having to be chipped out of the valve chests. A snifting valve was fitted to open when coasting; but as the oil quality improved this was done away with, for such a cure was almost as bad as the disease". Riddles said that Churchward, realising the likelihood of the oil carbonising and having the advantage of superior Welsh coal pursued a cautious policy. "In any case," Riddles added, "the Great Western locomotives were far and away better than most, so why invite trouble? The real culprits were his successors who should have realised the benefits of higher superheat with the advent of improved oils".

The arrival of superheating posed a rather different problem to French engineers. Most of them had designed or been concerned with compound locomotives and they tended to look at superheating as an alternative to compounding, rather than an addition to it.

In July and September 1907 the Paris-Orléans Railway put into service the first Pacific locomotives in Europe, Nos 4501 and 4502. They were designed by the PO and the Société Alsacienne and were intended to be developments of their very successful Atlantics (which were enlarged versions of those running on the Nord) and their 4-6-0s (which were six-coupled editions of the PO Atlantics). The Atlantics worked the easier main lines from Paris to Bordeaux and Nantes, whilst the 4-6-0s were used on the heavily graded Paris-Toulouse line. The new Pacifics of the 4500 class were needed to replace the 4-6-0s, which, with the increasing weight of the trains, were having difficulty over the steep banks between Argenton and Montauban – a stretch of 231 miles. They were four-cylinder compounds like the Atlantics and 4-6-0s, and had coupled wheels of 6ft diameter. They were not superheated. They had a Belpaire firebox of the trapezoidal type – wide over the frames at the rear and bending between them at the front – an arrangement that combined the advantages of a deep narrow firebox at its front end and a wide shallow one at its rear. In 1908-09 the class was expanded to a total of 70 engines, Nos 4501 to 4570. The earlier ones had a stovepipe chimney, but from No. 4530 onwards they had a shapely capped chimney, typical of British engines and which became characteristic of later PO engines. Another 30 of the class were built which were superheated, and others were superheated later.

At the same time that the 4500 class was being built for the Toulouse line, the Orleans company was projecting another Pacific of similar type but with larger coupled wheels of 6ft 5in diameter for the easier main lines to Bordeaux and Nantes. This became the 3500 class, of which the first 50 were constructed in 1909-10. Of these the first 20 were at first saturated, whilst the remaining 30 were superheated. The saturated engines were built by the Société Alsacienne, whilst the superheated ones were constructed by the firm of Fives-Lille. The 3500 class differed only slightly from the 4500s; boilers, cylinders, exhaust, and boiler pressure were identical. Like the 4500s, they were lovely looking engines and, indeed, even more attractive than their smaller wheeled sisters. They had a very English appearance and, with their graceful capped chimneys, they had a vaguely Great Central look.

In 1901-02 the Midi, like the PO, acquired compound Atlantics, though these were identical with the Nord engines. Also, like the PO, they experienced adhesion difficulties with the advent of heavier trains, and looked for bigger engines with more coupled wheels. In 1908, therefore, they put into service a class of compound Pacifics with many points in common with those of the PO, including the trapezoidal Belpaire firebox. The first 16 were superheated, but in 1910 four more were built which were superheated. There were originally to have been 15 superheated compounds in the 1910 order, but it had been decided to order some superheated simple expansion Pacifics instead.

The compound Pacifics worked the trains satisfactorily to the required schedules but, like those of the PO, their steaming was markedly less free than the preceding Atlantics. The CME of the Midi from 1907 to 1920 was A. Herdner. In his opinion the cause was due to the engines having four cylinders and a complex motion which affected adversely engines of this weight. In fact, the real reason (perceived only by du Bousquet, amongst French CMEs) was the inadequate cross sections of the steam circuit, which had not been increased in relation to the larger dimensions.

Herdner had been much impressed with the advantages of superheating, and in 1908-09 the Midi ordered 25 superheated tank engines. By 1910 this company had a bigger proportion of superheated locomotives than had the Nord, the PLM or the Etat. On 18th June 1914 the Société Alsacienne was asked to build four two-cylinder simple superheated Pacifics. The outbreak of war, however, delayed their construction until after 1919, in fact, the period 1910-21 was marked by the abandonment of the four-cylinder compound and by the appearance of new types with two cylinders, simple expansion, and superheating – all excellent examples of this type of locomotive. It was a trend reflected on other European railways, including the Prussian, Belgian, Etat, and the Midi's neighbour, the PO.

Herdner's view had a profound influence on the E. Solacroup, Ingenieur en Chef du Material et de la Traction (ie CME) of the PO from 1899 to 1918. He too came to believe that superheating had removed the need for compounding. In 1911-13 a series of two-cylinder simple

4-6-0 express engines were built in the hope that they would be cheaper both in first cost and maintenance than the compound Pacifics. They were, in fact, so successful that another batch was built in 1913-14. Though they too had the shapely chimney, they were not handsome engines, for their appearance was spoilt by high running plates and a 'hunched up' look.

In 1914 the PO, now firmly anti-compound, decided to build some simple expansion superheated Pacifics and preliminary studies were instituted. The First World War stopped design and construction, but during the war there arose the concept of a simple Pacific which could be constructed for all the large French railways, and preliminary designs were carried out by the firm of Schneider.

In 1920 the needs of the PO for large express engines had become urgent, and the Company ordered 50 simple expansion superheated Pacifics. At first these engines gave

PLM 231.D class Pacific No.231.D.43, with ACFI feed water heater. One of a class of 230 compound Pacifics delivered 1921-25. *(P. Ransome-Wallis Collection, Courtesy National Railway Museum, York).*

a good impression, as compared with the 3500 class compound Pacifics, which had become run down during the war, and they appeared less hampered in their running. But their riding was poor, due to balancing inferior to the four-cylinder engines. Their final consumption, at least when they were new, was a little less than the compounds, but maintenance costs, surprisingly, were rather higher. Nevertheless they gave good service and they were popular with the enginemen, because their free steaming enabled them to work overloaded trains.

It was to be on the PLM that the first true comparisons were made between simple and compound superheated engines. E. Chabal, who became CME of the PLM in 1907 answered the demands for greater power by designing a Pacific with a wide firebox. At this time, when superheating was spreading rapidly, current opinion favoured a low boiler pressure and superheating, rather than compounds with high boiler pressure, which some people thought posed problems in boiler maintenance. The PLM was thus persuaded to determine the question by building two Pacifics, one a saturated four-cylinder compound with a boiler pressure of 225psi and the other a superheated four-cylinder simple with 170psi pressure.

In 1909, therefore, the PLM built in its Paris works its first Pacific type express locomotives – the first, indeed, of 460 which were to be built over the next 23 years.

Of these two Pacifics, No. 6001, the four-cylinder compound, was completed in August 1909. It had a large boiler with a round top wide firebox. The four cylinders were staggered, following the de Glehn arrangement, with the high pressure cylinders outside, beside the second bogie axle and driving the middle coupled axle, and the low pressure cylinders inside, in the middle of the bogie, and propelling the leading coupled axle. There were piston valves to all four cylinders with Walschaerts valve gear. The maximum high pressure cut-off was 88%, whilst the low pressure cut-off was fixed at 63%.

The four-cylinder simple superheated Pacific, No. 6101, came out a month after the compound. Its four cylinders were in line and about the middle of the bogie; the outside cylinders driving the middle coupled axle and the inside cylinders the leading one. In other respects the two Pacifics were as nearly identical as possible.

Comparative trials between the two from January to March 1910 showed the compound consuming 13.07% more coal and 15.08% more water than the superheated simple. During the same months there were also trials between superheated and saturated compound 4-6-0s, otherwise identical, in which the superheated engines demonstrated an economy in consumption of 15%. From these trials the PLM deduced that compounding in addition to superheating did not confer any additional benefit. In consequence they had no hesitation in ordering 30 more of the 6100 class simple Pacifics in August 1910, and, in addition to these, another 40 were ordered in May 1911.

However, the compound Pacific, No. 6001, was so satisfactory in service and more easy running than the simples, that the PLM began to have some doubts, and in June 1911 they ordered 20 more compounds, but this time with superheaters. These were delivered in March and May 1912, some of them before the second batch of simples which arrived in April to July. The superheated compounds, Nos 6011-6030, immediately showed themselves very superior to the superheated simples, both in power and economy. To prevent a premature decision in favour of the compounds, however, the PLM ordered 20 more superheated simple Pacifics but with a boiler pressure of 205psi instead of 170. However, when they were compared with the superheated compounds they were found to consume 11.8% more coal. The PLM, therefore, concluded that all future Pacifics should be compounds, and that their existing Pacifics would be converted to compounds.

PLM Pacific No.231.D.199 at Dijon in 1929. (*P. Ransome-Wallis Collection, Courtesy National Railway Museum, York*).

Chapter 7

The Great Bear and the Baltics

It is likely that no locomotive in British railway history has excited so much speculation as to the reason for its construction as this big Great Western Pacific. G. J. Churchward, Chief Mechanical Engineer of the GWR, and the greatest of all British locomotive engineers, does not appear to have told anybody why he built it; but there is no doubt of the impression it caused when 4-6-2 No. lll *The Great Bear*, rolled out from Swindon Works in February 1908 – the largest steam locomotive built in Great Britain at that date.

It was not of course Churchward's habit to explain why he did things. Normally he would merely state what he intended to do and then listen to opinions as to the best way of doing it. When he had made up his mind, he would send for his Chief Draughtsman, G. H. Burrows, and give him an outline of the project. Burrows would then select a suitable draughtsman to get a scheme out on the drawing board.

The reason for the Pacific was a puzzle because the four-cylinder 'Star' class 4-6-0s were years ahead of any other express locomotive design in Great Britain and were doing everything required of them. But perhaps a clue can be obtained from a paper on *American Locomotive Practice* read before the Institution of Civil Engineers on 31st March 1903. In the discussion on this paper, Churchward said: "Probably, to English locomotive engineers, the part of the paper which deals with boilers is the most interesting; especially the reasonably wide firebox which the author has described. An express engine with a similar box has just been put on the Great Northern Railway by Mr Ivatt (ie the larger boiler Atlantic No. 251) and I trust it will have a good trial in England. I think English engineers are within a reasonable distance of adopting it, and I am sorry that the French Atlantic engine, which is to be put on the Great Western Railway, is not fitted with it – but I am taking the engine as it stands."

The point in Churchward's statement that merits particular attention is that he thought English locomotive engineers to be "within measurable distance" of adopting the wide firebox, and that must have included himself. His disappointment that the French du Bousquet/de Glehn Atlantics, which he was trying on the GWR, had not got the wide firebox, shows that he very much wanted to try it. But, in accordance with his customary cautious approach, any trials would be very lengthy and thorough before he concluded that big engines with wide fireboxes would or would not be suitable for the Great Western. As soon as he was satisfied that he had designed express locomotives that were adequate for all Great Western needs for some years ahead, he decided to experiment with a wide firebox.

There arose, then, the question as to the most suitable type of engine. It would obviously have to have a trailing truck because the firebox could not spread over big coupled wheels. An Atlantic would do, but he had already concluded that a four-coupled engine had not got sufficient adhesion to work express trains over the terrific gradients west of Newton Abbot. In any case he had to look ahead to the time when the 'Stars' would be stretched and more power would be needed. Indeed, the late K. J. Cook (who presented a paper to the Institution of Locomotive Engineers in 1950 on Churchward's Locomotive development on the Great Western Railway) wrote in a letter to the author that he had always believed that *The Great Bear* represented a quest for more power. To get an engine with a wide firebox which had sufficient adhesion, it would have to be a Pacific. The very big engine, that was thus emerging from his thoughts, might present a problem in axle-loading. At that time the principal main lines of the Great Western were limited to an axle load of $19\frac{1}{2}$ tons, and the big boiler that would be necessary to supply the power he wanted would probably bring the axle weight above this. On the other hand Churchward knew that J. C. (later Sir James) Inglis, when Chief Engineer of the Great Western, had in 1902 initiated a project to strengthen main lines to carry 22 tons. He was then on friendly terms with Churchward and there must have been discussion between them. Later, after Inglis became General Manager in 1903, considerable hostility arose between these two strong personalities, owing to Churchward's opposition to attempts by Inglis to bring the locomotive superintendent under the general manager, so depriving the former of his direct access to the Board. Perhaps, as a legacy of this hostility, the general managers who succeeded Inglis omitted to inform the chief mechanical engineers (as locomotive engineers later became) that the planned strengthening of the track had been carried out. In fact it never came out into the open until Collett, Churchward's successor, said to the then general manager, Sir Felix Pole, "If I could have an axle load of $22\frac{1}{2}$ tons I could give you a very fine locomotive".

As a result of Collett's statement, the then Chief Civil Engineer was asked what axle load he could accept, and the astonishing fact was then revealed that for over 22 years work had been going on to raise the $19\frac{1}{2}$ ton limit to 22 tons. In the light of the progress already made it was possible, says Sir Felix Pole in his book, to give Collett authority to go ahead with the 'King' class 4-6-0 locomotives of 1927. Churchward must have known that the line between Paddington and Bristol was ready to carry his projected Pacific. In addition, he probably forecast, from Inglis's plans, that by the time he had finished the very extensive tests he had in mind, the route to Plymouth would have been upgraded, and possibly also that to Birmingham. He could not foresee that both his plans for tests and the programme for track improvement would be upset by the outbreak of war in 1914.

Apart from the advantages to be derived from a large grate area, Churchward was undoubtedly well aware that his engines, with their long narrow fireboxes, depended on high grade fuel and skilled firing for their great success. In a letter to the author, W. N. Pellew (former Locomotive Running Superintendent of the Great Western Railway) wrote: "The quality of coal supplied

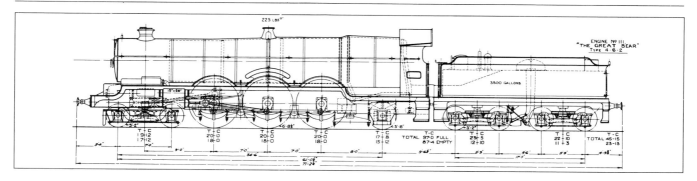

for locomotive use got gradually worse and worse, and I found on inquiry that the Pacifics of other regions, with their wider shallower fireboxes, were reported to be doing very well on the inferior fuel; while our firemen, with the long deep fireboxes of our standard boilers, had considerable difficulties with the fuel". Pellow, as Locomotive Running Superintendent, was the person most concerned with the problem.

The drawing office staff at the time that Churchward decided on his Pacific locomotive was divided into gangs, each of which was concerned with particular parts of locomotive design, and in charge of each gang was a leading draughtsman, styled 'chargeman'. When the job was sufficiently far advanced, Churchward would come and sit on the draughtsman's stool with, grouped around him, Burrows, O. E. F. Deverell (Assistant Chief Draughtsman), the chargeman of the gang concerned, and the draughtsman entrusted with the task. He would then listen while Burrows explained to him, point by point, the present situation of the job and how it had developed. When he had finished, Churchward would ask questions and perhaps make suggestions on which he would expect those around him to comment. As a result of the discussion he might want opinions on the practical aspects of the proposals and would send for the locomotive running superintendent or the foreman of the shops principally concerned. The matter would then probably be adjourned for a day or two whilst amendments or different approaches to the scheme were considered in the light of the discussion. When Churchward was satisfied that the various courses of action had been fully considered, he would summarise the favourable and adverse aspects of each and make his decision.

F. W. Hawksworth, who later succeeded Collett as CME, was the draughtsman entrusted with the general arrangement drawing of the Pacific locomotive. The late H. Holcroft (who gave the author the above description of work in the drawing office) was in the cylinder gang and was given the task of getting out the drawings of the cylinders. Churchward had said that there was to be no departure from the 'Star' class arrangement, other than an increase in cylinder diameter. But the diameter was limited by various factors. The longer wheelbase increased the bogie side movements; but the trailing bogie wheels were behind the outside cylinders, giving little clearance, and there was not much clearance between the leading bogie wheels and the inside cylinders. Holcroft found that

a diameter of 15 inches was the practical limit. On Churchward's next visit Holcroft told him this, but added that if the tyres were reduced from the standard Great Western width of $5\frac{3}{4}$ inches to $5\frac{1}{2}$ inches, as used on most railways, the cylinders could be increased to 16 inches. Churchward would not agree to the modification and seemed quite happy with 15 inches. It was apparent that it was increased boiler power in which he was interested. (His preference for boiler power was to be justified in the locomotive exchange between the GWR and the LNER in 1925, when it was assumed at the time that the GWR 'Castle' 4-6-0s had shown a marked superiority over the LNER Pacifics. So in most respects they had, but, though the tractive effort of the GWR engines was the higher, their boiler power was considerably less. The 'Castle' made the faster running in the short climbs of the LNER main line, but up the long gradients of the GWR, the Pacific with its big boiler was the faster of the two.)

The big Standard No. 6 boiler was, indeed, the principal feature of *The Great Bear*. Holcroft said that Churchward spent a lot of time on its development and that it was carried out on the board of W. L. Watson (later CME of the Irish Great Southern & Western Railway). Only one ring of the boiler was coned, the grate area was 41.8sq ft, and the firebox was Churchward's Belpaire pattern. The boiler tubes were 23ft long, which was exceptional, and their diameter was $2\frac{1}{2}$in, instead of the usual 2in, to compensate for the length of the tubes. Churchward was criticised on account of these long tubes, but, as he said in his paper on *Large Locomotive Boilers*, "The ratio of diameter to length of the tube undoubtedly has a most important bearing upon the steaming qualities of the boiler and upon the efficiency of the heat absorption". Once firemen got used to the wide grate, the steaming quality of the boiler was excellent.

The radial truck, with its inside bearings, was a weak point, because the axleboxes were difficult to lubricate efficiently and their surfaces were in a position where dust from the ashpans, and dust thrown up from the track, could reach them, with the result that there was frequent overheating. (Raven made the same mistake on the first two of his Pacifics for the North Eastern Railway. The subsequent three had outside bearings on the trailing truck.)

The Great Bear had an excellent bogie for it was the first British engine to be fitted with the type designed by Alfred de Glehn, the chief engineer of the Société

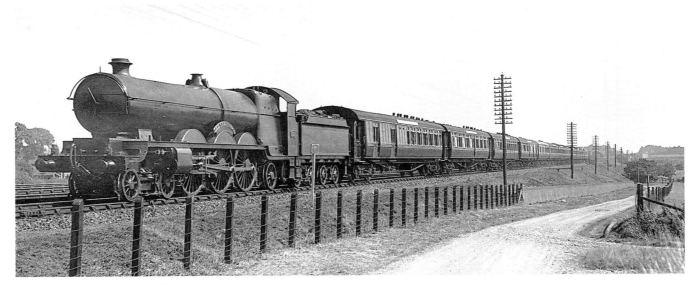

Churchward Pacific No.111 *The Great Bear*, **GWR, built 1908.**
(Courtesy National Railway Museum, York).

Alsacienne de Constructions Mécaniques, which eventually became standard on the Great Western, the London Midland & Scottish, and British Railways.

In the drawing office at Swindon a small team of men had been built up, known as the "Experimental Gang", whose principal task was to ride on locomotives in service, observing the effects of various experiments, and reporting on them to Churchward. "For Churchward," said Pellow, "was very cautious, and would not put any ideas or a new engine into general use until proved in practice over a period of general working." The prototype of a new engine was tested under all kinds of service conditions before he would recommend to the Board that a number of the type should be constructed. When Pellow went to the drawing office in 1912 the Experimental Gang were still testing *The Great Bear* and submitting their findings to an intensely interested Churchward. These lengthy tests were brought to an untimely end by the outbreak of war in 1914, and before normal working could be restored, Churchward had retired.

Unfortunately, records of the various trials do not seem to have survived. "Teething" troubles there were, as one might expect from such a revolutionary engine. Until firemen found the correct way to deal with the unfamiliar wide firebox, there were complaints about steaming. The late R. F. Hanks, who was a premium apprentice at Swindon at the time, told the author that the engine spent a lot of time in the Works having various devices tried in connection with the trailing axle, and that she was much given to de-railing when traversing sharp curves, "but", he added, "we loved her and very often I would go up to Swindon station to see her go through on a Bristol express about 8pm". *The Great Bear* worked all sorts of trains between Bristol and Paddington, from express passenger to fast goods. J. N. Maskelyne, in the

Model Railway News of February 1947, mentions an occasion in 1909 when the engine left Swindon with a fast goods train weighing no less than 2,375 tons, which it hauled non-stop to Acton at an average speed of 24.5mph.

The axle load, after sundry re-adjustments, was 20 tons 9cwt per coupled axle, which was above the limit at the time for any line other than that between Paddington and Bristol. Churchward would no doubt have dearly loved to have seen his great Pacific working over a much wider range; for, when shortly before his retirement he heard that Gresley was building a Pacific, he said (according to a tale that Pellow says "went the rounds") "Gresley could have had our *Bear* to play with if only we had known in time". Indeed the lessons that could have been learned from running *The Great Bear* on the Great Northern main line would have been invaluable to both companies. Gresley might have adopted Churchward's long travel valves from the start and Collett might have built Pacifics. The further development of *The Great Bear* was carried out by one of Churchward's most enthusiastic disciples, but Stanier built his Pacifics for the LMS, not for the Great Western.

The end of this famous and fascinating engine is stated in the following extraordinary minute of a meeting of the Locomotive Committee on 1st May 1924, which is recorded in the British Transport Historical Records (GEN 3-62-6):

"Engine 111 *The Great Bear* Reconstruction.

The above engine was built at Swindon in February 1908, and had a tractive effort of 27,800lb and weighed 142tons 15cwt. Owing to its extreme weight, it was necessary for the Hanwell Viaduct (a pencilled correction in the margin says: "the old iron skew bridge over the Uxbridge Road – not the viaduct) to be rebuilt before the engine could be allowed to work between London and Bristol, to which route it has been limited the whole 16 years on account of the enormous expenditure that would be necessary to strengthen the bridges to carry it on other main line routes. Mr Grierson has estimated the cost of doing so at over £500,000. The 'Castle' class of four-cylinder engine has now been produced and proved successful, the engines of which have a greater tractive effort than *The Great Bear* by 13¾% viz 31,625lb, and as they weigh only 119 tons 17cwt, or 22 tons 18cwt less than *The Great Bear*, no alterations are necessary to any of the bridges. There is, therefore, no longer any reason for the continued existence of *The Great Bear* and as it recently came into the shops for general repair and needed new cylinders and a new boiler, advantage has been taken of the occasion to reconstruct it, so that it will be similar to one of the 'Castle' type.

"In the past, reconstructions of engines have been dealt with in the same way as repairs and have not been reported to the Directors, but it is thought desirable to do so in this case owing to the notoriety of the engine and to the fact that several British railways followed our example in adopting the Pacific type and are still building them. They have not produced a more powerful engine of less weight."

Collett must bear ultimate responsibility for this misleading and inaccurate document. No competent engineer would assess the relative power of express engines on the basis of their starting tractive effort. The statement that several British railways were building Pacific locomotives was quite untrue. Only the Great Northern and the North Eastern had built them, and of these only the Great Northern type was still being built (for the LNER) at the date the minute was written. Finally, as three years later the main lines of the GWR could take the 'King'' class, with a 22½ ton axle load, it is clear that the statement about the enormous expenditure necessary to strengthen bridges was false, and that Grierson, the Chief Engineer, must either have been withholding information or had been incorrectly briefed by his own department.

A curiously similar fate befell the last locomotives designed by Churchward's great contemporary, du Bousquet of the Nord. In 1907 he tried out a water tube boiler on one of his Atlantics, No. 2741. Because of difficulties in mounting such a boiler on a locomotive chassis, a 'mixed' solution was adopted. The firebox was water tube and the boiler barrel had smoke tubes. As the weight at the rear end was heavy, a bogie was substituted for the trailing axle and the engine thus became a 4-4-4. Leaks developed, so that, in spite of the excellent performance of the water tubes, the boiler was removed and a new one of similar type was constructed. With this new boiler the engine ran satisfactorily for 25,000 miles in ordinary service, and was exhibited at Brussels in 1910. However, leaks started again and in 1913 No. 2741 was rebuilt as a conventional 4-6-0.

Although other French railways, in search of greater power for their express trains, had chosen the Pacific type of locomotive to succeed the Atlantic, du Bousquet, looking further ahead decided on the Baltic, or 4-6-4 wheel arrangement, because he believed it would facilitate the distribution of weights and the installation of the boiler and firebox he wanted, without having to resort to a trapezoidal grate or to a combustion chamber to move the centre of gravity further forward.

In 1909, therefore, the Nord carried out a design project for a 4-6-4 locomotive with a cylinder horsepower which should be greater than that of the Atlantics by 50%; that is, about 2,300 as compared with 1,500. In 1910 the La Chapelle Works of the Nord built two prototypes of a high powered express locomotive, Nos 3.1101 and 3.1102. They were superheated four-cylinder compounds, similar except that No. 3.1102 had a water tube firebox of the same type as that currently undergoing trials on the 4-4-4 No. 2741. The two engines were put into service in April and July 1911 respectively. No. 3.1101 had a wide Belpaire firebox of great volume, a Schmidt superheater, and a very long smokebox. The high pressure cylinders were outside with piston valves and the low pressure inside with compensated slide valves. No. 3.1102 was similar except for the water tube firebox.

These two remarkable engines surpassed in power and performance the Pacifics recently placed in service on the PO, the Midi, the Ouest, the PLM, and the Etat. They had been designed with the object of hauling a 400 ton train at an overall average speed of 75mph (the legal limit). In fact they proved capable of working a train of 800 tons at that speed. No. 3.1102's boiler with water tube firebox gave the same trouble as that of the 4-4-4 and was in due course replaced with a boiler and firebox similar to that of its sister engine in 1913. André Chapelon told the author that these two great engines (which du Bousquet insisted were Baltics and not Hudsons) proved capable of developing 2,800 ihp – and this in 1911!

Unfortunately du Bousquet died before the engines came into normal service, with the result that they were never given thorough trials. From the time that they were completed until September 1924, when the 3.1200 class Pacifics were produced, they only ran about 300,000 miles. One or two notable runs were recorded, including passing St Denis, four miles from Paris, with 600 tons at 72mph, and No. 3.1101, at the head of a freight train of bogie stock weighing 1,200 tons, reaching 70mph down the slight gradient at Neufchatel.

After the First World War they worked heavy expresses, with frequent stops, on the main line to Belgium. In 1926, owing to firing difficulties, they were fitted with mechanical stokers, but the type was unsatisfactory and they were taken out of service in 1934 and stored at Compiègne. In November 1936 they were withdrawn.

Asselin, who succeeded du Bousquet, did not like them. He said they were too powerful, and the fact that over certain parts of the Nord network the maximum axle load was 16½ tons, gave him a good excuse for relegating them to secondary main line services. He replaced them by an indifferent class of Pacifics, originally designed by the Société Alsacienne for the Alsace-Lorraine lines.

Chapter 8

Gresley's Beauties

To many people, who regard streamlining or 'air-smoothing' as being somewhat akin to the cosy that conceals the outline of a teapot, Gresley's A1 and A3 class Pacifics were some of the most beautiful engines that have ever graced railway tracks. They were obviously Great Northern engines, for they inherited the Doncaster lines which had been instituted by Patrick Stirling. They were all curves – firebox with round top, typical Doncaster flat 'S' curves to the running plate, slight taper to the boiler, and sweeping curves to the firebox sides – there was hardly a straight line or a sharp angle. Furthermore, to an engineer, as T. C. B. Miller (former CME of British Railways) said to me, they looked right, as Raven's contemporary North Eastern Pacifics somehow did not. Their achievements matched their looks, and though there are arguments as to whether the Great Western's *City of Truro* really did surpass 100mph, as timed by Charles Rous-Marten, there is no doubt that *Flying Scotsman* was the first steam locomotive to reach an *officially* recorded 100mph, and that *Papyrus* held the British record of 108mph before the streamlined era.

famous conjugated valve gear. H. Holcroft, when in the Drawing Office at Swindon, had patented a three-cylinder valve gear in 1909, and Gresley, in producing an improved version of his original design, was accused by some people of poaching on Holcroft's scheme, the patent of which had run out. I asked Holcroft if this was true. He replied, "No; we collaborated". (Holcroft later showed me an ingenious design of his own, and asked me if I would send it to Chapelon with a request for his comments. I did so, and Chapelon asked for further information, but Harry Holcroft, then aged 91, died before he could send it).

Gresley did not like a divided drive because, apart from the greater load it imposed on the axle boxes, he preferred the leading coupled axle to be straight, especially on heavy express engines. Very little information was available regarding the flange forces on such wheels when an engine was travelling at high speed round a curve, and a straight axle was less likely to give trouble than a crank axle in this position. Thus, the drive from all three cylinders was taken by the second pair of coupled wheels.

Gresley A3 class Pacific No.2750 *Papyrus* LNER. One-time holder of the British speed record.
(Courtesy National Railway Museum, York).

In his paper read before the Institution of Locomotive Engineers in 1947 on *The Development of LNER Locomotive Design 1923-1941*, B. Spencer said that "Gresley was a firm advocate of the three-cylinder simple expansion locomotive, but contended that if two, instead of three, main valve gears could be used, as in certain four-cylinder engines, one of the principal objections which from time to time has been urged against three-cylinder engines would be removed". The upshot was Gresley's

Spencer, in his paper, said that: "Other distinctive features were the fitting of a 6ft 5in diameter tapered boiler with combustion chamber, and the use of nickel-chrome steel for the piston, coupling rods and connecting rods". The use of this steel gave the motion a light and graceful appearance. The final development of Gresley's valve gear owed much to G. J. Churchward, who's valve design was still the standard at Swindon.

I first saw No. 4472 *Flying Scotsman* at the Wembley Exhibition in 1924, shortly before I sailed for Burma to join my regiment on first commission. I thought her the most magnificent engine I had ever seen, and I still regret that I did not pay similar attention to her beautifully

Gresley A3 class Pacific *Flying Scotsman* as BR No.60103 on the 9.52am King's Cross to York "Westminster Bank Railway Society" special, climbing Holloway Bank on 3rd April 1955. *(Philip J. Kelley)*.

turned out neighbour, No. 4073 *Caerphilly Castle*.

As originally built, Gresley's Pacifics had 8in diameter piston valves with $1\frac{1}{4}$in lap and a maximum travel of $4\frac{9}{16}$in at 65% cut-off. The short lap valves resulted from experience with the conjugated valve gear on the three cylinder K3 class 2-6-0s, which were built with 8in

diameter piston valves, $1\frac{1}{2}$in lap, and a maximum travel of $6\frac{3}{8}$in at 75% cut-off. During trials with the first of these big 2-6-0 locomotives, No. 1000, on express trains in Great Northern days, the centre steam chest cover was damaged by contact with the valve spindle crosshead. "This", said Spencer, "had been caused by over-running of the

Collett 'Castle' class 4-cylinder 4-6-0 No.5043 *Earl of Mount Edgcumbe* GWR. *(G.H. Soole Collection, Courtesy National Railway Museum, York)*.

centre valve which had occurred as a result of the engine being put into full gear when coasting at high speed with the regulator closed. " It was as a result of this trouble that Gresley decided on the above valve arrangements for his Pacifics, to minimise the possibility of valve overtravel. With this valve gear the Pacifics performed the duties required of them very well. Then in April and May 1925 came the exchange tests with the Great Western Railway in which the LNER Pacifics were matched against the GWR 'Castle' class 4-6-0s.

The 'Castles', produced under the Collett regime, were really Churchward 'Stars' with a larger boiler, and were therefore extremely good engines. The arguments about this locomotive exchange still continue; but whilst the 'Castle' scored easily with its low coal consumption and ran very fast up short gradients, the Pacific, owing to its big boiler, could out-run the Great Western engine up the long climbs of the GWR – a result which showed how right Churchward had been in wanting a Pacific with its big boiler and ample grate.

Nevertheless, it was clear that Swindon had got something that Doncaster had not. Gresley's technical assistant, Spencer, had suggested a long travel for the Pacifics, but Gresley had been doubtful. However, before the trials began there was apparently an opportunity at Doncaster to inspect the valves of a competing engine, *Pendennis Castle*, and on 23rd April Gresley gave instructions for one of the Pacifics to be fitted with long travel valves. The valve gear of No. 4477 *Gay Crusader* was modified and trials were conducted with valves having a $1\frac{5}{8}$ in lap. Spencer says in his paper that the results were most satisfactory; though it has been reported that his comments at the time were that a much better job could have been done. But the modest success with *Gay Crusader* led to the fitting of the completely redesigned valve gear that Spencer had himself suggested in 1924. The first engine to be fitted with this gear, in 1927, was No. 2555 *Centenary*, and in competition with other Pacifics which had the original short valve travel, the coal consumption, with trains of 500 tons, was reduced from 50 to 38lb per train mile. In the light of this performance, all the other 51 Pacifics were similarly modified, and it was the consequent reduction in coal consumption that made it feasible to run the "Flying Scotsman" express non-stop between London and Edinburgh from 1st May 1928.

Meanwhile, the economics which might be achieved with a higher working pressure were being considered. These A1 class Pacifics had a boiler pressure of 180psi and cylinders 20in by 26in. Two engines, No. 2544 *Lemberg* and No. 4480 *Enterprise*, were given new boilers carrying a pressure of 220psi. *Enterprise* retained the original cylinders, but *Lemberg's* were reduced in diameter to $18\frac{1}{2}$in. *Enterprise*, with its higher pressure, proved very successful. The increased power, as compared with the original A1s, enabled it to work the heaviest trains with relatively early cut-offs. *Lemberg* was tested in comparison with standard A1 class No. 4473 *Solario* between King's Cross and Doncaster. Of coal per mile *Solario* consumed 38.3lb and *Lemberg* 35.37, and the respective water

consumptions in lb per mile were 317.5 and 288.8. Both engines had the new valve arrangement and there was little to choose between them. However, *Solario* did more work than *Lemberg* because during its runs it had to compete with a greater wind resistance. Though the results were thus inconclusive, it was stated that *Lemberg* had struck a bad patch and her running was not truly representative. This is not convincing because the driver said that he had difficulty in holding *Lemberg* back; for it had been stipulated that both engines should run with a full regulator opening, and to do this, *Lemberg's* driver had, at times, to reduce his cut-off to 12%!

From these tests Gresley was satisfied that the increased boiler pressure would give a greater margin of power, and he directed that all future Pacifics should have the higher boiler pressure, whilst cylinders were fixed at 19in diameter. Engines so modified were classified A3. Later on, A3 class engines, beginning with No.2500 *Windsor Lad*, had a steam collector in the form of a steel pressing, integral with the dome, and fed by a series of slots $\frac{1}{2}$inch wide in the top of the barrel plate through which steam was passed to the regulator. This type of collector had advantages on the large diameter and high pitched boiler of the Pacifics, because the very low dome made it difficult to apply any form of centrifugal steam separator. Rather strangely *Lemberg*, with its smaller cylinders, was always noted as particularly free-running, with a reputation for speed.

A demonstration of what the A3 Pacific could do came in 1934. In 1933 the diesel-electric "Flying Hamburger" was running between Berlin and Hamburg, covering the 178 miles in 2 hours 18 minutes, at an average speed of 77.4mph. This performance caused considerable interest on the LNER, with the speculation as to whether similar trains could run on their own system. Gresley went to Germany in 1934 and travelled on the "Flying Hamburger". Following his report, he was authorised to discuss with the German constructors of the train the possibility of their building a similar three-coach train to run between London and Newcastle. The German engineers, after studying the LNER main line, calculated that one of their trains would need at least $4\frac{1}{4}$ hours to cover the 268 miles. Each train would seat 140 passengers, but not with the LNER standards of comfort, and meals would be restricted to a cold buffet service.

Neither the LNER General Manager nor Gresley were impressed with this report. Gresley undertook to try what one of his Pacifics could do, hauling a train of 147 tons, which, at four coaches, would be one coach better than the diesel. The trial train consisted of the LNER dynamometer car, a restaurant car, and two standard carriages. On 30th November 1934 the train left King's Cross for a run to Leeds and back, with the famous A1 class Pacific, No. 4472 *Flying Scotsman*, at the head and with Driver Sparshatt and Fireman Webster on the footplate. O. V. S. Bulleid was also on the footplate and Cecil J. Allen was in the train to record the trip. On the 'down' run the maximum speed was 95mph and Stoke summit was passed at 81mph. The 185 miles to Leeds took

151 minutes 56 seconds. For the return journey two more coaches were added at Leeds. The maximum speed, as recorded in the dynamometer car, was exactly 100mph near Little Bytham. The test run showed that Gresley's Pacifics could do better than the German diesel train and with double the number of coaches, offering far greater comfort and a full meal service.

Some months later, in March 1935, another test run was made this time from London to Newcastle and back. A3 class Pacific No. 2750 *Papyrus*, in the hands of Driver Gutteridge, had six coaches and a restaurant car behind it. The object this time was to do the run in the schedule proposed for a high speed service of four hours. In spite of a few miles of slow running and a dead stop for 19 seconds, due to a derailed goods train, Newcastle was reached three minutes early.

At Newcastle the engine crew changed, Sparshatt and Webster coming on again. On the return journey 105mph was attained at little Bytham, and C. J. Allen recorded a sustained 105.4mph thence to Essendine with a maximum of 108mph. Over the 12.3 miles from Corby to Tallington the speed was constantly over 100mph. The four-hour schedule was beaten by 8 minutes 12 seconds, and diesel haulage of express trains was not to be considered in Great Britain for another twelve years.

Gresley A3 class Pacific *Flying Scotsman*, as restored in LNER apple green livery with the number 4472. It approaches East Croydon station on 17th September 1966 with a special from London, Victoria to Eastleigh via Brighton.
(Peter Nicholson)

Chapter 9
The Nord Super-Pacifics

Asselin, who succeeded du Bousquet, having dispensed with the services of his predecessor's Baltics, found that new heavy express locomotives were needed badly. The Nord drawing office, on Asselin's direction, designed a light Pacific. But this project was abandoned and 20 compound Pacifics, of a type constructed for the Alsace-Lorraine Railway, with a deep firebox, were ordered from the Société Alsacienne. These, with some differences from the Alsace-Lorraine engines, were delivered in 1912. Numbered 3.1151-3.1170, they were much less powerful than the Baltics. They had poor steam passages with restricted admission ports, but gave reasonably satisfactory service because of the Nord's excellent fuel and very careful maintenance. Another fault was that the rear carrying axle was insufficiently loaded, resulting in derailment on sharp curves at locomotive depots. On the whole they performed as well as contemporary compound Pacifics on the other French railways, which had wide, or semi-wide, fire boxes in contrast with the narrow fireboxes of the Nord. However, as already pointed out, the other Pacifics were not particularly brilliant.

In 1913-14 it was apparent that the increasing weight of express trains would soon be beyond the capacity of the Asselin Pacifics, particularly when bad conditions necessitated working at the limit of their power.

The Nord drawing office produced a design for a new compound Pacific. Rather than returning to the wide firebox of the Baltics, they preferred the Nord's traditional narrow firebox, though rather longer, and they increased the diameter of the boiler. It was in effect a development of the Alsace-Lorraine Pacific, with an axle weight of $18\frac{1}{2}$ tons. However, the drawing office (under Ahend) had not forgotten du Bousquet's practice on the steam circuit, and the sections of the steam passages were increased. The drawing office thus produced the design for a remarkably good engine; for when the design was eventually translated

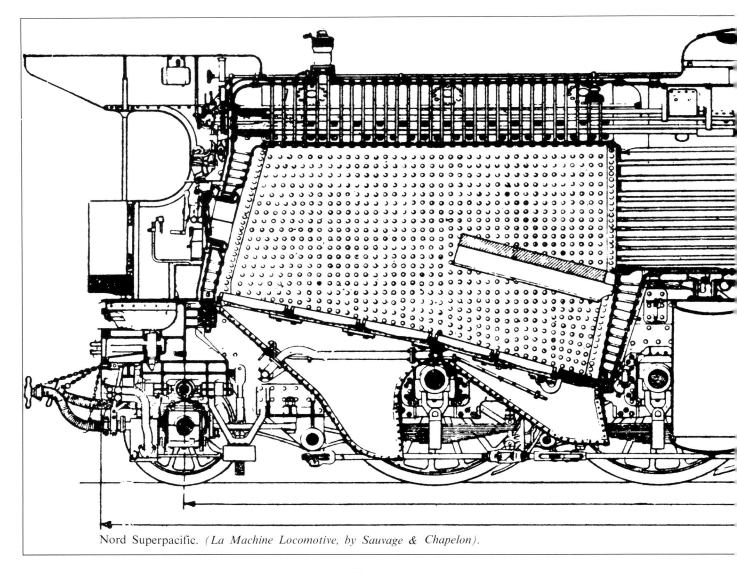

Nord Superpacific. (*La Machine Locomotive, by Sauvage & Chapelon*).

into production, the new Pacific, with a grate of only 37.6sq ft (as compared with the 42.5 to 43sq ft of the other French Pacifics) easily developed 2,700 indicated horsepower, which was greater by some 30% than the approximate 2,000ihp of any other French express locomotive of this type.

The design was very advanced when the outbreak of war in 1914 stopped further progress and it was not renewed until 1921-22. The new Pacifics, Nos 3.1201-3.1240, were ultimately completed in 1923-24 under the then CME, Bréville. They were immediately successful being powerful enough to allow the weight of express trains to be increased to 670 tons and to work trains of this weight over the easier gradients at the legal maximum of 75mph. Indeed, their outstanding performance led to them being unofficially designated "Superpacifics" – a name which stuck. Ten more were ordered, two of which were fitted with poppet valves – one on the Dabeg system and the other on the Caprotti. In 1933 these two were transformed into simple expansion engines with Cossart valve

gear. Again the aim was to achieve the same economic performance as a compound but without the latter's complexity and with a cheaper maintenance. Once again this hope was disappointed.

A minor drawback of the "Superpacifics" was the stress imposed on the actuating gear by the heavy balanced slide valves of the low pressure cylinders. A brilliant Nord locomotive engineer, Marc de Caso, produced a much lighter design of LP slide valve, almost halving the original weight, and valves of this type were fitted to a further eight "Superpacifics" built in 1929-30, as well as to 23 of the first series.

From 1923 until the early 1930s the "Superpacifics" were running the fastest and hardest express passenger trains in Europe, regularly hauling trains of 550-650 tons, at average start-to-stop speeds of 55-60mph, although the maximum speed was still limited to 75mph.

When George Collin, successor to Bréville as CME, decided to build a further series of 40 "Superpacifics", he and Léon Cossart, chief engineer for workshops and

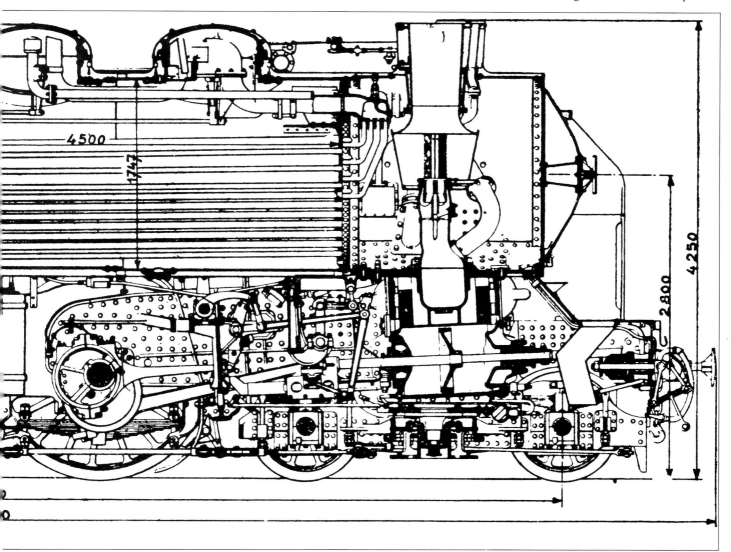

locomotives, gave Marc de Caso the task of redesigning the locomotive, within its overall parameters, where he considered it necessary to improve the robustness and layout of frames and mechanism to reduce maintenance. This he did. These 40, built 1931-32, had the LP slide valves replaced by 15in piston valves and the boiler pressure increased from 232 to 246psi. From 1935 these engines were fitted with Lemaître multiple jet blast pipes. This enabled the exhaust back pressure to be reduced considerably, and the maximum power was increased to 3,000ihp. On one occasion a 610 ton train was accelerated from 18mph to a sustained 66mph up a 1 in 200 gradient. The power output was little less than that of a Pennsylvania K4 Pacific with a 70sq ft grate area. Another engine, pulling a 667 ton train at 76mph on the Amiens-Boulogne section, on 23rd December 1932, developed 2,800ihp and 1,840dbhp. Ability to run fast was demonstrated during deceleration trials on 13th September 1935. No. 3.1290 reached a speed of 102mph with a train of 300 tons down a gradient of 1 in 250.

SNCF 4-6-2 No.231G42 heads the Locomotive Club of Great Britain "Calaise-Lille Rail Tour" on 14th May 1967, and is seen during a photographic stop at St Pol.
(Peter Nicholson)

Chapter 10
Steam Revolution

It is probable that André Chapelon, who was born in 1892, exercised more influence on steam locomotive design than any other engineer since George Stephenson. Not only did all French railways, besides his own Paris-Orléans, rebuild their principal existing locomotives, to a greater or lesser degree, according to the principles established so successfully by Chapelon, but in Great Britain, engines designed by Gresley, Stanier, Bulleid, and Riddles owed much of their success to them.

In 1921, after distinguished war service as an officer in the French Heavy Artillery, Chapelon returned to his pre-war technical studies, and, after graduating as Ingénieur des Arts et Manufactures, he joined the Paris-Lyon-Méditerraneé Railway as a probationer. During the time that he spent with the PLM, the aspect of the railway's handling of locomotives that impressed him most unfavourably was the drivers' habit of running their engines (particularly the four-cylinder simple expansion Pacifics) with 50% cut-off and partly opened regulator. This practice reduced the 170psi pressure in the boiler to about 57psi in the cylinders. It was soon apparent to him that there were few openings on the PLM for promotion and little scope for a disciple of Nicholas Sadi Carnot, founder of the science of thermo-dynamics. In the autumn of 1924 he left the PLM and joined the Société Industrielle des Téléphones, where his ability resulted in him being promoted Assistant Manager the following year. But he was not happy there because, as he told me, he suffered from "steam locomotive nostalgia".

His professor of thermo-dynamics at the Ecole Centrale, Louis Lacoin, had formed a high opinion of Chapelon's technical ability. He was a cousin of Maurice Lacoin, Engineer-in-Chief of Rolling Stock and Motive Power (equivalent to CME) on the Paris-Orléans Railway, and thanks to Louis Lacoin's help, Chapelon was appointed on 12th January 1925 to the Research and Development Section of the Paris-Orléans.

On the PO he came under the orders of a remarkable engineer, Paul Billet, who had created the Research and Development Section as an adjunct of the Design Office, which he had accused of being too absorbed by work in connection with existing equipment. At his direction Chapelon was put to work in connection with trials and charged particularly with improving the exhaust system of the Pacifics and other locomotives.

Indicator diagrams of the Pacifics' cylinder performance had shown throttling of the steam at the admission to the cylinders, high back pressure at the exhaust, and a considerable drop in pressure in the intermediate receiver between the high and low pressure cylinders. Superheating had increased the power of the Pacifics by 20%, but even then they could not develop more than 2,000 indicated horsepower, whilst the Atlantics could attain a peak of 1,600ihp, or even 1,900, and they were not superheated.

The PO's problem was how to provide sufficient power to haul the heavier trains. The normal solution would have been to build new engines of modern design, but this would have been expensive, and because the decision had already been taken to electrify the PO main lines, new locomotives could expect only a short life. It was resolved, therefore, to see what could be done to improve existing stock.

In 1919 a device to improve the exhaust of gas and steam had been invented by a Finnish engineer named Kylälä, and from this Chapelon developed in 1926 his Kylchap exhaust. This was so designed as to produce an adequate draught over the whole smokebox and to mix the gases so well with the exhaust steam that the mixture might be expelled with the minimum of effort. From the top of the exhaust standpipe, leading from the cylinders, the exhaust steam passed through a conical blastpipe nozzle fitted with four radial wedge-shaped inserts. These inserts divided the steam into four jets which, drawing some of the hot gases with them, passed into the four lobes of the Kylälä spreader which was mounted a short distance above. This division of the exhaust steam into four jets improved still further the entrainment of the hot gases above the exit from these lobes where most of the hot gases circulated; the mixture then being carried upwards through a petticoat to a final mixing with the remainder of the gases and out through the chimney.

A very large locomotive had insufficient height within the loading gauge to allow proper proportions to the draughting assembly. For such an engine two complete Kylchap exhausts with two chimneys placed one behind the other were usually provided; and on the most powerful locomotives there were three of such assemblies. The reason for these multiple Kylchaps was that, owing to the limit imposed by the loading gauge, the chimney of a large locomotive is necessarily very short. Ideally a chimney should have a height equal to three times its narrowest diameter; but it is generally less, even though its extension downwards into the smokebox may compensate for the lack of external height. Research having demonstrated that the chimneys in general use were inadequate for big and powerful locomotives, many large engines were provided with chimneys of almost double the normal diameter. But because this reduced the height to width ratio, the benefits, with the short chimneys which large boiler barrels dictated, were doubtful. To try to remedy this, Legein of the Belgian State Railways achieved considerable success in 1925 with double chimneys.

In 1926 trials of the Kylchap exhaust were carried out on compound Pacifics of the 4500 and 3500 classes, the simple Pacifics of the 3591 class, and other large PO locomotives. The results were most encouraging, for there was a significant improvement in steaming and a reduction of back pressure. On Pacific No. 4597 there was such an increase in draught that the exhaust pipe had to be so widened that the back pressure was reduced by 25%. On trial with the regulator wide open there was a cylinder pressure of 224psi instead of the previous figure of 112, and this was with cut-offs of 40% HP and 70% LP. In addition the engine showed an economy in coal consumption of 16%. Similar results were obtained with No. 4528 which, unlike No. 4597, was not superheated.

It was apparent to Chapelon that even better results could be obtained by increasing the cross-sectional area of the steam passages and, to be on the safe side, he believed it should be doubled. Also he would eliminate sharp bends in the steam pipes and increase the volume of the steam chests. By these means he would reduce the losses from throttling which were occurring in the steam circuit from the regulator through to the HP and LP cylinders. In 1897 the Nord Company had carried out experiments as a result of which the steam circuit proportions were established which ensured the success of the Atlantics. These included large steam chests to regulate the flow of steam between boiler and cylinders and so lessen the losses from fluctuations in pressure due to throttling. Chapelon deduced that to obtain the correct proportions in the LP steam chests of the PO Pacifics, it would be necessary to quadruple them in size to equal approximately the volume of the cylinders.

Chapelon calculated that his proposed improvements to the exhaust and to the steam circuit should (according to a theoretical diagram), with a 40% cut-off and at a speed of 60mph, result in an increase in the (obtained) indicated horsepower of a PO Pacific from 1,936 to 2,406; that is, a gain of 25% in both power and efficiency. But this was by no means the extent of the improvements that could be affected. Chapelon had measured the temperature in the intermediate receiver of one of the superheated locomotives and had found that the degree of superheat in the LP cylinders was practically nil. It was evident there-

fore that if the condensation in the LP group could be eliminated there would be a still further gain in the efficiency of the engines. The improvement in economy of the superheated over the original saturated engines was about 20%, and this was with 300°C (572°F) of superheat; but the gain was practically entirely in the HP cylinders. If the LP cylinders could be made to contribute their proper share it seemed reasonable to anticipate a further 10%. Chapelon estimated that to obtain such a result it would be necessary to raise the temperature of the superheat by 100°C (180°F) at the admission to the HP cylinders. The provision of oil and castings suitable for this higher temperature presented a potential problem, but he was able to solve it satisfactorily.

From these calculations Chapelon now assessed the overall improvement that could be expected from a PO Pacific locomotive rebuilt in accordance with the above principles. Taking the average indicated horsepower of a superheated Pacific of the large wheeled 3500 class running at high speed to be 1,850, he reckoned that his proposed improvements in the steam circuit would raise the ihp by 20% to 2,200, and that the increase in superheat should raise it a further 10% to 2,400. On top of this the improved draughting with the Kylchap exhaust should increase the boiler output by 25% above the previous limit and so raise the ihp to 3,000.

Put like this, as André Chapelon put it to me, the

Chapelon rebuilt Pacific No.231.E.31, purchased by the Nord Railway on the "Paris-Londres Ferry Boat de Nuit" on the way to Dunkirk on 8th June 1957.
(Philip J. Kelley).

whole process looks so simple that the brilliance of the reasoning can easily be overlooked. A very modest man, Chapelon maintained that he had only followed in the footsteps of eminent predecessors: Anatole Mallet, Henry of the PLM, du Bousquet of the Nord, G.J. Churchward of the Great Western, Nadal of the Etat, and Wilhelm Schmidt the superheater pioneer. Yet perhaps no other locomotive engineer since George Stephenson had produced such a revolutionary doctrine in steam locomotive design.

As a result of Chapelon's argument, and in the light of results obtained in putting it to the test, it was decided in November 1926 to rebuild one of the 3500 class Pacifics on these lines. Because of the high superheat entailed, the locomotive chosen was one of which it had already been intended to try the Lentz poppet valve system, and for which arrangements had been made with Messrs Paxman & Co. of London, licensees of the Lentz patent. Rotary cams were proposed at first, but Chapelon preferred to keep the existing Walschaerts valve gear to actuate oscillating cams. The engine chosen was No. 3566, regarded by the enginemen as the worst of the whole class, and so bad indeed that they had named it *Cholera*!

It was November 1929 before the rejuvenated *Cholera* emerged from the PO's Tours Works. The reason for this lengthy delay after the decision to rebuild the engine was the death of Billet and the retirement in 1927 of Lacoin, who was succeeded by Louis de Boysson. The two men who had faith in Chapelon's project had gone, de Boysson knew nothing about it, and others in authority had no confidence in it. At last Chapelon himself wrote a note to de Boysson, drawing his attention to the great interest that had been taken in the rebuilding plan when it had originally been approved. De Boysson sent for Chapelon and asked him for a full explanation of the whole project, and then sanctioned its completion.

In addition to the improvements outlined above, the rebuilt engine had an ACFI feed-water heater and a Nicholson thermic syphon. The purpose of this latter equipment was to improve the circulation of the water in the boiler and accelerate the increase in pressure after lighting up and after closing the regulator. The Kylchap exhaust was double with two chimneys.

No. 3566 ran her first trials on 19th November 1929, almost exactly a hundred years after the triumph of Stephenson's *Rocket* at Rainhill. By contemporary standards, the performance of the engine was just as astonishing. Chapelon's calculations were completely fulfilled, for No. 3566 developed about 3,000ihp at a speed of between 75 and 80mph hauling a heavy train, and with an economy over the unrebuilt engines of 25% at normal power outputs. The new locomotive sprang to immediate fame, not only in France but in most other countries of the Western world; for it was apparent that this was a quite revolutionary development in steam locomotive power – and one obtained not by a new engine but by rebuilding an existing one.

Extensive trials were carried out with the one-time *Cholera* on ordinary and special trains over the Paris-Bordeaux main line, south of the electrified section which ended at Les Aubrais (near Orléans). On 4th April 1930 the engine covered the 70.6 miles from Poitiers to Angoulême with a train of 368 tons at a speed which remained absolutely constant at the legal limit of 75mph, irrespective of gradient. On the engine was Edmond Epinay, who had just taken over from de Boysson (after the latter's short tenure as Chief of Rolling Stock and Motive Power), and who described the run as the most remarkable event of his career.

Another notable trial took place on 24th March 1931 to ascertain the practicability of a scheduled time of 5 hours 50 minutes over the 365 miles between Paris and Bordeaux. The train of 457 tons left Paris behind an electric locomotive, and No. 3566 took over at Les Aubrais. The whole run was completed in 5 hours 48 minutes at the overall average speed of 62.5mph without exceeding the 75mph limit, and included the change from electric to steam traction at Les Aubrais. From thence to Bordeaux is 286 miles and No. 3566 covered this in 4 hours 26 minutes, including a stop of 8 minutes at Poitiers. In spite of numerous slacks imposed by the permanent way department, average speeds included 65mph between Les Aubrais and Poitiers, and 64.4mph between Poitiers and Bordeaux. Passengers on the train included Marcel Bloch, Engineer-in-Chief of Rolling Stock and Workshops (under Epinay), who said on arrival at Bordeaux, "Chapelon you have certainly achieved something (*Vous avez fait quelque chose*)".

This run was undertaken to ascertain the practicability of a scheduled time of 5 hours 50 minutes between Paris and Bordeaux and it was clear that not only was this possible with the power available to the locomotive but that other accelerations of from one hour to one and a half hours could be made between Paris and Bordeaux. Indeed, Epinay, having experienced such timings himself, insisted on them being put into effect as more engines became available. For, in the light of the startling success of these trials, it had already been decided to rebuild Pacifics Nos 3501-20 of 1909, which were still using saturated steam. All were rebuilt at Tours in 1931-32 and were ready for the summer service. No. 3566 was renumbered 3701, as the first of a new 3700 class, and the other engines became 3702-20 (though not consecutively in their original numerical order). There were slight differences from the rebuilt *Cholera*, including a boiler pressure raised from 232psi to 246 and the replacement of the Robinson superheater by the Houlet pattern which gave higher superheat. All these effectively new engines were allocated to Tours depot and worked heavy express trains and "Rapides" between Les Aubrais and Bordeaux, and over the PO's other easily graded main line from Tours to Nantes.

Trials over this latter line had taken place in 1932. On 12th March of that year No. 3701 took over a train from Paris to Redon (317 miles) at Les Aubrais. Departure was delayed owing to a faulty coach, which had to be detached from the train, reducing the load from 475 tons to 345. Redon, some 40 miles beyond Nantes, is an

important junction on the way to Brest. In spite of four stops and 15 slacks, the overall average speed from Paris to Redon was 61.3mph. The average running speed between Les Aubrais and Redon was 78.8mph, with a specially authorised maximum for the trial of 84.3mph. Jean Lancrenon, CME of the Nord, was on the train and as a result of this run he decided to order 20 similar rebuilt engines from the PO and to have another 28 built new by private industry. This is probably the only occasion in railway history of express locomotives being built new for a railway, which were copies of rebuilds of another company – and this from the Nord! Truly the "Superpacifics" had lost their crown.

Left: Southbound "Blue Train" near Pont de Briques, hauled by Chapelon rebuilt Pacific No.231.E.6. (231.E was the Nord classification of these engines)
(P. Ransome-Wallis Collection, Courtesy National Railway Museum, York).

This decision by Lancrenon was confirmed by trials carried on the Nord later in 1932. The locomotives participating were Chapelon Pacific No. 3715, a Nord "Superpacific" of the 3.1250 class, a PLM Mountain (4-8-2) and an Est Mountain. It would have been difficult to collect more interesting engines for comparative tests, each supreme on its own railway, and probably together regarded as the best that France had.

The Nord Pacific belonged to a class of 1931 which was a modified version of the 3.1200 series built in 1923 and (as previously mentioned) at the time some 30% more powerful than any other French Pacifics. Certain defects, however, had led to costly maintenance and the modifications introduced in the 3.1250s were designed to rectify these. The Est 4-8-2 was one of a class built in 1925. In 1928 the Etat Railway wanted to run their boat trains over the very difficult 231 miles between Paris and Cherbourg (with one intermediate stop) in $4\frac{1}{2}$ hours and to load them to 600 tons. As they had no engines that would do the job, the Etat arranged trials with a 3.1200 class Nord Pacific and one of the Est Mountains. Its substantially larger grate and increased adhesion favoured the Est engine and the Etat accordingly ordered 40 of this type – a very considerable order, for the Est themselves had only 41. The PLM Mountain, No. 241.C.1 was a solitary example which had been completed on 30th December 1930.

Left: Nord Chapelon Pacific No.231.E.5 at Paris (La Chapelle) ready to work the "Flèche d'Or" express to Calais on 23rd March 1957.
(Philip J. Kelley Collection).

It was a successor to the earlier 241.A class of 1925 (but with 6ft $6\frac{3}{4}$in coupled wheels instead of 5ft 11in) and the prototype of the later 241.P class built for the SNCF in 1948, though the latter embodied many modifications due to Chapelon under whose authority they were produced.

There was a particularly interesting aspect of these engines in that, as Baron Gerard Vuillet has pointed out in his book *Railway Reminiscences in Three Continents*, they represented two schools of locomotive design. The main lines of the Est and the PLM mostly follow the valleys of the great rivers and are therefore routed in long sweeping curves. In consequence these railways always built their locomotives with rather thin frames so that they could flex to the curves. In addition, because their gradients were long but not severe, short periods of high power working were not required of them. The main lines of the Nord and the PO, on the other hand, generally cut across the valleys and were characterised by a number of short steep climbs and consequent difficult starts from many of their stations. Their locomotives had thick frames and were strongly built to meet the heavy demands of power over their often switch-back routes.

The trials took place in the winter of 1932-33 and entailed the haulage of special trains with frequent stops between Paris and Boulogne, firstly of 650 and later of 750 tons, and also the working of the "Flèche d'Or" ("Golden Arrow") service between Paris and Calais, with its load increased to 650 tons. On the footplate of No. 3715 were Head Driver Réné Gourault and Fireman Léonce Miot.

As had been foreseen, the Mountains showed to advantage with trains of 750 tons making frequent stops, their eight-coupled wheels giving them an advantage over the Pacifics. Nevertheless, even with 750 ton trains, No. 3715 put up a very good performance, returning from Boulogne in a time five minutes quicker than No. 241.C.1 and 16 seconds faster than the Est engine. The Nord "Superpacific" was unfortunately below form for its class and was not therefore tried on the 750 ton trains. The Est Mountain was not only inferior in power to the Chapelon Pacific but had the heaviest consumption of all the competing engines. Actually three of the Est Mountains took part in turn, for first one and then another fractured those long slender frames on the gruelling Nord main line.

The big PLM Mountain produced the highest drawbar horsepower but at the cost of double the expense in running maintenance as compared with the other competing locomotives. Chapelon's engine was by far the best. Its consumption of coal and water was the lowest of all, and it recorded the finest performance in the haulage of the "Flèche d'Or", passing the summit of the 24.9 miles long Gannes bank (1/333-1/250) at 74.6mph. The Nord locomotive men were very impressed with the engine, particularly Locomotive Inspector Cugnet, who was with Chapelon on the footplate during this run.

Cugnet had not been able to conceal his enthusiasm when the Gannes summit was passed at this speed with 650 tons. The engine had its regulator fully open, cut-offs were 60% in the HP cylinders and 58% in the LP, the pressure was high, and the water level held. It was a great triumph for Chapelon, and also for those two enthusiasts, driving and firing, Gouralt and Miot. After the trials were over, the Nord went ahead with its order for 20 rebuilt Pacifics from the PO, and in 1936-37 it ordered the other 28 built new by private firms.

PLM Pacific No.231.K.27 rebuilt on Chapelon lines, at the head of the "Flèche d'Or" express, passing Hesdigneul in 1968. A number of the 231.K class were sent to the ex-Nord lines of the SNCF.
(P. Ransome-Wallis Collection, Courtesy of National Railway Museum, York).

The PO also rebuilt ten more of its Pacifics for its own needs, and these embodied certain improvements in the light of experience. On trial one of these produced 3,700ihp and 3,400 dbhp at 87.5mph on the Vitry test bank. As Chapelon told the author, these figures proved that he had succeeded in the aim of most designers of compound locomotives in getting as much work out of the LP as the HP cylinders. Eventually there were 102 of these engines, of which 31 were rebuilt for the PO, 23 were rebuilt for the Est, and 48 were rebuilt or built new for the Nord; so the Nord finished up with having considerably more of them than the PO itself!

The performance of Chapelon's rebuilt Pacifics aroused great and immediate interest in Great Britain, and in no person more than Gresley. During the trials with the Kylchap exhaust, before the rebuilding of *Cholera*, Gresley had sent O.V.S. Bulleid, his principal assistant, to Tours to watch some of them, and before the end of 1925 he went himself to France and visited Chapelon. As an immediate result of this visit Gresley decided to try the Kylchap exhaust on one of his 'Shire' class 4-4-0 engines. Chapelon supplied the drawings and a single Kylchap exhaust was fitted at Darlington to No. 251 (the same number as the first of Ivatt's large Atlantics) *Derbyshire*. In 1930 Chapelon came to England and rode on the footplate of No. 251. The engine rode quite well, but a mistake had been made in the construction of the Kylchap assembly, so that the

performance was not as good as it should have been. The four lobes of the Kylälä spreader, instead of being entirely separate from each other, had been connected just below the top by iron ties, thus creating an obstruction which impeded the gas flow through the centre of the apparatus and preventing it from functioning properly. Chapelon pointed out the defect and suggested that it should be put right. No. 322 *Huntingdonshire*, one of the engines fitted with Lentz poppet valves, had been similarly fitted in 1929. Probably due to prejudice (for Kylchap exhausts were regarded with enthusiasm by the LNER in later years) the Kylchap was removed from both engines in 1930, but Chapelon never knew this.

Many locomotives of other French railways were rebuilt between 1932 and 1936 on the lines advocated by Chapelon. Even the mighty PLM, which did not follow lightly in the steps of other French railways, rebuilt many of its Pacifics on Chapelon lines. The first to be taken in hand was Pacific No. 231.F.141, which was given an improved steam circuit and new cylinders with piston valves. A double blast pipe was fitted; the dimensions being the same as Chapelon's, but with a variable double clover exhaust instead of the Kylchap device. There was a new boiler, pressed to 292psi, with an improved superheater and an ACFI feed water heater. The engine was renumbered 231.H. 141, and its performance was so good that it became the prototype of 30 231.H class Pacifics, rebuilt from those which had already been converted to compounds from the original simple expansion engines.

Other PLM Pacifics were also rebuilt, though on a more modest scale than the 231.Hs. Of these, twelve were classified 231.K and no less than 118 became Class 231.G. As compared with the 231.H class, the 231.Gs retained the

Above: Nord Chapelon Pacific No.231.E.16 on the northbound "Fléche d'Or" near Pont de Briques.
(P. Ransome-Wallis Collection, Courtesy National Railway Museum, York).

Below: Chapelon Pacific No.231.E.9 on a Paris-Calais boat train near Pont de Briques 1958.
(P. Ransome-Wallis Collection, Courtesy National Railway Museum, York).

original and larger HP cylinders, as well as the original boiler with its pressure of 232psi, whilst the 231.Ks were similar to the 231.Gs except that they had a slightly shorter boiler and independent HP and LP valve gears. In the later days of steam a number of these engines, displaced by electrification, were transferred to the Nord. At Calais I stood on the footplate of a 231.K, waiting to pull out the "Flèche d'Or" express, and chattered to the driver and fireman, who were well satisfied with their PLM engine.

On the Etat, Raoul Dautry was so enthusiastic about Chapelon's achievement that he stopped existing development on his own railway and gave orders that existing Pacifics were to be rebuilt exactly on Chapelon lines and ordered new engines to the same design.

Above: PLM Pacific No.231.K.58 on a Boulogne-Paris train near Pont de Briques.
(P. Ransome-Wallis Collection, Courtesy National Railway Museum, York).

Below: PLM 231.K.51 on a train from Tergnier entering Paris, (Gare du Nord) in 1961.
(P. Ransome-Wallis Collection, Courtesy National Railway Museum, York).

Above: PLM Pacific No.231.K.8 and other locomotives at Paris (La Chapelle) on 23rd March 1957.
(Philip J Kelley).

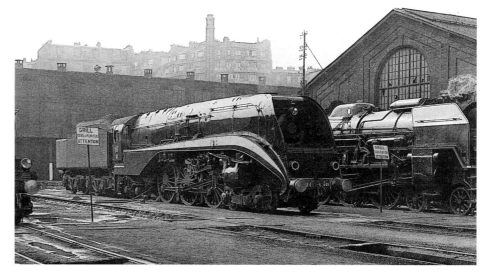

Right: De Caso 3-cylinder compound 4-6-4 No.232.S.001 at Paris (La Chapelle) on 23rd March 1957. (De Caso built eight 4-6-4 locomotives for the Nord Region of the SNCF, the last in 1949, all incorporating Chapelon techniques; four were 3-cylinder compounds of Class 232.S, three were 3-cylinder simples of Class 232.R, and one a 4-cylinder compound, Class 232.U.)
(Philip J. Kelley).

Right: Etat Railway 231.G class 4-cylinder compound Pacific No.231G.780 (originally 231.500 class built 1914 onwards). All of these engines were rebuilt as classes 231.D, 231.F, 231.G, or 231.H, the first three classes being on Chapelon lines. This engine is shown at Paris (Batignolles) on 23rd March 1957.
(Philip J. Kelley).

Chapter 11

Stanier's Pacifics

After the Grouping of the old railway companies in 1923 to form the large London Midland & Scottish Railway, it was the erstwhile Midland Railway of the Group which became dominant in locomotive affairs. Midland men believed that the Midland practice of frequent and light trains would be suitable for all the main lines of the LMS and that the Midland Compound was the primary engine for the task. But it was soon found that the trains over the old London & North Western route between London and Carlisle remained just as heavy as in pre-Grouping days. A LNWR 'George' or 'Prince' (and of course a 'Claughton') could haul them, but a Midland Compound (in LNW hands) could not. The reason that the Compounds performed indifferently on the lines of the old LNWR was that the drivers had not been trained in compound working.

and immediately wound the reversing gear to notch 6, halfway to mid-gear. We had a full boiler and were blowing-off. Naturally, our progress was extremely slow.

After a few hundred yards I persuaded the driver to push the regulator right across and drop down into full-gear. He was apprehensive as to what would happen to the water level in the boiler – but I was able to reassure him. With one injector on, the regulator wide open and in full gear we sailed up the bank in great style to the pleased astonishment of the driver." Here at least was one Western Division convert to the Midland Compounds. R.A. Riddles told the author that the Midland Compounds were good engines up to a load of 350 tons; but a 'George' or a 'Prince' could take 420 tons on the fastest schedules. A Compound had a greater thermal efficiency than a 'George', but a 400 ton train would

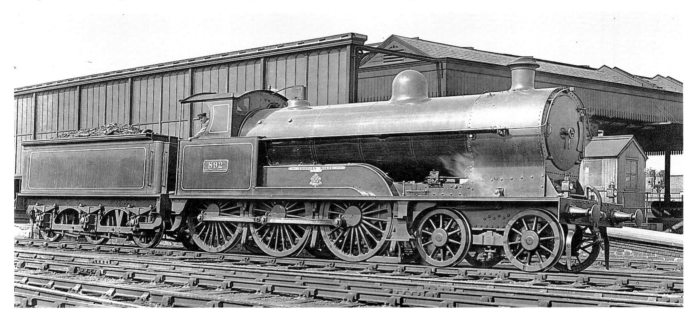

Bowen Cooke's 'Prince of Wales' class 4-6-0 No.892 *Charles Wolfe* **LNWR. (Riddles told the author that these were the finest express engines on the LNWR – he drove one during the General Strike of 1926.)**
(Courtesy National Railway Museum, York).

In his book, *A Lifetime with Locomotives* (Bath, Goose & Son, 1975, p56), R.C. Bond writes: "Compound working on these engines depended on the regulator being opened on to the second valve to shut off the auxiliary live steam supply to the low pressure cylinders. This was not often understood. Nor was the fact appreciated that every notch on the reversing gear of a Compound denotes a much greater overall ratio of expansion than on a simple expansion engine. I recall one journey very clearly. It was from Liverpool, Lime Street to Crewe with one stop at Runcorn. Starting away from Runcorn at the bottom of the two-mile bank at about 1 in 115 up to Sutton Weaver the driver opened the regulator on to the first valve only

require two Compounds which burnt more coal than one 'George'. (Both Robert Riddles and Roland Bond were my great friends, but the former, of course, was North Western and the latter Midland.)

The need for more powerful express locomotives was ultimately met by the 4-6-0 'Royal Scot' class, the first of which appeared in August 1927. The design of these had been mainly entrusted to the North British Locomotive Company, with whom the LMS placed an order for 50. There were some Midland features and Derby did manage a Midland appearance. All the engines were in service before the end of 1927. They were an immediate success and their advent was accompanied by an attractive little booklet by S.P.B. Mais, *Royal Scot and her Forty Nine Sisters*, illustrated by photographs and by the badges of the regiments which they commemorated or by drawings of the old engines after which they were named. Amongst the relevant poetic extracts quoted by Mais was an anonymous

LMS 'Royal Scot' class 3-cylinder 4-6-0 No.6115 *Scots Guardsman*.
(P. Ransome-Wallis Collection, Courtesy National Railway Museum, York).

one from *Punch*: "The liners of the land, the clippers of the clay, the great big blazing thundering things that ply the permanent way". It was probably the most striking publication that has ever paid tribute to a steam locomotive.

At last the LMS had a stud of fast and powerful express passenger engines that could bear comparison with those of the other big companies. Fast and heavy expresses were once more, in the North Western tradition, steaming in succession out of Euston with one engine at the head. Another batch of 20 'Royal Scots' was built at Derby in 1930. The Works Superintendent at Derby was H.G. Ivatt and the Assistant Works Superintendent was R.A. Riddles. The latter had much to do with their construction and had a very high opinion of them. He told me that, perhaps owing to the rapidity with which they had been designed and constructed, certain faults developed, resulting in heavy coal consumption, rough riding, and hot boxes; but that modifications were produced which corrected these troubles.

All the 'Royal Scots' were ultimately rebuilt with new tapered boilers and double chimneys from designs prepared under Stanier, though appearing under his successors Fairburn and Ivatt. The rebuilds proved to be, in the opinion of many commentators, the finest express passenger 4-6-0s ever built in Great Britain. In the 1948 interchange trials they outclassed the Great Western 'Kings', and in drawbar horsepower they equalled the Pacifics taking part in the trials. In the rebuilding, much

of Chapelon's teaching had been followed, particularly in internal streamlining of steam ports and passages, and it was to these improvements that the superiority of the rebuilds over the original 'Royal Scots' was primarily due. T.S. Coleman, Stanier's chief designer, had been particularly interested in Chapelon's work and had obtained Stanier's permission to rebuild two 'Jubilee' class engines which, in effect, became the prototypes of the subsequently converted 'Royal Scots'. Though the metamorphosis was not so complete, the change which Tom Coleman's design effected in the 'Royal Scots' was somewhat similar to Chapelon's revolutionary improvement of the PO Pacifics.

The above has, of course, gone far ahead of events. In January 1932 W.A. Stanier came from the Great Western Railway to be Chief Mechanical Engineer of the London Midland & Scottish. In 1931 Riddles had been transferred back to Crewe as Assistant Works Superintendent to F.A. Lemon, and he had not been in his new post long before Stanier arrived. "And," said Riddles, "we started on the 4-6-2 *The Princess Royal* – new ideas, new methods, an anxiety to please the new CME – all absorbing and exciting!"

The background to this big new engine lay in the conditions of the times. Trade depression and strenuous competition from road transport were affecting railway revenues seriously, and many different schemes were being studied for retaining the existing traffic on the railways and for tempting back from the roads some of that which had been lost. For passenger traffic the LMS had decided on a programme of more trains, faster trains, and more attractive trains; and the question was being asked whether, as a commercial proposition, it would be possible to run through from Euston to Glasgow, a distance

Right: LMS 'Patriot' class 3-cylinder 4-6-0 *Royal Signals*, rebuilt from a LNWR 'Claughton' class 4-cylinder 4-6-0 on a 'Royal Scot' class type chassis. Engines of this class were known as "Baby Scots" in their early days. *(LMS Railway).*

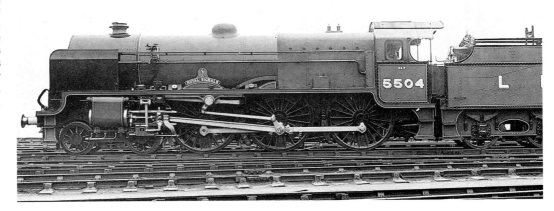

Above: Stanier rebuild of the 'Royal Scot' class, as BR No.46158 *The Loyal Regiment* at Bletchley on the 'up' "Manxman" express in 1954. *(P. Ransome-Wallis Collection, Courtesy National Railway Museum, York).*

Left: Rebuilt 'Royal Scot' class 4-6-0 No.46168 *The Girl Guide* at Crewe Works 29th August 1962. *(Philip J. Kelley).*

GWR 'King' class 4-6-0 No.6001 *King Edward VII* leaving Westbury on a Paddington-Penzance express. It was from this class that Stanier took many of the dimensions for his 'Princess Royal' class Pacifics.
(G.H. Soole Collection, Courtesy National Railway Museum, York).

of more than 400 miles, without an intermediate stop. Before 1933 no locomotive on the LMS, not even a 'Royal Scot' could do such a journey as a regular performance.

"Stanier," remarked Riddles to the author, "faced the task of providing one". He no doubt had memories of *The Great Bear*, and the success of Gresley's Pacifics persuaded him to set about the task of designing a large Pacific type engine. The result was *The Princess Royal* with four cylinders, 250psi pressure, and a tractive effort of 40,300lbs." Riddles said that they worked literally day and night to get the engine ready by the date fixed for inspection by the Directors at Euston. The boiler was the biggest ever yet built at Crewe and presented a continual problem, even to the clothing.

The old North Western boiler covering, to which Crewe was accustomed, was merely a poor quality felt, which was whitewashed on one side and which after a short time was completely scorched away between the lagging bands. The lagging for the Pacific was derived from Great Western practice. It was a kind of loose asbestos, covering firebox and barrel; but it arrived in this loose state and the problem was to get it on. Riddles said that he went down to the boiler testing shop late one night to find them all in despair. They had been told to put the covering on whilst the boiler was hot under test, but it would not stick. Riddles was at a loss to know what to do. Then he remembered an occasion during the war when, as a Royal Engineer officer he was constructing quarters on Salisbury Plain with a batch of German prisoners of war at his disposal. Some of the quarters

were stucco finished and he had been intrigued to see these Germans standing with buckets of stone and gravel and throwing handfuls with such force that they stuck. He wondered if this could provide the answer to the problem, and told one of the men to bring him a bucket of the stuff. He said, "I took a handful and threw it at the barrel and to my delight it stuck there. By 2.30 in the morning the barrel was beautifully and evenly covered."

Work continued night and day and the great occasion for its journey to Euston arrived all too soon. There was no time for any preliminary trial, for, hard as they had worked, they could not get the engine ready to leave the works until the day before the inspection. At 5am, therefore, the Pacific left the works, without any previous trial in steam, to run the 158 miles to Euston 'light engine' in the gentle time of ten hours – none too long a time for an untried engine that was the first of its class. It had been arranged that Riddles should ride on the footplate as far as Rugby where he would hand over to the Works Superintendent, F.A. Lemon. Buckets of oil were carried on the footplate and frequent shops were made 'just in case', whilst examinations were carried out and much oil was poured on. The news of the new engine had got around and even at that early hour they were accorded something of a triumph. Every station on the route had heard of the engine's journey and it appeared to Riddles as if the whole railway had turned out to cheer them as they went slowly past.

From Rugby Riddles returned to Crewe, and there he saw at the top of the station the materials van "with lots of pieces in it". This turned out to be the special tackle for drawing the crosshead of *The Princess Royal* and he wondered what on earth had gone wrong. He soon found out that the crosshead had overheated and the metal run out twelve miles beyond Rugby. It was a design fault which was put right eventually, but the engine had to go back to Rugby to have the slide block re-metalled –

a task which entailed a somewhat hectic night for all concerned. Nevertheless the engine was on view at Euston the following day. I can remember my own intense interest in the photograph of the engine which appeared in *The Times* that morning – noting particularly, as I had somehow expected, that there was a distinctively Great Western look. It was a lovely engine, which could even stand comparison with Gresley's Pacifics. According to Riddles, F.G. Carrier, a section leader in the Development and Design branch of the Derby Drawing Office, was largely responsible for what both Stanier's and Riddles' engines looked like.

There was one aspect of the design which Chapelon told me with great glee had amused him. When Churchward had copied the cylinder layout of the du Bousquet/de Glehn Atlantics, he had preferred two sets of valve gear to the four of the Atlantics. But Stanier, whilst retaining the de Glehn position of the four cylinders, had gone back to their four sets of valve gear.

On 1st July 1933, shortly after *The Princess Royal* had been turned out from Crewe, Riddles was transferred to London as Stanier's assistant.

The boiler of the new Pacifics required some modification. Stanier had insisted on following the Great Western practice of limited superheat, and it soon became clear that this did not suit LMS conditions. I discussed this with R.C. Bond who told me that Great Western firemen had been trained in the skills necessary to fire an engine with a low degree of superheat, but no such training had been given to LMS firemen, who were used to engines with high superheat. Early in 1935, therefore, the two existing Pacifics, No.6200 *The Princess Royal* and No.6201 *Princess Elizabeth* were fitted with boilers having 32 superheater flues instead of the previous 16.

C. Read, who was brought to the LMS from the Great Western by Stanier, had some interesting comments on the riding of Stanier's first Pacifics. He mentioned hunting as the most serious trouble encountered with them, and this could be frightening. It was cured by fitting stronger controlling springs. Read says: "Incidentally, in retrospect, I always considered my greatest service to W.A.S. was to persuade him that instant action was necessary". There were a number of other faults which needed correction on these engines. Distortion of the heavy crank axle gave rise to trouble in the leading driving wheel axle boxes, but rebuilding of the crank axle effected a cure. There was some crosshead trouble, but this was cured by allowing more clearances. Other troubles were fractured eccentric straps caused by heating from a high peripheral speed, and fractured piston heads due to the omission of internal ribs in the hollow heads. However, these Pacifics always rode better than the 'Royal Scots' which Read says never rode well and rolled badly. Rebuilding did something to improve them in this respect, as did also alteration of axle boxes and springing. Riddles thought that they did not ride too badly when first turned out from shops, but that they got very rough after a comparatively short mileage.

The difference in riding by apparently similar types

of engines was frequently strange. Riddles, who drove both 'Georges' and 'Princes' of the LNWR during the General Strike of 1926, regarded the 'Georges' as rough and the 'Princes' as riding very well.

At a time when Stanier was away, a run to Crewe and back behind *The Princess Royal* was arranged for the Press. E.J.H. Lemon, a Vice-President of the LMS, rode on the footplate whilst Riddles leaned out of a carriage window. Some ten miles south of Stafford the train came to a stand. Riddles jumped onto the track and went up to the engine, to find the left hand driving box aflame. The driver had sensed it was running hot and got forward to it by climbing through the cab window and creeping along (though how he managed it puzzled Riddles). He then poured oil on it from the top, and this became so hot that it burst into flame. Lemon asked Riddles what they were to do. It was a nasty problem, for they had all the Press on board and it would take at least an hour to get another engine coupled up. On the other hand if they ran the engine as it was, anything might happen. Riddles decided to risk running the train at a reduced speed and gave the necessary instructions. Luck was with them, and they arrived at Crewe 45 minutes late, but at least they had arrived, and the newspaper correspondents were very good about it. The axle, however, was badly scored and had to be scrapped. The only engine available for the return journey was a 'Royal Scot' which was ready for overhaul in the works. Riddles said: "A *Daily Telegraph* man asked me if he could ride the engine. "Certainly", I replied, trying to pour oil on the troubled waters. Then I said to the driver, "Go like hell; you have a clear road". And he did. The expression on the face of the *Daily Telegraph* correspondent on our arrival at Euston was far from happy. "I've no guts left", he said; and the poor chap had indeed suffered an appallingly rough ride."

Probably Stanier's greatest success, in Riddles' opinion, was his very efficient boiler. Stanier himself though, gave credit for the detailed design of this to J.L. Francis, a draughtsman at Crewe who started his apprenticeship in the same month as Riddles.

The third of Stanier's Pacifics was turbine driven. I only travelled behind it once. Sometime in 1948 I believe, I had changed at Crewe and was waiting there for my London collection. When the train came in, it was hauled, to my delight, by the turbine Pacific, No.6202 which I had never ever seen before. The start from Crewe, as compared with her conventional sisters, I can only describe as somehow 'silky'. R.C. Bond had a very close connection with the construction of this engine and he told me how fond he was of it. In his book, *A Lifetime with Locomotives* he wrote that it was, he thought, "the most successful unconventional steam locomotive ever to run in this country . . . The turbine locomotive covered nearly half a million miles in revenue earning service. This might well have been very much more but for long periods out of service during the war years when absolute priority for munitions production made it impossible to undertake repairs to the turbines and transmission . . . In 1952 Riddles decided that the cost of new turbines, which by

Stanier turbine-driven Pacific No.6202 LMS, with a double chimney fitted in 1937, but discarded after a comparatively short time.
(Courtesy National Railway Museum, York).

then were needed, could not be justified. The decision was therefore taken to rebuild No.6202 as a normal four-cylinder locomotive."

In June 1935, after the first two Pacifics had been fitted with the modified boilers, a test run was made from Crewe to Euston by No.6200 *The Princess Royal* with Riddles on the footplate. The train concerned was the 'up' Liverpool express booked to cover the 152.7 miles from Crewe to Willesden in 142 minutes, but with a load increased to 453 tons the run was made in 129 minutes 33 seconds at 70.7mph. This was one of a number of test runs made prior to trying out a schedule of six hours for the 401 miles between London and Glasgow.

The run to Glasgow was finally arranged for Monday 16th November 1936, and the second Pacific, No.6201 *Princess Elizabeth* was selected. The whole of Sunday, the day preceding the run was taken up in getting the locomotive ready. The story of what happened was told me by Riddles and was reproduced in the biography I wrote of him (*The Last Steam Locomotive Engineer: R.A. Riddles, CBE* (George Allen & Unwin, 1970). This was a good many years ago now and it is probably worth repeating here. Riddles' account of what happened from that Sunday onwards is as follows.

"In the morning at Willesden I watched the coaling-up with nine tons of hand-picked coal. No.6201 was fitted with a speedometer specially for the occasion and was gone over with the proverbial tooth-comb. Similar treatment was given to No.6200 *The Princess Royal*, which

was being prepared as a stand-by engine. Calculation was made of the best possible train-loading consistent with the high average speed demanded. I was to ride on the footplate and had had a continuous diagram made, on two small rollers, covering the whole of the journey. This diagram showed gradients, speed restrictions (amounting to fifty, all of which had to be strictly observed) and a theoretical curve of speeds which would be needed to maintain the six-hour schedule. This apparatus was suspended from my neck in a special case, so that by turning a screw I could wind the diagram from one roller to another as the journey progressed.

"Before leaving Willesden I had impressed on the Mechanical Inspector that he must make sure that all steam pipe joints were tight in the smokebox. Judge my consternation when at 5.15pm he telephoned me to say that the left-hand main steam pipe joint had failed! This was a special stainless steel coned joint and was not available locally. It was too late to transfer all the special test fittings to No.6200. I telephoned R.C. Bond, Assistant Works Superintendent Crewe, at his home and asked him to get a spare fitting from the Works and send it to me by the driver of the 6.46pm which was the last that day from Crewe. (The next one did not leave till after midnight.) I was extremely anxious, in fact, as to whether Bond would be able to get the part in time, because the works would be closed and in darkness, and the store was an immense place containing thousands of spare parts. However, Bond went straight to the house of a retired storekeeper called Frogatt who knew the place intimately and where everything was kept. Frogatt was fortunately in and led Bond straight to the right rack, where they found the joint; and Bond was just in time to hand it to the driver of the 6.46. I met the train at Euston about

10pm, rushed the joint out to Willesden, and by 2.30am the job was done and the fire lit.

"At 9.50am we were given the "right-away" from Euston. The run which followed was remarkable, as extracts from the official records show. With seven vehicles weighing 225 tons tare we covered the 401.4 miles between Euston and Glasgow in 353 minutes 38 seconds non-stop, at an average speed of 68.1mph. The maximum speed reached was 95.7mph and 83mph was sustained for twelve miles on practically level track. The ascent from Carnforth to Shap summit was a record – 31.4 miles to an altitude of 916 feet at an average speed of 70.5mph; and the ten miles of Beattock incline was covered in $9\frac{1}{2}$ minutes without the speed dropping below 56mph. Our arrival at Glasgow, $6\frac{1}{2}$ minutes early was a great thrill, and to my relief the Inspector, on going round the engine pronounced everything to be in order and cold.

"We had tea at the Central Hotel in Glasgow, and the train passengers, LMS officials, and the Press were most enthusiastic over their day's experience. After tea E.J.H. Lemon, a Vice-President, got hold of me and suggested that we ought to try to run even faster on the return to London the next day. But I was opposed to higher speeds and suggested adding an extra coach. Lemon agreed to this.

"Later in the day we all sat down to dinner with the Scottish Directors – chief officials of the Company, Press representatives driver and fireman – and all seemed set for a happy celebration. Halfway through dinner I was tapped on the shoulder and told I was wanted on the telephone. A voice at the other end said, "I am sorry to tell you that my examining fitter has found all the metal out of the left-hand slide block". This was an awful blow; what on earth was I to do? We were due to leave again next day at 1.15pm and I was told that they had not even a 'Scot' in good order. I said, "Get the engine to St Rollox;

Below: Stanier 'Princess Royal' class Pacific No.46212 *Duchess of Kent* on the 'down' "Mid-day Scot" express passing Bourne End on 30th July 1953.
(*Philip J. Kelley*).

Right above: LMS 'Princess Royal' class Pacific No.46211 *Queen Maud* near Lockerbie on a 'down' Perth express.
(*A.C. Cawston Collection, Courtesy National Railway Museum, York*).

starting stripping down; I will be there as soon as I can." An hour later, I having been sitting without saying a word to the by now happy company, Lemon looked at me and said, "You look tired; you had better go to bed; a big day tomorrow."

"Yes, Sir," I said. "I would like to go"; and made my escape. But what a job faced me at St Rollox! We had already experienced a lot of trouble with crossheads, and I had arranged some months before for a centre line to be marked right round them to avoid taking out the pistons each time. This precaution saved the day; for even with this advantage it was not until 5.30am that we were coupled up again, and then had to be hauled off to the shed for firing up and preparation.

"As we were about to leave Glasgow Central on the return journey, one of our publicity men came up and asked me to warn the driver that the film people would have very brilliant lights on the platform at Euston. I was wondering if we would ever reach Beattock with a newly metalled slide-block! But just an hour later we swept over Beattock summit at 66mph and, despite bad weather, went on to reach Euston 16 minutes inside the six hours, an average speed of exactly 70 miles an hour. In the two days we had run an aggregate distance of over 800 miles at a mean speed of 69mph, which was a world's record for

steam traction. When we got to Euston, Lemon came up to me and asked, "Riddles, why did you lose a minute to Beattock?" There was no appropriate answer!"

This amazing run gained great praise for the locomotive and immense prestige for the LMS. A horse that wins the Derby is rightly credited with the victory, but ridden by a less able jockey or prepared by a less competent trainer, it would probably have lost. There was fortunately a brilliant team on the footplate of the engine, but without Riddles' careful preparation of No.6201, and the drive and determination with which he overcame tiredness and two successive nights with little sleep, the run could never have been undertaken or completed.

It had, of course, been established that the projected high speed service was practicable, given some attention to the track. For there were over fifty speed restrictions which both reduced recovery time and increased the consumption of coal. The problems facing the civil engineers were the correction of such things as badly designed curves, poor alignment, indifferent packing, and irregular super-elevation. It was a matter of producing a track suitable for speeds of 75-90mph, rather than 60-70. There were only six months before the new fast services were scheduled to begin, so the poor engineers had a difficult task. However they did it and 1,820 yards of new points and crossings were installed.

I was at this period the Regular Army adjutant of a Territorial Army Signal Regiment (the London Corps Signals). Some months after the above event, on 28th June 1937, there was a call on my office telephone. It was Robin Riddles. "We've got a new engine at Euston", he said; "would you like to come round and see it?" There was no hesitation in my reply! Riddles met me at Euston and

it had been done. "Because," he replied, "the public like it." This was the engine that had been designed to haul the high speed service for which Riddles' exploit with *Princess Elizabeth* had been the pioneer.

As compared with the 6200 class, there were some modifications. The boiler was bigger and so were the cylinders, and there was an interesting reversion to Churchward practice in having two sets of Walschaerts

LMS 'Coronation' or 'Duchess' class Pacific, streamlined, No.6220 *Coronation* at South Kenton on the "Coronation Scot" express. (*A.C. Cawston Collection, Courtesy National Railway Museum, York*).

took me to the main departure platform where a big blue streamlined Pacific stood at the head of a long line of similarly coloured carriages. It was an impressive engine, but I did not like the streamlining and asked Riddles why

valve gear instead of four. In addition the coupled wheels were larger, and this was due to Riddles. He told me: "To my shame, I suggested to Stanier that the wheel diameter be increased to 6 feet 9 inches. My reasons were based on a remark by J.E. Anderson that beyond a given piston speed the locomotive lost considerably in efficiency, and, as presumably only light loads were to be hauled, longer legs would be able to run faster. This I suppose is true, but I had forgotten that the engine had to start from a stand; and could those big wheels slip!"

The decision to build the *Coronation*, as she was

called, and her sisters, stemmed from the rivalry between the LMSR and the LNER over the services to Scotland – the traditional rivalry between the West and East Coast routes, which had survived the railway amalgamations of 1923.

On 27th September 1935 (as is discussed in a later chapter) Gresley's streamlined Pacific No.2509 *Silver Link* had, on a trial run, reached a speed of 112½mph, and in 1936 a sister engine, *Silver Fox*, had raised this to 113mph whilst working the LNER's "Silver Jubilee" express. Most locomotive engineers, certainly those of the LMS, heartily disliked this new practice of concealing the lines of a beautiful locomotive behind a streamlined casing, and Stanier loathed it. Nevertheless it did appear that for the sake of Press publicity and public appeal it would be necessary to streamline the engines intended to haul the fastest services if the LMS was to attract custom from the LNER, and the Directors accordingly so decided. Wind-tunnel tests had proved that streamlining had no worthwhile effect at speeds under 80mph. No one was bothering about side winds, though streamlining might even increase their pressure on the locomotive. In fact, it was only the publicity which could justify the extra expense incurred in streamlining each locomotive. In addition, many parts of the engine that needed daily attention were covered up and this did not make streamlining popular in the running sheds.

The form of the streamlining had been designed by Coleman and approved after careful experiments with models in the LMS Research Department's wind-tunnel at Derby. The fixing of the streamlined casing presented quite a problem, as did also the access to the smokebox. There was a discussion on this latter difficulty between Stanier, Riddles, and Coleman. Coleman produced a scheme for the shape of the doors of the casing, but not the method of fixing them. Eventually, Riddles, using his building experience, suggested a solution which was adopted.

As I walked back along the train with Riddles, he told me that the next day engine and train were going on a test run to Crewe, but that he could not offer me a seat because every one had been alloted either to railway officials or the Press. As I was not expecting a seat I was not disappointed, but I would have been had I known what was to be attempted. Riddles gave the following account of this epic journey:

"On 29th June 1937, at 9.50am we set out from Euston with the new "Coronation Scot" train on its Press demonstration run. Again I was fortunate to be on the footplate, and, with my diagrams laying down the projected speeds, all was set to make an attempt on the world's maximum speed record at Whitmore, where, after a short rise, there is a falling gradient down to Crewe, 10½ miles away. We had decided not to pick up water from the troughs at Whitmore, and so avoid reducing speed. The exhaust was humming with a continuous roar like that of an aeroplane engine. The white mileposts flashed past and the speedometer needle shot up through the '90s' into the '100s' to 110-111-112-113-114 miles per hour; but

beyond it – No! Basford sidings 1½ miles away now; spectators from Crewe coming into view at the lineside, and the train still hustling along at 114mph. On went the brakes; off the regulator; but on we sailed with flames streaming from the tortured brake blocks. To my horror the signal was set for Platform No.3 at Crewe, which has a 20mph speed restriction. We were doing 60 to 70mph when we spotted the platform signal: down to 52mph through the curve, the engine riding like the great lady she is: there wasn't a thing we could do about it but hold on and let her take it. And take it she did; with the crockery smashing in the dining car: past a sea of pallid faces on the platform; till we ground to a dead stand – safe and sound and still on the rails. We had set up a new world's speed record for the steam locomotive!"

As they entered the reverse curve, back in the train, F.A. Lemon, sitting opposite Stanier, had said: "We're for it now!", and put his feet up on the seat to steady himself. Some appalling misjudgement at Crewe had led to the train being switched to this difficult platform road, and it is probable that only the excellent de Glehn bogie (copied by Churchward from the French Atlantics and brought to the LMS by Stanier) had saved the train from disaster.

The LMS had now secured the speed record from the LNER, but only by a narrow margin. The engine was still accelerating when Riddles had to halt further effort. Nobody knows what speed could have been reached if there had been some miles more of suitable track. But the LMS did not have it, so should the LNER, with a longer stretch of track suitable for very high speeds, regain the record, there would be no possibility of reply. And this, as related later, is what actually happened. The return journey from Crewe to Euston was another distinguished run. A speed of 100mph was reached at one point and the 158 miles were covered in 119 minutes at a shade under an average speed of 80mph.

The American railroads had taken a keen interest in the "Coronation Scot" and had persuaded Lord Stamp, Chairman of the LMS, to send a complete train to the United States to tour the Eastern part of the country and appear as an exhibit at the World's Fair in New York. The new and magnificent train consisted of eight coaches, and its locomotive was numbered and named No.6220 *Coronation*; but actually the name and number plates of the original 6220 had been changed with those of a newer streamlined Pacific, No.6229 *Duchess of Hamilton*.

Riddles was detailed to travel with the train to America, with responsibility for its operation during the whole tour. The driver and fireman selected were F.C. Bishop and J. Carswell, both of whom had been presented with watches by King Boris of Bulgaria after that railway enthusiast monarch had been at the controls of the *Coronation*.

The train was to visit 38 American cities and towns and would cover 3,120 miles in the process. The tour was scheduled to start at Baltimore on 21st March and end at New York on 14th April. This lengthy journey would entail running over the tracks of eight American railroads.

After crossing the Atlantic, it was 24th February 1939 by the time that the train was assembled on Baltimore & Ohio Railroad tracks and ready for movement. It was then run to the B&O shops to be prepared for the long trip. It was subsequently taken on a test run. Bishop, the driver, was feeling unwell at the time. The next day he was ill with pneumonia, and was in hospital for most of the tour. In this emergency, Riddles decided that he would take over the duties of fireman while Carswell became driver; though actually Riddles did most of the driving whilst Carswell carried out his proper job as fireman.

The details of this run have already been described in my previous book mentioned above, and it will suffice to mention one or two incidents connected with the locomotive. At Philadelphia, Carswell had given the American Press his first reactions to United States railway conditions. He gave high praise to the American road bed; it was, he said, almost as good as the British. But he was scornful of the coal; the stuff they had given him at Baltimore was so dirty that they had had a hard job cleaning the firebox. The *Greencastle Banner* of Indiana complained that the "Coronation Scot" lacked the thrill in its movements and appearance that was anticipated. "There was no noise or bluster about it as it moved, such as is displayed by the common sort of trains with which Greencastle is familiar. The Terre Haut *Star* commented on Riddles taking over the job of fireman and said that "This and the fact that the locomotive is constructed with such care that gaskets are unknown in the pipe fittings probably tells a better story of the British than all the excellent fittings and arrangements for comfort on the train".

At Chicago, on 2nd April, Riddles received an American locomotive whistle which was presented by the

Stanier 'Duchess' class non-streamlined Pacific No.6234 *Duchess of Abercorn*, **the first of these engines without streamlining.**
(P. Ransome-Wallis Collection, Courtesy National Railway Museum, York).

Model Railroad Builders of America. The presentation took place in front of the "Coronation Scot" with a Baltimore & Ohio diesel locomotive on the adjoining track. The *Courier* of Buffalo said that the train had been travelling at moderate speeds due to lack of American braking power, but had been let out on a few occasions, due, it was said, to "Mr Riddles, the executive turned fireman who is reported to be a 'speed demon'. The Rochester *Democrat and Chronicle* quoted Riddles as saying, apropos of his temporary job, "Somebody had to shovel. A bloody dirty job, I'll say, but we managed." On the arrival at New York Riddles said, "I must admit that I was thankful to see the World's Fair ground and relieved that we had got to it all in one piece. I had lost seven pounds in weight – but we were there!"

With its streamlined covering thankfully removed

and with its proper number and name restored, *Duchess of Hamilton* now belongs to the National Railway Museum and, fully restored, is frequently (at the time of writing) working special trains over British Rail – and what locomotive more deserved preservation?

Roland Bond told me that the riding of the 'Duchess'

class (as they were later termed) Pacifics was "superb", and he regarded them as the best of all Class 8 express locomotives on British Railways. When he was CME of British Railways, he wanted to transfer some of them to the Southern Region, and was most disappointed when clearances prevented this.

Stanier 'Duchess' 4-6-2 No. 46229 *Duchess of Hamilton* works the "150 Anniversary Mail by Rail Tour" special at Manchester Victoria on Tuesday 11th November 1980. *(Gavin Morrison)*

Chapter 12

Water-Tube Boiler

I n strict chronological order, Gresley's engine with a water-tube boiler should have been dealt with earlier in this book; but this would have interrupted the narrative of the LNER Pacific development. It preceded Gresley's streamlined Pacifics, but in its rebuilt form it had a close affinity with them.

The idea of an express engine with a water-tube boiler had occurred to Gresley as early as 1924, when the A1 Pacifics were proving heavy consumers of coal and the LNER was keen on securing economies. In that year Gresley approached Harold Yarrow, head of the Clyde shipbuilders of that name, and suggested to him the design of a water-tube boiler that might be applied to locomotives. It will be remembered that du Bousquet had tried water-tube fireboxes on an Atlantic and on one of his two Baltics. In 1924 the American Locomotive Company, at its Schenectady Works, had constructed for the Delaware & Hudson Railroad a 2-8-0 freight engine with a high pressure water-tube boiler, No. 1400 *Horatio Allen*. This was a two-cylinder compound with a steam pressure of 350psi. Initial trials were successful, and ALCO built three more for the same company, the last of which was a 4-8-0 with a pressure of 500psi – a four-cylinder triple expansion compound with poppet valves. All were freight engines and could haul heavier loads than the Company's simple expansion engines of the same size and with conventional boilers. But they were desperately slow and their maintenance costs were heavy enough to absorb most of the undoubted economies in fuel consumption.

When Gresley approached Yarrow the first of ALCO's engines was under construction, and it may have given him the idea of incorporating a water-tube boiler in an express locomotive. On account of the high steam pressure planned for the engine, it was decided that compound expansion should be adopted.

The water-tube boiler consisted basically of one steam drum and four water drums. The steam drum was at the top and extended the full length of the boiler. The four water drums were disposed with two outside the engine frames on each side of the grate, and two further forward and placed between the frames. All four water drums were connected to the steam drum by tubes, through which the water circulated.

There were four cylinders, of which the two high pressure cylinders were inside and driving the leading coupled axle, and the two low pressure ones were outside, impelling the middle coupled axle. The wheel arrangement was 4-6-4, but with two independent carrying axles at the trailing end instead of a bogie.

As completed, the engine had 12in by 26in high pressure cylinders and 20in by 26in low pressure; the grate area was 34.95sq ft, the boiler pressure at 450psi, the coupled wheels 6ft 8in in diameter, and the tractive effort was 32,000lb.

The so-called "hush-hush" engine was turned out at the end of 1929, painted grey, and numbered 10000. (The next time this number was used was on the first British diesel express passenger locomotive, which emerged lettered LMS, just before that company ceased to exist.) The bulbous outside casing of the LNER engine was extended forward in two wings to lift the smoke clear of the chimney, which they obscured from view. The singularly unlovely appearance of the water-boilered 10000 horrified me when I saw the first photographs, and earned it the nickname of the 'Galloping Sausage' from irreverent footplatemen.

Right: LNER 4-6-4 No.10000, Gresley's water-tube boiler locomotive; built with such high hopes but a great disappointment. Seen here at Dunfermline Lower.
(R.D. Stephen Collection, Courtesy National Railway Museum, York).

Extensive trials were made with test trains early in 1930, the engine working from Darlington to King's Cross and return, and then to Edinburgh and on to Perth. Some minor modifications were made, but there was trouble with the steaming. Gresley sent for the drawings of the last batch of Stirling 'eight-foot singles', and remarked that they steamed all right though they had no boiler to speak of. After studying these drawings, Gresley directed Darlington Works to alter the diameter of the blastpipe and the taper of the liner above the choke. After various other modifications had been made, No. 10000 entered traffic on 20th June 1930. On 15th August, as a result of experience in service, it was returned to Darlington for further modifications. On 17th January 1931 it was returned to ordinary service, but was soon back in Darlington Works. Performance was patchy for the remainder of the year, with further adjustments and tests. During 1932 and on into 1933 there were further tests and modification, with the engine spending only a moderate time in traffic. In May 1933 it was taken into Darlington Works for its first general repair. It had then run a total of some 70,000 miles. It was over a year before it once more returned to service, and during that time a number of major modifications had been carried out.

By this time Chapelon's rebuilt compound Pacifics were producing their outstanding performances, and Gresley, who had a great admiration for André Chapelon's work, consulted him about the problems that he was encountering with No. 10000. Chapelon, after going into the details of the design, said that the degree of superheat was insufficient to prevent condensation in the low pressure cylinders and that it should be considerably increased. He added that even better results could be obtained by re-superheating; that is to say, not only superheating the steam before its entry into the high pressure cylinders, but also during its passage to the intermediate receiver, on its way from the high pressure to the low pressure cylinders. This entailed reserving an adequate number of superheater tubes for the low pressure superheater. He also recommended the fitting of a double Kylchap exhaust. Bulleid visited Chapelon for detailed

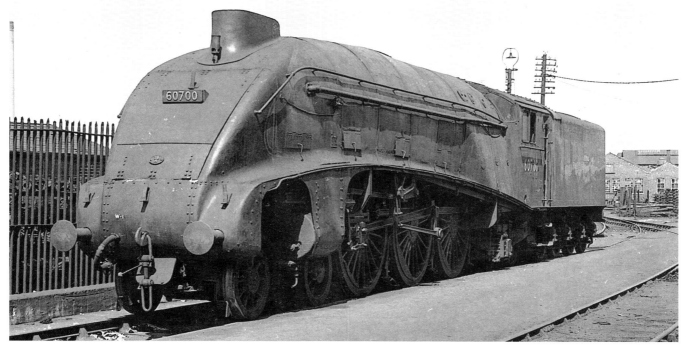

LNER No.10000 rebuilt with a conventional boiler and A4 type streamlining. At Doncaster Works on 23rd May 1957 as BR No.60700.
(Philip J. Kelley).

conversations about these recommendations.

Chapelon told me more than once what a great admiration he had for Gresley as a locomotive engineer, and how keen he had been to help find a cure for No. 10000's problems.

All Chapelon's recommendations were in due course put into effect, and there was a considerable improvement in performance and efficiency. But problems such as lack of air tightness in the boiler walls and short circuiting of gases with consequent lowered boiler efficiency remained unresolved, and No. 10000 never produced economies or performances to justify the expenditure on its unconventional design. At least two thirds of its life had been spent under repair or being modified, and Gresley, like du Bousquet before him, had failed in his attempt with water tubes to modify successfully the conventional steam locomotive established by George Stephenson's *Rocket* of 1829.

In 1937 No. 10000 was rebuilt with a normal tubular boiler as a three-cylinder simple expansion 4-6-4 with a double Kylchap exhaust and streamlined in the same fashion as Gresley's A4 class Pacifics. In its new form it was a successful engine and popular with the enginemen; but it is sad that such an imaginative venture had not better success.

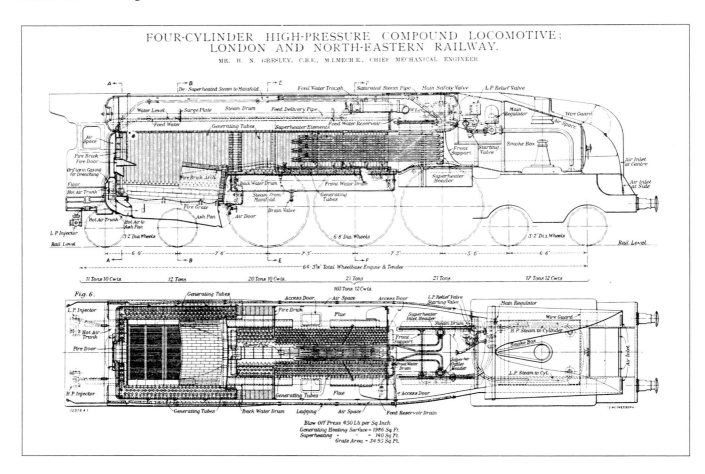

FOUR-CYLINDER HIGH-PRESSURE COMPOUND LOCOMOTIVE; LONDON AND NORTH-EASTERN RAILWAY.

MR. H. N. GRESLEY, C.B.E., M.I.MECH.E., CHIEF MECHANICAL ENGINEER.

Chapter 13
Gresley's Streamlined Finale

Gresley's, 2-8-2 No. 2001 *Cock o' the North* was the first of the only eight-coupled express locomotives ever built in Great Britain. The object of their construction was to provide a class of locomotives with sufficient adhesion to work heavy trains at express speeds over the difficult main line between Edinburgh and Aberdeen, with its steep gradients and curving tracks. Maximum trailing loads of express trains could reach 530 tons, and for trains of this weight double-heading had been necessary. The engine could have been of the Mountain (4-8-2) type, but, to keep down the overall length Gresley decided on a two-wheeled pony truck instead of a bogie.

After various alterations from the original concept,

and Calais and hauling three 40 ton wagons (loaded with the coal with which it was normally fired), a van carrying spares, and a guard's van to make up the little train. Bulleid was on the footplate of the engine during the run from Calais to Vitry-sur-Seine.

The results at Vitry were unexpectedly disappointing for the British team, for *Cock o' the North* could not be driven hard on the test bank without the axle boxes heating. However, it was explained to Bulleid that this was not an uncommon occurrence with French engines. When Gresley was informed he came over to France and visited Chapelon in his Design Office, where he showed him the plans of the engine and asked for his advice. Chapelon,

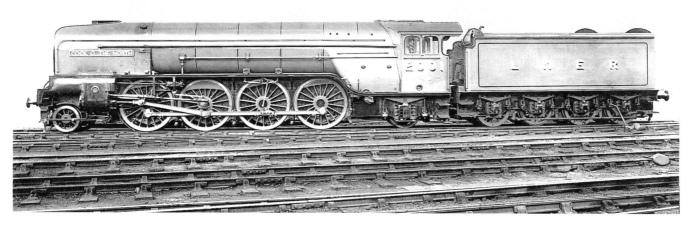

LNER Class P2 2-8-2 *Cock o' the North*. This was the first eight-coupled British express engine, and was deliberately given the number of the first British six-coupled express engine, 4-6-0 No.2001 of the NER.
(Courtesy National Railway Museum, York).

the first engine was completed on 22nd May 1934. It had the Lentz arrangement of rotary cam poppet valve gear, three 21in by 26in cylinders, a grate area of 50sq ft, and a boiler pressure of 200psi. Preliminary trials were carried out in england, and then, after discussions with André Chapelon, *Cock o' the North* went to France for trials on the Vitry test plant. The engine incorporated various Chapelon features: the double Kylchap exhaust, wide stream passages, and high superheat – all copied from the rebuilt PO Pacifics. Indeed, Gresley, in his second Presidential address to the Institution of Locomotive engineers in 1936, said: "I did not hesitate to incorporate some of the outstanding features of the Paris-Orleans Railway's engines, such as the provision of extra large steam passages and a double blastpipe. There was no real novelty in these features but the French engineers had worked out the designs scientifically and had proved them by the results obtained in actual service".

In December 1934 *Cock o' the North* was despatched to France for the Vitry trials, travelling via Harwich

who had himself seen engines perform badly on the test bank, suggested that a trial on the line with a test load would probably be more satisfactory. The normal PO test load for line trials consisted of a dynamometer car and three 'dead' (ie out of steam) four-cylinder compound counter-pressure brake locomotives (in which water was admitted to the cylinders and pumped against pressure in the boiler). The engine was tried hauling such a train between Les Aubrais and Tours and was completely satisfactory: axle boxes remained cool and *Cock o' the North* produced a drawbar horsepower of 2,000 at 80mph. But this was considerably lower than Chapelon's own eight-coupled engines (described in the next chapter). Two factors contributed to this. The firing was carried out in turn by the LNER fireman and Léonce Miot, who had been fireman on PO rebuilt Pacific No. 2566 during its trials. They agreed that the firebox door was too small for them to cover properly the back corners of the wide grate. As a result, the steaming was hampered so that the pressure in the boiler fell whilst the steam production rate remained practically constant. The other factor was an apparent design fault in the cylinder block. Unlike the second engine of the class, No. 2002 *Earl Marischal*, No. 2001 had poppet valves, and it was necessary with these to increase the diameter of the exhaust pipe by 50% to avoid having too great a draught. Chapelon believed that this could be attributed to the excessive temperature of the exhaust steam, which probably arose from its being re-heated by contact with a partition separating it from the live steam. The efficiency of the engine was thereby lowered. If this diagnosis was correct, a re-design of the cylinder block would be necessary to rectify it. All this was explained to the author by Chapelon, and the same comments were apparently included in his report to Gresley.

In a discussion at the Institution of Locomotive Engineers in 1947, Bulleid claimed that *Cock o' the North* compared favourably in its coal consumption per drawbar horsepower with the French engines. However, this discussion took place many years after the event, and Bulleid's memory must have failed him. Chapelon sent me the figures compiled from comparative tests between *Cock o' the North* and one of his own rebuilt Pacifics, which showed that Gresley's engine was far from being as economical in coal and water as his own compounds. The former was, of course, a simple expansion locomotive, and Chapelon suggested that perhaps the poppet valves may not have been perfectly steam tight.

The comparative figures were:

	PO Pacific		Cock o' the North
Speed	68mph	56mph	68mph
dbhp	1,900	2,700	1,910
water per hp/hr	7.5kg	8.2kg	10.45kg
coal per hp/hr	1.05kg	1.22kg	1.48kg

(I might add here that the very large number of letters written, in French, to the author by Chapelon on Locomotive design and performance have been deposited in the National Railway Museum.)

Chapelon said that the design of the leading pony truck resulted in *Cock o' the North* being very hard on the track, because the first coupled axle of the rigid wheelbase encountered any change in the direction of the track too roughly. He had noticed this during the trials,

particularly at the junction of Montlouis, which was taken rather harshly even by his rebuilt PO Pacifics. This weakness could have been eliminated by using the Italian bissel bogie (in which a displacement of the leading two-wheeled truck was followed by a lateral movement of the leading coupled axle), which Chapelon had fitted to SNCF 141.P class 2-8-2. These rode as well as his Pacifics, whilst having all the advantages of superior adhesion. It is worth noting, too, that in both the WD and BR 2-10-0s designed by R.A. Riddles, he got over the disadvantages of the long fixed wheelbase by having flangeless centre coupled wheels, and flanges of reduced thickness on the second and fourth pairs of coupled wheels, together with frames capable of slight flexing; and these engines could run through a $4\frac{1}{2}$chain curve without even the 'grind' normally experienced with the average 2-8-0. As the 9F 2-10-0s ran satisfactorily at over 90mph, either of the above arrangements would probably have suited Gresley's eight-coupled express engines.

Gresley and Bulleid both stayed in France while these tests were being conducted on the LNER engine. Although Gresley had incorporated many of Chapelon's ideas in the design of his 2-8-2, it was clear that he had failed to build an engine equal in either performance or efficiency to the French rebuilds. Indeed, he told the Institution of Locomotive engineers that the first *Cock o' the North* would be the last and that any subsequent P2 class engine would incorporate the lessons learned in France. The second of the class, No. 2002 *Earl Marischal,* was completed, however, in October 1934, before the despatch of No. 2001 to France, and differed from it only in having Walschaerts valve gear with piston valves. The final four, Nos 2003-2006, had the even larger steam passages that were being fitted to his A4 class Pacifics and

No.2001 *Cock o' the North* with altered valve gear and A4 type streamlined casing.
(Courtesy National Railway Museum, York).

***Cock o' the North* as ruined by its conversion into an indifferent Pacific by Edward Thompson.**
(Courtesy National Railway Museum, York).

they were streamlined in similar fashion. To these, the first two were modified to conform, but the life of all six P2s, in their final form, was short, for when Thompson succeeded Gresley he rebuilt them, turning very fine Mikados into very bad Pacifics.

The A4 class Pacifics, of course, astounded the locomotive world by the speed records they achieved, and remarkably trouble-free running immediately they were put into service. In his paper on *The Development of LNER Locomotive Design* presented to the Institution of Locomotive engineers, B. Spencer gives an admirable resumé of the purpose and success of the A4s. They were intended to work the "Silver Jubilee" express which went into service on 30th September 1935, providing a four hour service between Newcastle and London, with one intermediate stop at Darlington. Over the 232 miles between London and Darlington it was intended that the booked average speed of 71mph should be maintained by running fast on the rising gradients, rather than by very fast speeds downhill.

It was considered of great importance that not only air resistance to high speed should be reduced, but that measures to effect this should also carry steam and smoke clear of the cab front windows. Experiments had been carried out at the National Physical Laboratory with scaled models of an ordinary Pacific engine and one which had been streamlined to determine the comparative head-on wind resistance, and, from the results obtained, to calculate the horsepower required at various speeds to overcome it. With the horizontal wedge form front end of streamlining, which, as experiments showed, would meet the need to prevent smoke obscuring the cab windows, a table was worked out to show the savings in horsepower which it could effect against high air resistance over various speeds, as compared with unstreamlined engines. At 60mph it was 41hp, at 90mph 138hp, and at 110mph 253hp. However, travelling head-on into a gale,

it was necessary to take into account the speed of the wind as well as that of the train, so that calculations were worked out to a combined speed of 150mph, and at this the saving was no less than 639hp – 1,521hp for an unstreamlined Pacific as against 822hp for the streamlined engine. But these figures related only to head-on air resistance and not to side winds. Nevertheless, in still air there would be a saving of over 100hp continuously at the average speed at which the "Silver Jubilee" was required to operate. In relation to the total horsepower which the engine would require to develop at these speeds, and also because it was ineffective against side winds, many locomotive engineers did not consider the extra cost of streamlining to be worthwhile.

A number of modifications were made to the A3 class Pacific design to ensure freer running and an ample reserve of power for uphill work. The boiler pressure was increased from 220psi to 250psi, and the distance between the tube plates was reduced and the combustion chamber length correspondingly increased. The piston valve diameter was increased from 8in to 9in diameter and particular attention was paid to the size and shape of steam and exhaust passages, in the light of Chapelon's achievements. Also, following Chapelon, in the castings all passages were carefully examined and all roughness removed.

The result of these alterations was, undoubtedly, one of the finest British express locomotives that had yet been built. To admirers of the conventional steam engine, the appearance was a disappointment. I remember looking at *Silver Link* at King's Cross, in its silver-grey livery. Another bystander asked me what I thought of it. "It looks", I replied, "like a tea cosy", comparing the streamlined covering to the woollen monstrosity which hides the contours of a teapot. Later, one got used to it – or nearly used to it – but many agreed with me at the time.

From 1935 to 1938, 35 of these new Pacifics were built, and they worked not only the high speed trains but also took their part on the normal Pacific-hauled main line expresses. Four of them were fitted with the double

LNER class A4 streamlined Pacific No.4489 *Dominion of Canada* in Garter blue livery on the down "Coronation" express at Hadley Wood in 1937. To mark Coronation year the LNER had announced that streamlined trains would be introuced between London and Edinburgh, doing the journey in six hours. Five engines had been selected for this service, Nos 4488-92, which were to be given names of the major countries of the Empire and painted Garter blue. (*Philip J. Kelly*).

Kylchap exhaust, and the value of this was shown when one of them, No.4468 *Mallard,* hauling a load of $236\frac{1}{2}$ tons, attained a world speed record for steam of 126mph, which has not yet been beaten. The event took place during brake trials on 3rd July 1938. It appears that Gresley was not able to obtain approval to fit Kylchap exhausts to all the A4 Pacifics on account of the royalty payments involved.

The bogies originally fitted to the A1 Pacifics were very similar to those used by Ivatt on his Atlantics. Ivatt brought this bogie from the Great Southern & Western Railway of Ireland. It was developed from that designed by Alexander McDonnell for his 0-4-4 tank engines of 1870, when he was Locomotive Superintendent of the GS&WR. It proved very satisfactory and he accordingly fitted it to his notable little 'Kerry' 4-4-0 passenger engines of 1877 – so called because they were designed for the twisting Mallow-Killarney-Tralee line. (The Kerry engines had a remarkably long life. In the 1930s I saw one of them at Sligo station at the head of a passenger train bound for Limerick over the line of the old GS&WR.) McDonnell was a very able locomotive engineer and it is unfortunate that he seems to be remembered chiefly for his rapid departure from the North Eastern Railway, over the alleged unsuitability of the engines he designed for it. J.A.F. Aspinall kept the bogie when he succeeded McDonnell; and so did Ivatt when he succeeded Aspinall at Inchicore.

Side movement of the McDonnell bogie was controlled by swing links, and, as fitted to the A1 Pacifics, these links allowed a side movement of $3\frac{1}{2}$ inches, which had been that used on the Atlantics. But, owing to the longer wheelbase of the Pacifics, this had to be increased to 4 inches.

The detailed design of Gresley's D49, or 'Shire' class 4-4-0s had been carried out at Darlington, and for these engines the Darlington Works designed an entirely different type of bogie, which had helical side spring control instead of swing links. Gresley was impressed with this bogie and in 1931 he tried it on one of the Pacifics. The trials were so satisfactory that he directed that it should be fitted to all the Pacifics, though with some slight modifications.

When the A4s were designed, they too had this D49 type bogie. The initial loading on the side control springs was 2 tons, and the maximum loading 4.55 tons. Excessive wear on the flanges of the leading coupled wheels showed that this loading was insufficient, and it was therefore increased to an initial 4 tons and a maximum of 7 tons.

The D49 bogie had one disadvantage as compared with the McDonnell swing link in that it did not prevent excessive rolling. Roland Bond told me that at Gresley's invitation he rode on the footplate of an A4 Pacific from King's Cross to Newcastle and back. He was impressed with the A4 as a very fine engine, but he told Gresley that it did not ride as well as Stanier's Pacifics, because it occasionally rolled so badly at high speeds that the driver had to brake. Gresley was somewhat taken aback, and Bond thought that perhaps nobody had dared to tell him. On Gresley asking him what he thought the reason was, Bond suggested that it probably lay in the bogie, and explained the system of side checks that they had on the LMS bogie. Gresley thereupon sent a request to Stanier, through Bond, for drawings of the LMS bogie. Tests made on an A4 in 1938 confirmed Bond's diagnosis and the LMS type bogie was adopted. On these bogies horizontal check plates were fitted to the undersides of the main frames and the tops of the bogie frames on both sides of the engine. There was normally a gap of $\frac{1}{16}$ in between the check plates, but any roll to one side was checked by the plates coming into contact with each other.

As stated above, only four of the A4s were fitted with the double Kylchap exhaust, but this was due to LNER reluctance to pay the royalties for this patented equipment, and the others therefore had Churchward's jumper top to the blastpipes.

Blastpipes have excited more controversy in locomotive design than any other aspect, from the rivalry between Stephenson's Rocket and Hackworth's *Sanspareil* of 1830 onwards. Colonel K.R.M. Cameron remarked to the author: "There has probably been more steam blown off in the metaphorical sense than ever passed through the blastpipes themselves!" His own experience was that any well-designed blastpipe system was good, provided that the smokebox was kept airtight, the tubes and brick arch were kept clean, and the fuel was of good quality. "The Kylchap", he said, "proved itself superior when fuel quality fell off from first class standard." At King's Cross, he got into official hot water for clamping down the jumper tops, even though this did improve the steaming on several single-chimney A4s. He said that the A4 was a magnificent machine; provided that it was kept in first class order it was brilliant; but if it was not well maintained it could be "bloody awful". It was like a racehorse, in that it demanded attention if you were to get the best results.

On double blast pipes, André Chapelon told me that he was quite puzzled by the type that was fitted to the three-cylinder 4-6-0s of the Great Southern Railway of Ireland; for the two outside cylinders exhausted into a blastpipe placed below the rearward chimney and the single inside cylinder exhausted into another blastpipe situated under forward chimney.

At the time that he was Assistant District Motive Power Superintendent at King's Cross, P.N. Townend had no doubt about the value of the double Kylchap exhaust. In a letter to the author he says that when he went to King's Cross in 1936 the A4s were, and had been for some time, at a low ebb in performance. The depot had either bolted down the jumper top blastpipes or fitted their own fixed tops of various heights and sizes, none of which was satisfactory nor could compare with the double Kylchap exhaust borne by three A4s at King's Cross. Townend accordingly submitted a request for all the A4s to be fitted with the Kylchap exhaust. This request was received with little enthusiasm; instead, Townend was asked to report on the effects of having the chimney cowl, etc., altered to the proportions used on the Western Region. Townend's report concluded that the Western Region arrangement compared unfavourably with the Kylchap exhaust, and this was what he wanted. The response to this was to send him another set of Western Region proportions. These varied only slightly from the first lot, and both were based on the proportions used on the admirable Great Western 2301 class 0-6-0 goods engines designed by Dean in 1883. (One of these had shown up remarkably well against a Class 2 2-6-0 mixed traffic engine designed by Ivatt for the LMS and adopted by British Railways). About this time King's Cross was asked if it was true that the A4s with the Kylchap did not steam properly, and if so would they like them removed. A long-suffering Townend replied that on the contrary these engines steamed excellently and that they would like all A4s converted to this system. However, no comment was received on this suggestion, and it was not until nearly the end of their career that the remaining A4s were given the Kylchap.

Chapter 14
Chapelon's Favourite Engines

Chapelon's revolutionary rebuilding of the large-wheeled PO Pacifics has already been described; these were the engines designed for the more easily graded of the PO main lines. But by 1930 the Company needed to seek means of both accelerating and increasing the weight of the trains on the Toulouse main line, particularly over the difficult section between Chateauroux and Montaubon, with its long 1 in 100 banks. Here the smaller wheeled Pacifics, built for this line, had reached the limit of their capacity in the haulage of 500 ton trains on the existing schedules. An engine was required that would work a train of 700 tons at the accelerated schedules which the PO envisaged.

Edmund Epinay, the Chief of Rolling Stock and Motive Power, at first considered buying big Mountain type locomotives, like the PLM C class 4-8-2 (which two years later took part in the previously mentioned trials over the Nord main line between Paris and Boulogne); for a Mountain, with its eight coupled wheels, would have the extra adhesion needed. An alternative solution which came to his mind was the rebuilding of the PO's two-cylinder simple expansion 2-8-2s as three-cylinder 4-8-2s. He discussed the problem with André Chapelon, who suggested that a way out of the difficulty might be found in rebuilding the small-wheeled 4500 class Pacifics in the same fashion as the large-wheeled 3500 class, but to convert them into 4-8-0s. Epinay accepted this idea enthusiastically, and, in October 1931, instructed Chapelon to carry it out.

It was obvious that the existing 4500 class boiler

would not do because the trapezoidal grate would not fit over the rear coupled wheels, and a long narrow firebox would be necessary. Chapelon decided that the excellent boiler fitted to the Nord "Superpacifics" of the 3.1200 class, and which had the characteristic Nord long narrow firebox, would meet his requirements and he asked the Nord Railway for the drawings. But he chose the similar but larger Belpaire firebox of the earlier Nord Asselin Pacifics with its grate area of 40.4sq ft, instead of the modified 1923 pattern with only 37.7sq ft grate area, and he incorporated a Nicholson thermic syphon. The 3.1200 class of the Nord had always been able to produce performances that were some 30% superior to those of pre-Chapelon Pacifics of the PO, and, indeed to the Pacifics of any other French railway and also of the LNER, in the early 1920s. They had better valve gear arrangements and a better designed steam circuit. Rather unexpectedly, perhaps, the narrow firebox, Chapelon said, contributed to their improved performance. In conversation with me, Chapelon insisted that a well designed narrow firebox was every bit as good as a wide one. The original frames of the 4500 class engines were cut behind the third coupled axle, and then prolonged to the rear by plates of the same thickness, welded on.

Chapelon's first rebuild of a Pacific into a 4-8-0, Paris-Orleans Railway No. 4521.
(P. Ransome-Wallis Collection, Courtesy National Railway Museum, York).

After being given the task in October 1931, Chapelon started on the task in the same month at Tours Works, and it was finished six months later, in April 1932, when No. 4521, rebuilt as a 4-8-0, emerged from Tours and ran its first trials.

It was the general opinion that the maximum length of a firebox, which a fireman could manage, was 10ft. However, Chapelon opted for one of 12ft 6in, because he was satisfied, from practical tests, that a narrow firebox of this length would not present a fireman with any great difficulty. Furthermore, he had established that this type of firebox could enable a combustion rate higher than that of a wide firebox of similar grate area. (This is extremely interesting, and one wonders whether similar comparative evaluation was ever carried out on a British railway. It would be typical of Churchward if it was.) As regards firebox length, Chapelon said that it was easier for a fireman to maintain a good fire on a narrow grate than on a wide one, on account of the difficulty in reaching the back corners of the latter – a difficulty that became apparent on the trials in France with the small firebox door of *Cock o'the North*. An additional advantage of the narrow firebox is that the automatic trimming forward of the coal tends to stop any clogging of the grate, whilst with a wide firebox the fireman has to watch every point of the grate to stop this happening.

On the engine's first run it was apparent that here was a paragon amongst locomotives, for the performance was superior even to that achieved by Chapelon's rebuild of the 3500 class Pacifics.

During the first public demonstration of No. 4521's ability, there was an amusing incident. The engine was at the head of a train weighing 730 tons between Vierzon and Limoges. Amongst the passengers were a large number of observers from other French railways, as well as Press correspondents. The former had already condemned the grate area as being too small to meet the stated requirements. At Chateauroux, as already planned, the load was reduced to 642 tons before tackling the heavily graded section on to Limoges. There was some delay before the train started again. Then, after a fast run over the level stretches to Argenton, the train was faced with the formidable banks; but here the steaming suddenly became superabundant and so remained, to the confusion of the hostile critics; for they had learned that the delay at Chateauroux had been due to steaming troubles and they had happily anticipated a late arrival at Limoges, But No. 4521 surmounted these heavy gradients at such a speed that Limoges was reached at the scheduled time, wiping all the delay that had been incurred up to the time of leaving Chateauroux. The trouble had been caused by poor functioning at low cut-offs, and it was while running in that condition that the poor steaming had occurred. A minor adjustment had put the matter right.

A short time later No. 4521 carried out another test run on the same route at the head of a 575 ton train. This time the heavily graded 125 miles between Vierzon and Limoges were surmounted at an average running speed of 61.25mph; and on subsequent tests the engine demonstrated its ability to maintain continuously an indicated horsepower of 3,800 at 56mph, and 4,000 at 70mph. These were powers never obtained by any British express engine and were even considerably in excess of the power available, many years later, to the diesel-electric 'Deltic' class locomotives of British Railways – at that time rated as the most powerful single engine diesel locomotives in the world. Seeing an illustration of this remarkable engine and reading an account of its performances in the *Locomotive* magazine remains a vivid memory. I was astounded at the, to me, almost unbelievable power output by an engine of this size. It became an ambition to meet one day the designer – an ambition that was ultimately realised some 40 years later.

The PO thus had a locomotive that more than fulfilled its traffic needs and eleven more of the 4500 class were rebuilt in the same way. No. 4521 was renumbered 4701 and the others became 4702-4712. They were put into service at Brive depot to work the heavy expresses between Vierzon and Narbonne. On this service they easily met the PO objective of hauling 700 ton trains on the new fast schedules. They also proved remarkably capable over a wide range of duties; for they were equally at home with fast and heavy passenger trains at speeds up to 94mph over the more easily graded sections, or with the 700 ton passenger trains on sections having a ruling gradient of 1 in 100 and 500 yard radius curves at 30 to 50mph, or even with freight trains over these same difficult routes, of heavier weight and at faster speeds than those taken by the 6000 class four-cylinder compound 2-10-0 locomotives of 1910. In this flexibility of operation they could be roughly equated with the Class 9F 2-10-0 engines designed by R.A. Riddles for British Railways twenty years later.

Tried at a constant speed and cut-off, the first of the class, No. 4701, maintained 3,030 horsepower at the drawbar when running at 62.5mph. On this occasion the redoubtable Fireman Marty, refusing the aid of an assistant fireman, and in the space of a single hour, shovelled four tons of coal into the firebox – a feat which could well merit inclusion in the *Guinness Book of Records!* Not only did he move this astounding quantity of coal, but he retained such a mastery over his fire that the boiler was steaming perfectly the whole time.

Both the Nord and the Etat Railways were taking a keen interest in these trials, for the Nord had already purchased some of Chapelon's rebuilt Pacifics, and the Etat were rebuilding some of their own Pacifics on similar lines. In 1935, therefore, No. 4707 (but by now renumbered 240.707) was loaned to both railways for trials, on which it confirmed the reputation the class had established on the PO. It went first to the Nord, and on 18th February 1935 hauled a train of 650 tons from Paris Nord to Calais Ville, with one stop at Amiens, at an overall average speed of 68.8mph. The average *running* speed was 74.4mph, but the especially authorised maximum speed of 87.5mph was maintained over the whole $72\frac{1}{2}$ miles between Amiens and Etaples. The average running speed on the return journey to Paris was 77.25mph. The engine was then tried on a

750 ton Paris-Boulogne train, making frequent stops and steam-heated. On this run the power output by No. 240.707 was remarkable, including 3,200dbhp at 53mph on the Neufchatel gradient of 1 in 143, and a sustained dbhp of more than 2,750. In comparison with this latter figure, the much bigger Mountain type engine No. 41.C.1 of the PLM had managed 2,350-2,450dbhp on a similar train during the Nord-Est-PLM-PO trials in 1932; whilst the Est Mountain had registered 1,960-2,000 and Chapelon's rebuilt Pacific 2,150-2,250dbhp.

Chapelon's 4-8-0 then went to the Etat, where it worked several times over the steeply graded and sinuous main line between Paris St Lazare and Cherbourg at the head of a 14-coach train weighing 607 tons. The best recorded time for the 231 miles was 212 minutes, and this included a stop for six minutes at Caen.

No. 240.707 then returned to the PO, where it was put on to the haulage of a 1,000 ton train to run from Bordeaux to Angoulème at the schedule of the "Sud Express", which was timed 13 minutes faster than the heavy express trains – a schedule that it had no difficulty in keeping.

The Est Railway, which had sent Mountains to the trials on the Nord, was also interested; so the following year the same engine was sent to them and tried on the *rapides*, heavy ordinary express trains, stopping passenger trains, and even heavy freight trains. On all of them it had no difficulty in gaining considerably on the scheduled timetable. Particularly noteworthy were the arrival on a 823 ton express from Chalons 26 minutes before time, and a gain of 38 minutes with a freight train weighing 1,228 tons over the 98 miles from Paris to Troyes.

In 1938 the conservative PLM, always reluctant to believe that any other railway could produce something better than their own products, at last condescended to express interest and asked the PO for the loan of one of its rebuilt 4-8-0s. No. 240.705 was accordingly despatched and tried on the main line between Paris and Lyon. The trains it was allotted were the No. 11 'down' and the No. 12 'up', which were the fastest on the railway and scheduled to cover the 332½ miles between Paris and Lyon without change of engines. No. 240.705 worked these trains for nine round trips, 2,992.5 miles, without a single hitch. The average running speeds for the 'down' and 'up' journeys were 67.4 and 66 mph respectively, as compared with the 61.5 and 61.2mph required by the timetable. The standard weight of the train was 345 tons, but on all except one journey the dynamometer car was added, increasing the weight to about 400 tons. On 6th July Blaisy Tunnel, at the top of the 1 in 125 bank, was passed at 71mph, registering an average drawbar horsepower, corrected to the equivalent on the level, of 2,600, and a maximum of 2,840.

In 1938 all the old railway companies in France were nationalised, and, as a result of these trials, the new SNCF decided that another 25 of these 4-8-0 locomotives should be built for the PLM (now the Sud-Est Region). In these new rebuilds Chapelon incorporated a number of improvements. These included an increase in the volume of the low pressure cylinders of 10%, the fitting of a mechanical stoker, and strengthened frames. In addition, external pipework was largely concealed within an enlarged boiler outer casing, the running plate was raised above the coupled wheels so that wheel splashers were eliminated, and the cab was fixed to the boiler instead of the chassis, thus reducing vibration and providing more comfort for the enginemen. Chapelon had obtained the services of the artist Emile André Schefer to assist him with the external outline and so produced a most attractive looking engine; for André Chapelon was most particular about the appearance of his engines. These new engines were classified 240.P and numbered 240.P.1 to 240.P.25. They were put into service from the beginning of June 1940, when the evacuation of the British Expeditionary Force (including the author) from Dunkirk and its surroundings had just been completed. All were in service by the end of 1941, hauling fast and heavy trains on the Laroche-Dijon-Lyon section of the old PLM main line.

One of the 240.P class engines, No. 240.P.5, with Driver Chartier and Fireman Jarry on the footplate, recorded what is probably the finest steam locomotive performance on a power-to-weight basis ever produced in any country. The train hauled weighed 800 tons and consisted of 17 coaches. With this load, on 31st May 1941, and under the scrutiny of the senior motive power officials of the Sud-Est, the engine maintained an average speed 66.3mph and developed 3190 equivalent drawbar horsepower up the 19½ mile climb between Les Laumes and Blaisy, with an average gradient of 1 in 138 and a maximum of 1 in 125. A speed of 71mph was reached up the 1 in 213 immediately after Thenissey, and Blaisy at the summit was passed at 61mph. The gross power (ie neglecting acceleration and gradient) developed at the drawbar, as registered in the dynamometer car, increased steadily over the whole section; it was 2,500 passing Les Laumes, 2,900 at Thenissey, 3,300 at Verrey, and no less than 3,300 at Blaisy. The last two kilometres, on a rising gradient of 1 in 125, were covered at a speed of 61.25mph with a dbhp of 3,175, corresponding to *3,600*dbhp at a uniform speed on the level. The pressure in the boiler was kept constant during the whole of this run, and the water level in the gauge still stood at 6cm when the regulator was closed at the end of this effort.

Chapelon told me that the 240.Ps were his favourite engines, and he presented me with a signed photograph of one of them. As a class, they were probably the most brilliant steam locomotives ever built. Some English writers have said that there was too much power packed into these engines and that they suffered from broken frames. Chapelon was most indignant at this allegation and told me that it was quite untrue, and that no 240.P ever had a broken frame. It was a tragedy that when electrification came they were broken up in 1952 – none being saved for preservation. It has been suggested that PLM outrage at a 'foreign' locomotive demonstrating its superiority over the native Mountains may have had something to do with it.

Chapter 15
Bulleid's Deviation

O. V. S. Bulleid was one of those engineers of genius who produced brilliant ideas that are put into practice before they are thoroughly thought out. Many aspects of the locomotives that he designed, therefore, embodied deviations from the generally accepted practice in construction that generations of engineers had developed from the experiences of their predecessors. Bulleid's engines were loved by the men who drove and fired them, which showed that the theory was sound; but they were loathed by the men who had to maintain them, which demonstrated the gap between theory and practical application. Bulleid cannot be omitted from the list of eminent locomotive engineers, but the locomotives that he built were so separate from the main stream of development that they had no influence. The steam circuit of his engines was excellent because he had adopted the ideas of Chapelon, whom he greatly admired; but his own ideas did not influence any other locomotive engineer. He had, indeed, introduced too many untried features at once, and Chapelon himself once commented to me with a smile that Bulleid's engines were *"un peu compliqué".* That Bulleid's special features marred a truly great design, was shown by the record of his Pacifics when they had been modified into a more conventional form.

The immediate problem facing Bulleid when, on 20th September 1937, he arrived at Waterloo and took over from R. E. L. Maunsell as CME of the Southern Railway, was to meet the demands posed by increasing weight of the Company's express trains on the non-electrified routes. This would need an express locomotive with increased boiler capacity and tractive effort as compared with existing stock, without exceeding the main line axle load limit of 21 tons or the restrictions imposed by the Southern Railway composite loading gauge.

On 2nd March 1938 the Locomotive Committee authorised the construction of ten steam locomotives for main line use, but did not mention the type. Bulleid decided that his engine must be able to haul a train of from 550 to 600 tons on the main lines of the old London & South Western Railway at 70mph and a Continental boat train of similar weight on the more difficult South Eastern & Chatham section at 60mph. The existing 'King Arthur' class 4-6-0s, good engines though they were, were limited to eleven coaches, or approximately 350 tons, on the LSWR routes; whilst on the SECR section the more powerful four-cylinder 'Lord Nelson' class 4-6-0s were having difficulty in running the 460 ton "Golden Arrow" Pullman car express because of the slow initial running from Victoria imposed by the frequent suburban electric trains. The "Night Ferry" London-Paris sleeping car express, incorporating the heavy Wagon-Lit coaches, had to be double headed, generally by SECR rebuilt D or E class 4-4-0s.

The wheel arrangement of the engine Bulleid wanted presented difficulties. A 4-8-2 seemed the ideal, but he found that this would be too long for the existing turntables. Then, in the light of his experience with

Gresley's P2 classs, he suggested a 2-8-2; but here he came up against the Civil Engineer, who was opposed to a leading pony truck on an express engine because of the disastrous accident at Sevenoaks to an express headed by a 2-6-4 tank engine (even though it had been proved that it was the track not the engine that was at fault). A trailing truck was needed because Bulleid wanted a wide firebox (though Chapelon with his 4-8-0s had shown this was not necessary). There was only one choice left and that was a Pacific, which the Civil Engineer accepted.

Bulleid may well have felt aggrieved over the opposition to a leading pony truck for express work, for express trains were being worked by engines with such trucks without incident on the three other main line companies in Great Britain, and the type of Southern tank engine that had been hauling the train in the above mentioned accident had been approved by Gresley as perfectly satisfactory for fast running, after trials on the London & North Eastern Railway.

The upper portion of the new Pacific was covered by a light plate casing. Bulleid did not believe in streamlining and his casing was not intended to have that effect. He described it as 'air-smoothing', and the shape of the engine and tender was meant to merge with that of his flush-sided carriages. The effect was rather ugly, but artistry in design was not one of Bulleid's strong points. The casing did, indeed, dispense with the need for the wheel splashers, running plates, and boiler lagging plates used in the conventional superstructure, but any advantages that may have resulted were more than overshadowed by the ensuing penalties, as will be described later. Bulleid did not like a round-top firebox, because when the final Great Northern K2 class 2-6-0 was subjected to a pressure test there had been a slight bulging, and transverse boiler stays had to be fitted. He therefore chose a Belpaire firebox, the flattened top of which determined part of the shape of the casing from cab to smokebox. A Lemaitre blastpipe was adopted, but it was modified, probably to avoid the payment of royalties. The chimney, therefore, was of wide diameter and of a plain stovepipe pattern because it was hidden from view by the casing.

The magnificent boiler was perhaps the most notable feature of Bulleid's engine. Chapelon influence was apparent in the grate area of 48sq ft, which was unusually large by British standards, for Bulleid was determined that the engine should never be short of steam. The boiler pressure of 280psi was higher than previously used on a class of locomotives in Great Britain, and Chapelon's practice on his rebuilt locomotives was copied in the high superheat temperature of 400°C. With these high figures, a copper firebox was not considered suitable, and one of all-welded steel was provided. This had the additional advantage of saving weight. Two thermic syphons were fitted in this firebox, connecting the lower part of the tubeplate to the crown. Their syphonic action added to the circulation of the water in the boiler and increased the heating surface within the firebox and above the fire bed, which is the most effective part. They also conferred the further advantages (in no way connected with their functional purpose) of making the firebox more rigid and of helping to keep the crown sheet from collapsing in the event of a serious drop in the water level. (Indeed, these thermic syphons did save at least one disaster, by keeping the firebox crown up when all six fusible plugs went.)

The diameter of the coupled wheels was 6ft 2in. Bulleid's experiences on the LNER had shown that wheels of this diameter were no bar to high speed, and they did provide a higher tractive effort than the normal 6ft 7in wheels of Southern express engines. Also, they helped to keep the engines within the restricted 13ft 1in height of the Southern Railway loading gauge. Further weight was saved by the use of steel plates, joined by welding, instead of the usual heavy castings.

Bulleid decided on three cylinders to enable him to omit reciprocating balance and he selected a stroke of 24in to avoid unduly high piston speeds when running fast. The diameter was 18in in order to obtain the tractive effort he wanted. So that the passages from the valves to the cylinders should be as straight as possible (André Chapelon again), outside admission valves were used instead of the inside admission customary with piston valves.

A major innovation was to enclose the motion in an oil bath between the frames, to improve on traditional methods of lubrication and eliminate wear in motion details caused by grit. An added advantage was a reduction in the large number of oiling points required (a reduction much appreciated by drivers). As it would not be feasible to fit three sets of normal Walschaerts valve gear within the limited confines of the oil bath, Bulleid designed an ingenious miniaturised version. He replaced the outside return cranks and inside eccentric, of the usual

Walschaerts arrangement for three cylinders, by a three-throw crankshaft, driven by two inverted tooth chains which actuated the expansion links. One chain was horizontal, running from crank axle to an intermediate sprocket wheel, from which the second chain ran downwards to the three-throw crankshaft. This intermediate sprocket wheel was adjustable, so that chain tension could be adjusted during repairs. Each valve was actuated by an arm and link between the valve heads, where there was room for them in the exhaust cavity.

Although outside admission cylinders were used, the valve gear was arranged for inside admission, and so the movement of the arms was reversed by a rocker shaft. All three rockers were connected to a shaft passing transversely through the three cylinders. So that the three sets of valve gears could fit into the space between the frames, there was an ingenious arrangement. The full throw of the expansion links was made less than that required for a full travel of the valves; but to compensate for this, the rocker arms were made of unequal length in the proportion of 3 to 8, so that a $1\frac{1}{2}$in movement of the radius rod gave a valve travel of 4in. The oil bath contained the three sets of valve motion, the inside cross head and slide bars, inside connecting rod, crank axle, big and little ends. Oil was delivered over all these parts by two gear pumps, driven by a chain off the three-throw crank shaft, by means of perforated pipes.

Three mechanical lubricators looked after front end lubrication, one for each cylinder; and these were sited in an enclosure below the smokebox door – the lubricator ratchets being driven off the valve rocker shaft. There was

Bulleid's 'air-smoothed' Pacific of the 'Merchant Navy' class, No.21C4 *Cunard White Star*.
(Courtesy National Railway Museum, York).

a steam reversing gear.

Another Bulleid speciality was the coupled wheel centre. With the normal spoked wheel centre there is a tendency to distortion and the spokes sometimes crack. In conjunction with the Sheffield firm of Firth Brown, Bulleid designed a type of wheel centre very similar to the American 'Boxpok' pattern, which he called the 'BFB' (Bulleid-Firth Brown) wheel.

Bulleid was rightly proud of his cab, which was more comfortable and better protected from the weather than that of almost any other contemporary British locomotive, and the springing was designed to give the engine crew as comfortable a ride as possible. He had indeed designed an engine which was destined to be a footplateman's dream – but a fitter's nightmare!

Soon after the testing of the Pacifics started, various faults began to occur. There were changes in power output, which it was afterwards discovered could be corrected by lengthening the cut-off and opening the regulator. The cause was found to lie in the steam-operated reversing gear, which frequently crept away from the position in which the driver had set it. A frequent cause of complete failure on the road was a broken rocker shaft, and the enclosure of the motion made it difficult for the driver to detect impending failure by stopping for examination. A driver learned that a rocker shaft had broken by the engine missing two beats. The main cause of broken rocker shafts was traced to an unbalanced steam chest pressure, that is a pressure difference between the two ends of the piston valves. The immediate solution arrived at was to strengthen the rocker shafts by increasing their diameter. Later the steam chests were redesigned, with a balancing cavity included.

Erratic running was another problem, and this was due to the type of valve gear, and was caused by backlash in the many joints, which was amplified by the unequal arms of the rocker shafts. The wear of the pins and holes of the chain links and also of the teeth in the intermediate sprocket wheel, made it quite impossible to operate the valve gear with any degree of precision.

The oil sump, though excellent in theory, could not remain oil tight because it was fabricated as part of the main frames, and unlike a car sump (from which Bulleid had got the idea) it was subject to frame flexure. In addition, the steamy conditions and large changes in temperature resulted in condensation serious enough to make the oil emulsify and thus corrode the valve gear components.

Oil consumption was appallingly heavy. Oil escaped from the valve spindle guides in front of the sump; getting on to the driving wheels and causing the engine to slip, and on to the boiler lagging where it caught fire. It was impossible, too, to prevent oil leaking where the driving axle passed through the frames, as well as through joints in the structure of the bath and through cracks in the metal caused by vibration and flexing of the frames on curves.

The sumps did indeed reduce considerably the amount of oiling that drivers normally had to do, but the fitters had to top them up daily and also drain off the water deposited by condensation. Furthermore, the customary inspection by drivers was difficult on these engines, and this, together with fault finding had to be left to the fitters.

But in spite of all these difficulties the Bulleid Pacifics were a joy to drive and fire – in fact firing was so easy that with an unconscientious or unskilled fireman there could be a very large consumption of coal.

Named after vessels in the Merchant Navy, these big Pacifics had been intended to meet all Southern express passenger traffic needs on the principal non-electrified main lines; and so they did, but there were a number of secondary main lines, including all those west of Exeter, over which long distance passenger services ran, but over which engines with an axle load over 18ton 10cwt were prohibited. For these the "Packets" (a nickname derived from the first of the class, *Channel Packet*) were too heavy. Most of the passenger trains over such routes were worked by Maunsell's U and N class 2-6-0s, and these admirable engines did sterling work on the lighter trains, but they were sorely taxed on the long heavy trains to the West Country during the holiday seasons.

In April 1941 Bulleid instructed Brighton Drawing Office to design a suitable engine to take over from Maunsell's Moguls west of Exeter. The Drawing Office first suggested an engine of the same wheel arrangement, 2-6-0, as those it was to replace, but a three-cylinder engine somewhat similar to the LNER K4 class which Gresley had designed for the West Highland line. Bulleid did not like this idea; the quality of the coal was deteriorating and he thought that a wide firebox was necessary to deal with inferior fuel. (Chapelon would not have agreed with him; his 240.P class 4-8-0s produced astounding results with some pretty awful coal in their long narrow fireboxes!) The Drawing Office went back to its drawing board and returned with a 2-6-2, again a three-cylinder, with three sets of Walschaerts valve gear and BFB wheels. Bulleid gave this modified approval, but thought that a leading bogie, instead of a pony truck, would be better suited to the many curves on the West of England lines (doubtless, also, with a thought of possible objections from the Civil Engineer to the pony truck!). This meant a Pacific, and one sufficiently light to meet the axle load restrictions. Owing to wartime production difficulties, it was desirable that it should embody as many of the 'Merchant Navy' parts and features as possible. As one might have expected, the result was a Pacific which bore a close resemblance to a 'Merchant Navy' – so close, indeed, that to a casual observer it was difficult to tell the difference. All the new engines were named after towns in the West Country and were officially known as the 'West Country' class, though they acquired a nickname among the footplate men as the "Lightweights". The first of them was completed in May 1945, and from then on (though the original authority had been for 20 engines) they were turned out almost continuously up until January 1951, by which time they had attained the astounding number of 110. Their route availablity was such that they were

Bulleid SR 'West Country' class Pacific No.21C101 *Exeter.*
(Courtesy National Railway Museum, York).

acceptable almost anywhere on what was now the Southern Region of British Railways, except for a few branch lines. Forty four of the light Pacifics were given the names of personalities, headquarters, squadrons of the Royal Air Force, etc., associated with the Battle of Britain and were rather stupidly referred to as the 'Battle of Britain' class; for they were identically the same engines as those in the 'West Country' class – a differentiation that has been misleading railway enthusiasts ever since!

Naturally the "Lightweights" inherited all the troubles of their bigger sisters, but in spite of these problems both 'Merchant Navies' and 'West Countries' were brilliant performers. They had a tremendous reserve of boiler capacity which was just what was required to enable rapid recovery from the numerous signal checks in the dense traffic areas in the Eastern Section of the Southern with its difficult gradients.

Drivers were spared the occasional anxious glance at the boiler pressure gauge, for with these excellent boilers there was never any shortage of steam, even with the most

'Merchant Navy' class Pacific as BR No.35008 *Orient Line* **on the 1.30pm Waterloo to Bournemouth express leaving Basingstoke on 29th March 1955.**
(Philip J. Kelley).

ham-handed of inexperienced firemen; nor was the setting of the cut-off critical, so that the vagaries of the steam reverser gave no cause for concern, even though they could be prodigious. With worn valve gear the cut-off setting could read anything between 50% and full gear! Heavy spark throwing at the chimney top did serve as a notice to the driver that the lever needed easing back. Although both classes were liable to slip, not only at starting but also at speed, it is unlikely that there has ever been a British locomotive that could be driven in such an almost light-hearted manner without losing time, steam or water. Of their performance during the Interchange trials of 1948, Cecil J Allen wrote: "The most uniform standard of performance throughout the tests were put up by the Southern engines, behind which it was a joy to travel".

The various troublesome features of the Bulleid Pacifics, together with a number of cases of broken or fractured crank axles, led to a decision to rebuild them. The major alterations carried out in the rebuilding were the removal of the oil bath and chain driven valve gear, and their replacement by three independent sets of normal Walschaerts valve gear; the removal of the 'air-smoothed casing' and its replacement by normal boiler clothing; the substitution of a screw reversing gear for the steam one; and the fitting of the following: a circular smokebox, standard BR piston heads, new mechanical lubricators, a regulator designed to reduce the tendency to slip, new ash pans, and new sandboxes. It will be observed that the locomotives remained substantially as Bulleid designed them.

They were rebuilt, under the general direction of Roland Bond, the CME, by R. G. Jarvis. Bond had insisted that in their rebuilt form they should conform to that designed for British Railways; and indeed a rebuilt

Bulleid Pacific looks very like a 'Britannia'. In their new guise they were extremely good and handsome engines; but many enginemen felt that they had not got quite the sparkle of their early days. All the 'Merchant Navies' were rebuilt, but the rebuilding of the 'West Countries' stopped in 1961, when 60 had been dealt with. The remaining 50 remained in their original condition until withdrawal.

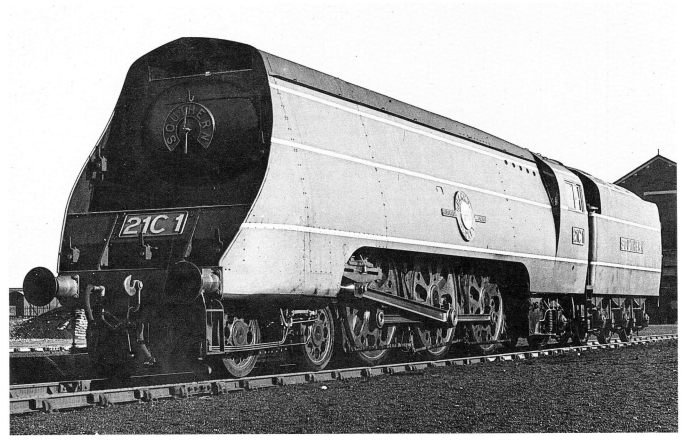

The first Bullied Pacific, No .21C1 *Channel Packet* as originally built, and posed for official photography in 1941.

Chapter 16
The Mountains

Tender engines with a 4-8-2 wheel arrangement were not, of course, part of the British railway scene, but *Les Mountains* (pronounced as if the word were French) figured largely amongst the latter day French heavy express locomotives, and they are mentioned in connection with the Nord trials in Chapter 10.

During 1921 and 1922 the Est and PLM Railways foresaw that their existing express locomotives would soon be insufficiently powerful to work express trains over the heavily graded lines of their systems owing to the increasing weight of the load behind the tender, particularly as both administrations were considering an acceleration of some of their services.

On the Est the requirements was for a locomotive capable of working the trains proposed at 80mph over the switchback route between Paris and Belfort. The PLM wanted engines more powerful than their Pacifics to run the heavy expresses over the difficult sections Laroche-Dijon, Marseilles-Nice, and Dijon-Vallorbe. Both companies opted for a 4-8-2, and in January 1925 prototypes were constructed by the Epernay Works for the Esty and by Schneider-Creusot for the PLM.

The Est engine, No. 41001, with an axle load of 18.5 tons, could run on most of the Company's main lines. It was a four-cylinder compound and, when it appeared on

10th January 1925 for trials between Epernay and Chalons-sur-Marne, it was hailed by the Press as the most powerful locomotive in Europe.

Expensive trials were carried out for five years with this engine under Robert L'éguille, who was in charge of design work on the Est, and several modifications were made before further orders were placed for another 40 engines in 1930.

From 2nd to 11th October 1929 No. 41001 of the Est was lent to the Etat Railway for trial on its 600 ton trains between Paris and Cherbourg with a scheduled time for the journey of $4\frac{1}{2}$ hours. Its performance so pleased the Etat that it ordered 29 similar engines for its own use from the Fives-Lille Company in 1932, and, two years later, another 20 from two other private builders. No. 41001 was renumbered 241.001 in December 1930 and all subsequent 4-8-2s built for the Est and the Etat were numbered on this new system of preceding the engine number by its axle arrangement. With the additon of a letter after the axle notation to denote the class, this system was eventually adopted on all French railways.

Two of the Est Mountains took part, as already stated, in the trials over the Nord main line in competition with the Nord "Superpacific", a PLM Mountain, and Chapelon's rebuilt PO Pacific.

On 24th October 1933 Etat Mountain No. 241.022, hauling a Cherbourg-Paris express, was derailed while crossing the St Helier Viaduct. The engines had proved powerful and free-running and rode well with the original bogie springs which had eight tons initial control value.

Est Railway Mountain 4-cylinder compound No.13 at Troyes in 1929.
(P. Ransome-Wallis Collection, Courtesy National Railway Museum, York).

Est Mountain No.241.A.7 with double blast pipe and chimney at Troyes in 1952.
(P. Ransome-Wallis Collection, Courtesy National Railway Museum, York).

For some reason the 'crack-off' value had been reduced from eight tons to four, after the retirement of the Etat CME, Duchatel, and hence this disastrous derailment. The result of this accident was an unnecessary reduction in the maximum speed permitted with these engines from the standard 75mph to 70mph. After the formation of the SNCF (French National Railways), the substitution of springs with a 6 ton crack-off value gave very steady riding at the original 75mph when this altered bogie was tried on one of the Mountains. But no further action was carried out by the Etat until 1949, when large numbers of PLM 231.G and 231.K class Pacifics, which were allowed to run at 75mph, became available after the PLM electrification.

The reduction of their permitted speed led to Etat Mountains being removed from the Le Havre and Cherbourg main lines and transferred to the lines running through Le Mans to Rennes, Quimper and Brest. On 22nd May 1937 the lines between Paris and Le Mans were electrified at 1,500 volts, which reduced the field of action available to the Mountains. A number of them became redundant and were accepted by the Est. Although they were basically the same as the Est's own Mountains, they had not received the same modifications as the latter and were consequently received with little enthusiasm by the Est enginemen.

On the Est, Robert Léguille was responsible for many modifications to the Mountains, including double

admission and exhaust valves to the low pressure cylinders and a six-jet trefoil exhaust. The maximum cylinder horsepower was thereby raised from about 2,900 to 3,600, which was about equal with the second series of Chapelon's rebuilt PO Pacifics. One can understand why the Est driver's had a poor opinion of the Etat Mountains! The Est Mountains in their final form were, indeed, very fine engines.

During the Second World War several Etat Mountains were removed to Germany, and others suffered from Allied air attacks on the French railways.

The last of this class of Mountains was withdrawn on 18th February 1965. It had started life on the Etat in 1932 and was transferred to the Est in 1947.

The story of the PLM Mountains is very different. At the beginning of 1921 the company was running short of Pacifics to haul passenger trains and some of its Mikados were accordingly made available to haul the heavy expresses between Paris and Dijon. With the great adhesion of their eight coupled wheels they proved more successful than the Pacifics over the steeply graded line between Laroche and Dijon, and they could easily sustain the required speed of 56mph.

The PLM concluded that it would be better to have a bogie in front of eight coupled wheels for an express engine, and a design study was accordingly undertaken for a 4-8-2. The PLM requirement was for a four-cylinder compound with cylinders of the same dimensions as those of the Mikados. In the approved design the low pressure cylinders (on account of their large size) were outside and driving the leading coupled axle; the high pressure cylinders were inside, at the rear of the outside cylinders, and drove the second coupled axle, being located suffi-

Est (ex-Etat) Mountain No.241.A.83 at La Vilette 1955.
(P. Ransome-Wallis Collection, Courtesy National Railway Museum, York).

ciently high for the connecting rods to pass over the leading axle. The inside crank axle was of the 'bent', or 'Z', type, which was perhaps more popular on the Continent than the 'built-up' pattern. The coupled wheels were 6ft in diameter.

The first of the new Mountains, No. 241.A.1, was delivered in February 1925 and soon demonstrated its capacity. On 16th March it headed a passenger train weighing 571 tons, making numerous stops between Laroche and Dijon. The train was some 10% heavier than

that normally worked by a Pacific, but the Mountain displayed a capacity for rapid acceleration and easily maintained a speed of 50mph up the ascent to Blaisy. The PLM were so satisfied with the engine's performance that no less than 145 of the same type had been delivered by 1931. They proved extremely successful, and by 1932 they were working between Paris and Lyon, Dijon and Vallorbe, Paris and Nevers, and Avignon and Vintimille. They were stationed at Laroche, Dijon, Dôle, Marseille, Nice, and Les Laumes.

In service, however, some faults appeared. The 'Z' type crank axle, while perfectly satisfactory for moderate powers, got overheated due to the high powers developed by the inside high pressure cylinders; and at speeds in

PLM Mountain No.241.C.1, built 1930, at Dijon in 1952
(P. Ransome-Wallis Collection, Courtesy National Railway Museum, York).

excess of 60mph there were heavy vibrations owing to the chassis being insufficiently robust. Above all, after some 30,000 miles of running the 'Z' type cranks broke at the angles of the bend. This last trouble was eventually cured by fixing counter-weights at the bends.

In assessing their express motive power, the PLM reckoned that the 241.A class had all the power needed but that their speed was too limited; whereas the Pacifics had the speed, thanks to their larger wheels (they had not yet been rebuilt on Chapelon principles), but they lacked the requisite power on the more heavily graded sections. They decided, therefore, that they needed an engine that would have both the power and the speed. In 1929, accordingly, they invited the Schneider Company to design a Mountain type with 6ft 6in driving wheels and a pressure of 280psi. An engine to meet these requirements was constructed by the firm and completed on 29th December 1930 as No. 241. C.1. This engine, as already recounted, took part in the trials on the Nord in 1932 in comparison with a Chapelon rebuilt Pacific, a Nord Pacific, and an Est Mountain. It remained the sole example of its type, though being somewhat modified over the years. After the war it was put into the same link as Chapelon's 240.Ps. The advent of these latter had resulted in some of the PLM 241s as being withdrawn from service as redundant. Some of them, however, had been modified through the replacement of the cone-shaped boiler front by deflector plates and the fitting of a double exhaust, and had been reclassified 241.D.

Meanwhile a modification of the 241.C design had been undertaken and, with improvements due to Chapelon, the 241.P was produced. Tests showed it to be a very satisfactory engine. In 1945, immediately after the war, an order was placed for 35 of this class, of which

the first were in service in 1948. They never worked on the Paris-Laroche-Dijon section, for which they had been intended, because electric trains were running between Paris and Dijon by 1951, and the 240.Ps continued to work express trains between Paris and Dijon until electrification. The 241.Ps, therefore, hauled heavy express trains between Lyon and Marseille. Ultimately they went to other main lines of the SNCF, and the last were based at Le Mans, working over the old Etat routes in Brittany.

The 241.Ps were excellent engines, though they did not approach the brilliance of the Chapelon 240.Ps. It would seem, however, that the authorities in the South Eastern and Mediterranean Regions of the SNCF (the old PLM) preferred the 241.Ps because they regarded them as up-dated versions of 241.C.1, and therefore PLM engines, whereas the 240.Ps came from the PO, and that it must never be said that the last great trains worked by steam over the *Ligne Impériale* were headed by engines of one of the lesser companies! However, an engine was to come which surpassed even the 240. Ps in power.

In 1932 the Etat Railway asked the Office Centrale d'Etudes de Matérial (the central design office of the French railways) to design for them a 4-8-2 express locomotive. The OCEM accordingly produced plans for

Opposite: SNCF Mountain No.241.P.1 leaving Lyon (Perrache) on a Paris to Marseilles express in 1957.
(P. Ransome-Wallis Collection, Courtesy National Railway Museum, York).

Below: Two SNCF 241.P class Mountains at Marseilles (La Blancharde) in 1957. The nearer one is No.241.P.17.
(P. Ransome-Wallis Collection, Courtesy National Railway Museum, York).

a three-cylinder simple expansion Mountain which was intended to achieve expansion ratios equal to those of Chapelon's highly efficient compound locomotives.

This big engine was built by the works of Fives-Lille in 1932 and launched with great publicity, including an inaugural and well advertised display at the Gare St Lazare, for the awe-stricken admiration of the general public and officials of less fortunate railways. In 1935 it was on view at the Brussels Exhibition. The salient features of this locomotive were a boiler pressure of 292psi, Renaud poppet valves, driving wheels 6ft 4¾in, in diameter, a grate area of 53.8sq ft, and a mechanical stoker which reduced the effective area of the grate to 47.3sq ft. A trefoil exhaust was fitted at first, but before long this was replaced by a single Kylchap exhaust with six lobes.

asked the Locomotive Study Division of the SNCF for advice. André Chapelon seized the opportunity to submit a proposal for the rebuilding of the engine as a three-cylinder compound so that the potential power of its large boiler and other dimensions could be realised. The Directorate of Rolling Stock and Traction rejected the proposal, perhaps because they thought the expenditure could not be justified. Chapelon did not give up hope, but he had to wait until he found an acceptable reason in building a prototype for his projected range of high powered compound engines for the SNCF. In due course approval for the rebuilding of the Etat engine was given, but too late to do anything before the outbreak of war in 1939. However, in 1942 conditions in German-occupied France had become sufficiently stable for work to start.

This engine was allotted the number 241.101, and it was presumably hoped that it was to be the first of a class. Alas for such hopes! No. 241.101 was awful! It would not steam, the small cross section of its valves restricted its power output, and it rode so badly that it damaged the track. In 1936 it could be seen at the Achères depot as a stationary steam generator. In 1938 it was consigned to the sanctuary of Le Mans, from whence it made occasional sorties until serious damage to its inside cylinder terminated its active career.

One imagines that OCEM was distinctly unpopular. The Ouest region (which the Etat had by now become)

The frames of the Etat Mountain were only 1¼in thick, which was inadequate for the power that Chapelon expected from his rebuild of the engine. The chassis would therefore have to be strengthened, but strengthening on the existing wheel arrangement would raise the axle weight above the permitted maximum of 21 tons. He decided to replace the trailing bissel axle by a two-axle bissel truck. This altered the wheel arrangement to 4-8-4, and, strictly speaking, removed the engine from the Mountain category which is the subject of this chapter. However, the author has overruled this objection on the grounds that the original was indeed a Mountain!

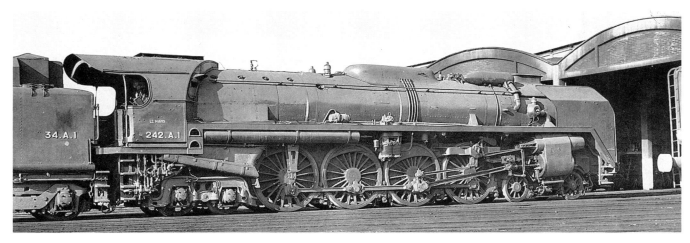

Chapelon's 3-cylinder compound 4-8-4 No.242.A.1 at Le Mans in 1952.
(P. Ransome-Wallis Collection, Courtesy National Railway Museum, York).75

Chapelon had wanted a monobloc construction, such as he had envisaged for the powerful SNCF locomotives of the future, of which this was to be the prototype, but under the occupation conditions this was impossible. He decided therefore to strengthen the chassis transversely by joining the frames with steel stays at convenient intervals along their whole length, and longitudinally by welding horizontal plates to the upper parts of the frames. This proved a sound solution to get the additional strength he needed.

A three-cylinder compound was a new conception in Chapelon rebuilds, for his Pacifics and 4-8-0s were four-cylinder engines; but in rebuilding one tries to make use of the existing cylinder arrangement. There were certain advantages in having three cylinders. In the four-cylinder arrangement the two inside cylinders needed, of course, two cranks on the driving axle, which inevitably detracted from its rigidity. A weakened rigidity promotes a tendency to flex at high powers, which in turn has an adverse effect on the seating of the axle boxes. Chapelon therefore decided to retain the engine's three-cylinder layout but to use the Smith-Sauvage compound system with one inside high pressure cylinder and two outside low pressure cylinders. With only one inside cylinder, the crank axle webs could be increased in thickness to 7.1in, as compared

Another view of No.242.A.1 at Le Mans in 1952 the most powerful European express steam locomotive ever built.
(P. Ransome-Wallis Collection, Courtesy National Railway Museum, York).

with the maximum of 4.1in possible in the 240.Ps. The inside high pressure cylinder drove the leading coupled axle and the outside low pressure cylinders the second. All three cylinders were in line between the bogie wheels; the same layout as in the original simple expansion engine. There was independent Walschaerts valve gear to all three cylinders and independent cut-off to HP and LP cylinders. (Chapelon had chosen the last because this was a trial engine, and the independent cut-off was only a temporary arrangement to enable him to establish the relationship, between HP and LP cut-offs, which divided power between the two cylinder groups in the best proportion. They could then be permanently tied in that relationship in the future production of similar engines.)

Chapelon, of course, paid particular attention to the steam circuit. The boiler was so big that even a double Kylchap exhaust would not have provided sufficient width of chimney, and Chapelon therefore fitted a triple Kylchap and chimney. The boiler pressure was 292psi and there were two Nicholson thermic syphons.

Now numbered 242.A.1, Chapelon's great engine was completed on 18th May 1946. Never had his brilliance as a locomotive engineer been displayed more impressively; for the fairy wand that changed Cinderella into a Princess scarcely equalled the genius that transformed this slut amongst locomotives into the most outstanding steam locomotive that ever ran upon rails.

During trials carried out on the Vitry bank and on the line with brake locomotives, there was, for the first time in Europe, a sustained 4,000 horsepower at the tender drawbar in continuous working (with pressure and water constant in the boiler). This entailed 800hp per square metre of grate area, corresponding to more than 5,000 cylinder horsepower. This result was achieved at 50mph, with cut-offs at 80%HP and 50%LP, and at 62.5mph, with cut-offs at 70%HP and 45%LP. At 75mph, with 60% cut-off HP and 40%LP, horsepower at the drawbar was 3,800. The fuel and water consumptions of this three-cylinder compound were comparable with the best obtained with Chapelon's four-cylinder compounds.

On trials there were many brilliant runs. It will suffice to mention one on the Ouest Region. The working was an 'up' train from Caen to Paris on 23rd April 1947. With 775 tons behind the tender, the engine tackled the Lisieux bank, which starts about $2\frac{1}{2}$ miles from Lisieux and is over 8 miles long with a gradient of 1 in 125. In spite of a strong wind of 25mph, the engine lifted its heavy train up the bank at an astonishing speed. An average

tractive effort of 10 tons was held throughout the climb, and the speed, which was 55mph when the climb began, after a previous rising gradient of 1 in 370, rose to and was maintained at between 56.2 and 59.4mph during the whole of the ascent, with a tendency to accelerate. The gross horsepower developed at the drawbar reached maximum of between 3,500 and 3,750; this latter, at the speed of 56.2mph, was equivalent to *4,300*hp on the level.

On 12th September 1952 a run behind No. 242.A.1 was arranged for a delegation of South American railwaymen who were on a visit to view French railways. The engine was booked to work a train of 26 coaches, weighing 810 tons, over the 131.1 miles from Paris to Le Mans at the schedule allowed for the fastest electric trains; though these were limited to 640 tons. This schedule was improved on by six minutes, No. 242.A.1 taking 1 hour 49 minutes, with an overall average speed of 72.2mph. The improvement was, in fact, even greater, for the electric locomotives made the journey non-stop; whereas Chapelon's 4-8-4 made a special stop at Chartres for ten minutes to take water, so the running time was cut by 16 minutes!

There was a rather amusing sequel to this brilliant run. Electric locomotives to work the express trains over the Paris-Lyon line of the old PLM were being designed, and their intended horsepower was 3,900. But when the account of this run and others by No. 242.A.1 became known the design was hastily altered and the horsepower increased by 1,000 to 4,900.

But to Chapelon's bitter disappointment his projected range of magnificent locomotives was never to be realised. A shortage of coking coal in France led to the Government ordering the SNCF to reduce their consumption of coal in order that sufficient should be available for the steel industry. It was in vain that Chapelon protested that his projected locomotives were to be fitted with 'stokers' and would use non-coking coal, which was useless for the steel works and of which France had ample resources. The plans for the electrification of main line railways were expanded and construction accelerated. It is conceivable that this temporary shortage of coking coal provided an excuse to stop the construction of steam locomotives which might have thrown doubts on the economic justification for spending a vast sum on main line electrification. Chapelon believed that they would, and his plans for these great steam engines are described in a later chapter.

Chapter 17
After Gresley

On 28th April 1941, during the darkest days of the Second World War, Edward Thompson became Chief Mechanical Engineer of the London & North Eastern Railway, following the sad and sudden death of Sir Nigel Gresley. It was not a happy succession, for Thompson had thoroughly disliked his predecessor, and, when he took over responsibility for the locomotive affairs of the LNER, he did his utmost to disparage and overturn his achievements. Engines built henceforward were to be obviously Thompson in both appearance and design, and would incorporate as little as possible of Doncaster's traditional Great Northern practice.

Not long after he became CME Thompson announced his intention to build a Pacific with 6ft 2in coupled wheels which would supersede a wide range of locomotives, mostly engaged on mixed traffic express freight work. These were the P2, or 'Cock o' the North', class 2-8-2s; the V2, or 'Green Arrow', class 2-6-2s; the Great Central four-cylinder 4-6-0s of class B7; the North Eastern B16 class three-cylinder 4-6-0s; and the Great Northern K3 class three-cylinder 2-6-0s.

Thompson elected to produce prototypes for his mixed traffic Pacifics by rebuilding Gresley's P2s. The ostensible reason for destroying these fine engines was that they had given much trouble on the Edinburgh-Aberdeen main line through hot boxes and other ailments. In fact, an investigation showed that these troubles were due to very bad repair work (perhaps as a result of wartime conditions) and a report to that effect had been submitted. Presumably this report had not reached the LNER Locomotive Committee in time to stop their consent to the rebuilding.

One of the great assets of these locomotives was, of course, the extra adhesion provided by their eight coupled wheels, and it was because, in Gresley's opinion, that such extra adhesion was required to work heavy passenger trains over the difficult route between Edinburgh and Aberdeen, that they had been designed. It was for the same reason that André Chapelon had designed his 4-8-0s for the Toulouse main line of the PO. After the conversion of the P2s to Pacifics it seemed unlikely that, in spite of their slightly smaller driving wheels, that they would be able to haul trains any heavier than those within the capacity of the A4s – and so it proved.

Thompson chose three cylinders, but decided on an inside Walschaerts valve gear for the middle cylinder in place of Gresley's conjugated gear. In the light of the lower standards of maintenance available in wartime, this was probably a wise decision. He also chose a divided drive, which was a perfectly reasonable preference.

In obtaining authority to rebuild the P2s, Thompson had assured the LNER's Chief General Manager that he would make full use of existing parts. As part of this undertaking, he retained the rather short connecting rods of the P2s, which drove on the second coupled axle, the cylinders being located between the pony truck and the leading coupled axle. But Thompson had decided on a divided drive for the rebuilds, with the outside cylinders driving on the second coupled axle of the Pacifics, which had been the third coupled axle of the Mikados. The middle cylinder drove on the leading coupled axle, previously the second coupled axle, and thus retained its old position. But on account of the short connecting rods, the outside cylinders had to be sited immediately in front of the leading coupled axle (the original second axle). As the outside cylinders of a three-cylinder engine of this power were too big to be mounted outside the trailing bogie wheels without fouling the loading gauge, the bogie had to be placed in front of them. A draughtsman remarked that one could almost say that the rebuilds were designed round the connecting rods. Thompson insisted that the live steam pipes connecting the superheater header to the cylinders should be as short as possible, though Churchward's designs had shown that this was quite unnecessary because (as Riddles has pointed out) of the speed with which steam travels. The outside cylinders being so far back, the boiler had to be shortened to give these short steam pipes sufficient clearance; the smokebox, therefore, was unusually long. The original boiler was retained, though shortened for the reason given above, but the pressure was increased from 220 to 225psi. The perforated steam collector was kept, as well as the banjo-shaped dome casing in which it was housed. Thompson disliked it but he had undertaken to use existing parts. The double Kylchap exhaust was also retained but the chimney was a rather unsightly stovepipe pattern, and flanked by small (and very ineffective) smoke deflectors mounted on the smokebox. The bogie was the type designed for the B1 4-6-0s.

The first of the P2s to be rebuilt was No. 2005 *Thane of Fife,* and on 2nd April 1943 it was returned to service in its new guise on the Edinburgh-Aberdeen main line, and by the following year all the others in the class had followed it. Troubles came immediately. T.C.B. Miller (conversation with the author) said that the frames flexed about three inches. J.F. Harrison (in a letter to the author) commented that "short connecting rods, for a start, are not good (as was shown by the Raven Pacifics) and between the cylinders and the coupled wheels there developed a serious frame weakness". The flexing was due partly to the inside cylinder being sited where on the Gresley Pacifics there was a frame bracing member. Over a certain speed the engine 'nosed' badly, and on one occasion the Chief draughtsman, who had taken a trip on one of the rebuilt engines, returned terrified at the experience.

During 1945 *Thane of Fife* had to return eight times to Cowlairs Works. The reason was the number of faults that needed correcting: these included cylinders working loose, exhaust system pipes breaking, live steam pipes torn from the header in the smokebox, and bolts breaking between the smokebox and the saddle. All these troubles arose from the frame flexing ahead of the outside cylinders.

The shed master at Peterborough reported that the riding of a later batch of Thompson Pacifics, of basically similar design, was very bad. It was not until after Peppercorn became CME that the reason for the bad riding was found to lie in the weakness of the bogie side control springs. This bogie was satisfactory for the much lighter B1 class 4-6-0s, for which it had been designed, but it could not supply the guidance required by the heavy Pacifics. It will be remembered that the derailment of an Est Mountain on the Etat had been caused by weakening the bogie control springs.

Before all the P2s had been rebuilt, Thompson had already planned the replacement of Gresley's V2 2-6-2s by Pacifics, and the last four of a batch of V2s were turned out from Darlington as Pacifics with the same type of front end as the rebuilt P2s. These, as might be expected, suffered from the same troubles as the ex-P2s. They retained the V2 boiler and rear end, and also the double Kylchap exhaust, which had proved its value. Thompson was sufficiently satisfied with them to order his standard A2 class Pacifics (later A2/3), which were in all major respects identical with the two former batches, which were classified A2/2 and A2/1 respectively. The 1945 Locomotive Construction Programmes authorised 43 of this new standard class, though in fact only 15 were ever built. All the A2 varieties had coupled wheels 6ft 2in diameter and were theoretically mixed traffic engines.

Thompson now turned his attention to a standard express engine to succeed Gresley's A4s. He decided to rebuild as a prototype for the new class, on similar lines to his A2s, a Gresley A1 class Pacific. Of the 18 of these engines that had not yet been modified into the A3 class, he chose the pioneer of all the LNER Pacifics, No. 4470 *Great Northern.* It was a selection that horrified many of those who had worked under Gresley both at Doncaster and on the footplate. J.F. Harrison wrote to the author that Thompson was determined to undermine Gresley's reputation and that there was no better way to do it than to take the first of his Pacifics and rebuild it without the conjugated valve gear. Harrison added that the conjugated valve gear was not satisfactory if not properly maintained and that during the war maintenance in all respects had been sadly neglected, and he believed that Gresley himself would have given it up for that reason. "All of us," wrote Harrison, "tried hard to persuade Thompson to take any other Pacific except the first; but he would have none of it!"

Thompson decreed that his new Pacific would be the first of a new Class A1, so all the remaining 17 original Pacifics were re-designated Class A10. Little remained of the great engine with which Gresley had astonished and delighted lovers of the steam locomotive – indeed, practically nothing apart from wheel centres and some axles was incorporated in the ugly thing that emerged from Doncaster in September 1945.

Practically all the features of the Thompson A2s were repeated, resulting, predictably, in the same weaknesses. The boiler of course was excellent, for it was the A4 type with a double Kylchap exhaust. The traditional apple green, which the Great Northern bequeathed to the London & North Eastern, had been replaced by the Great

Eastern livery which Thompson had admired when he was at Stratford – dark blue lined out in red, and his pre-Grouping allegiance was suggested by the letters NE, which were displayed on the tender sides. (On its first general repair after Thompson's departure, the engine was reclad in London & North Eastern green and lettered LNER.)

The cab was immediately unpopular; it was difficult to climb into and it swayed about at speed owing to inadequate staying. Two months after completion the engine was returned to Doncaster for modification. The opportunity was taken to deepen the cab sides to make them level at the bottom with those of the tender, and to restore the Great Northern flat 'S' curve at the rear end of the running plate, so that some grace of outline was granted this unlovely damsel. Smoke deflectors were fitted at the same time.

It had been Thompson's intention to rebuild all the A10 Pacifics in similar style and authority was obtained for this in the 1946 Locomotive Construction Programme; but by the time the work was due to start, Thompson had been succeeded by A.H. Peppercorn, and the eventual A1 class Pacifics were vastly different engines.

No. 500, the first of Thompson's standard A2s, was completed in May 1946, and, to mark this retirement as CME, it was named *Edward Thompson* at a ceremony at Marylebone station.

On the return of the ex-P2s to the Edinburgh-Aberdeen main line, it was soon found that they could manage no heavier loads than the A4 Pacifics; in other words, owing to their loss of adhesion in rebuilding, they could no longer tackle the work for which they had been designed. In fact, the A4s were so much preferred that they were hauling all the heaviest expresses, and the A2/2s were soon relegated to express goods, fish, and parcels trains.

Mileage between general repairs was poor for all the Thompson Pacifics, and in March 1957 all but one of both the converted P2s and the replacements for the V2s were laid up in Cowlairs and Darlington respectively. It is fair to say, however, that it was mainly as vehicles that these engines failed, because their steam circuit was excellent and they were very free runners. To the drivers, their tendency to roll at speed seemed positively dangerous.

The North Eastern section of the LNER got, for a time, the four A2/1s. They were received with little enthusiasm and were used mostly on slow passenger and fast goods workings. Two were sent to King's Cross in November 1944, where they were heartily disliked owing to their rough riding, their steam reversers, and the continual leakage from the expansion joints of the outside cylinder exhaust pipes. Having got rid of two of them to King's Cross, the North Eastern inflicted the other two on Edinburgh's Haymarket shed. Here they were equally unpopular and were never used on the principal express workings.

The rebuilt *Great Northern* went to King's Cross, where its arrival must have been regarded as something of an insult by that most 'Great Northern' of railway sheds. King's Cross tolerated it for nearly five years, before getting it moved to New England, where the disgruntled recipients ran it mostly on fast goods and parcels. In September 1951 Grantham got it and tried it for a time on its top link with regular drivers, but it was so unreliable that it was eventually used only as the spare engine.

Nine of Thompson's A2 (later A2/3) Pacifics went to the North Eastern area, five were allocated to the Southern area, and one to Scotland. Due to lack of maintenance during the war, many of Gresley's A4 Pacifics were badly run down, so five A2s in the Southern area were used for a time by King's Cross shed on the normal main line express duties. But as soon as the Peppercorn A1 class Pacifics became available, the A2/3s (as they had then become) were transferred rapidly to New England, where they were relegated to secondary passenger services and express goods.

The late Colonel K.R.M. Cameron had much experience of the riding of Pacifics during the latter days of LNER locomotive haulage. In a letter to the author he expressed his opinion of what he called "those Thompson monstrosities the A2/1, A2/2, and A2/3". He said that, with their long wheelbase, they "developed quite an alarming yawing motion which at times could be quite disconcerting, especially to those of us who did not ride on them very frequently".

When Thompson retired he was succeeded by A.H. Peppercorn, who had been Assistant Mechanical Engineer and who was, by upbringing, a Great Northern man and a disciple of Gresley. Another Great Northern man, J.F. Harrison, previously Mechanical Engineer at Gorton, became Assistant CME. It was not a partnership likely to be sympathetic to Thompson's innovations. Nor, indeed, was the Doncaster drawing office over-enthusiastic about the ideas of their late chief. Even before his retirement they had been thinking about the new engines and had determined to try to prevent them being built with the cylinders so far back. B.C. Symes, who was in the drawing office at the time, said, in a letter to the author, "The general layout of the first Peppercorn Pacific was in fact on my drawing board (except for the front end) before Pepp took over". Thompson, in his tours of the drawing office, was quite happy over the appearance of the back end!

When Peppercorn assumed office, he reinstated B. Spencer in the post that he had held under Gresley as Technical Assistant to the CME. Under Thompson the Chief Draughtsman, E. Windle, had been given many of the matters relating to locomotive design which had been Spencer's responsibility. The very satisfactory solution reached was that Harrison, Spencer, and Windle jointly discussed locomotive design policy and submitted their agreed views to Peppercorn. The CME then considered them, made his decisions, and instructed Windle to turn them into practical designs. Agreement was not a problem because all of them had been devoted disciples of Gresley and aimed at locomotives that would preserve the main Gresley features, whilst discarding those which post-war conditions had made difficult to maintain. Conjugated

valve gear, for instance, was so expensive in maintenance under these conditions by a largely inexperienced post-war staff, that it would be far better to have a separate valve gear for the middle cylinder.

Peppercorn had seen enough of the Thompson Pacifics to make a rapid decision that no more of the A2 (soon to be re-designated A2/3) Pacifics would be built than the 15 that had already been started, and that the remainder of these 6ft 2in engines, which had been authorised should be built to the new Harrison/Spencer/Windle design which he had already approved.

To the observer, the most obvious difference of the Peppercorn from the Thompson design was the restoration of the bogie to the conventional position with the outside cylinders between its wheels, and there was no need for the long and objectionable external exhaust ducts. Mistakenly, however, it was decided that the smokebox should be self-cleaning, and, because the smokebox was shorter than that of the A2/3, there was no room for the double blastpipe and Kylchap exhaust. The Peppercorn A2, therefore, had a single chimney. Nevertheless, those who had been horrified by Thompson's desecration of Gresley's *Great Northern* were delighted to see an engine which seemed to promise a return to the classic Doncaster tradition. It had been intended that there should be 35 of Peppercorn's A2 Pacifics, but the advent of British Railways had intervened and it was decreed that only 15 of them should be built.

The single chimney with self-cleaning smokebox strangles the steaming and on 6th May 1948 Doncaster Works were instructed to fit a double Kylchap exhaust pipe and chimney to the last A2 of the order, No. 60539, as well as to the new Peppercorn A1 class Pacifics, the first of which was approaching completion. As the length of the smokebox was not altered, there was no room for the self-cleaning apparatus. The steaming of No. 60539 far surpassed that of the single chimney engines, so in 1949 five more of the A2s were provided with the double Kylchap arrangement.

Thompson, having obtained authority for 16 Pacifics similar to his reconstruction of the *Great Northern* to be built under the 1945 programme, had secured permission for another 33 to be built in 1946, making a total of 40 engines. In 1948 Peppercorn was given authority for another ten in the 1949 programme, but all 49 successors to the *Great Northern* were to be of Peppercorn and not Thompson design. Peppercorn's A1 was identical to his A2 except for a longer coupled wheelbase on account of the larger coupled wheels, and a slightly longer smokebox for the same reason. To the casual eye the only difference in appearance from the double chimney engines of the A2 class lay in the small splashers over the coupled wheels of lesser diameter possessed by the latter.

When the first of his A1s were turned out from Doncaster in August 1948 Peppercorn had retired and the LNER had been swallowed up by British Railways, so that these LNER engines never bore their Company's initials on the tenders, but the first 30 were painted in LNER green to emphasise their paternity.

Peppercorn A2 class Pacific No.60539 *Bronzino* at Hadley Wood on 5th June 1950.
(A.C. Cawston Collection, Courtesy National Railway Museum, York).

Peppercorn A1 class Pacific No.60156 *Great Central* passing Greenwood, near Hadley Wood on 6th July 1954.
(A.C. Cawston Collection, Courtesy National Railway Museum, York).

Though excellent engines, there was something wrong with the riding of the Peppercorn Pacifics. They did not ride as smoothly as the A4s and were liable to give sudden lurches at the cab end. R.C. Bond told the author that an A1 on which he rode hunted badly, and J.F. Harrison, in a letter to the author, wrote: "The Peppercorn A2s, when first built, were liable to lurch in an alarming manner at speeds in excess of 90mph".

The trouble was eventually traced to the lightly loaded side control springs of the B1 bogie which were inadequate for the much heavier Pacifics. These bogies had been fitted to the Thompson Pacifics and had been continued on the Peppercorn engines under the impression that the alarming 'yawing' motion experienced with the former was due mainly to the flexing of the frames ahead of the outside cylinders, caused by the long gap between the bogie and the leading coupled wheels. This was indeed partially true, but it concealed a contributory factor in the weakness of the side control springs. Peppercorn's engines, through an oversight, had inherited an entirely unsuitable bogie. When the loading of the side control springs of the bogie was increased to a figure, which as far as Harrison remembers was 3.2 tons, riding of the Peppercorn Pacifics became comparable to that of any other express locomotives in the country.

In performance the double chimney engines were unsurpassed. J.F. Harrison wrote to the author: "I think it is right to claim that the Peppercorn A1s were the best express locomotives ever to run in this country. The word 'best' needs defining. It is not, as so often seems the case, a question *only* of the ability of a locomotive to pull this or that weight of train at a known speed, or of the amount of coal burnt per train mile in doing so, or even the maximum horsepower developed in this performance. All these factors are relevant, but at the time of Nationalisation differences recorded in respect of them by locomotives of the constituent companies were marginal, and from these figures alone one cannot draw any real conclusion as to which class of locomotive was the 'best'. The factor which is always omitted, largely because no one, official or otherwise, had any figures to prove the case one way or another, was the cost of shop and shed maintenance to both engine and boiler. However, the British Railways Board eventually decided that the collection of shop and shed maintenance costs should be assessed on a common basis. When the figures were finally produced the LNER A1s were found to be the cheapest of all the large locomotives."

In his Presidential address to the Institution of Locomotive Engineers in 1961, Harrison said (and quoted in a letter to the author): "In 1949 Doncaster produced, under the guidance of the late A.H. Peppercorn, five Pacific locomotives (part of an order for 50) having boilers pressed at 250psi, roller bearing axleboxes, and with separate valve gear drive to the middle cylinder, which we thought were the kind of locomotives Sir Nigel Gresley would have designed, had he been alive, to meet the changing conditions of maintenance. They were intended to give a better performance than any previous Pacific, to be cheaper to maintain, and to run an increased mileage per annum. These five locomotives, Nos 60153/54/55/56/57, have now been in service exactly twelve years during which they have run 4.8 million miles; one in fact having just completed 1,000,000 miles or 228 for every day since leaving Doncaster as a new engine. The average miles between "shopping" are 120,000, and these figures compare with figures given by Mr Bond in his paper to the Institution in 1953 showing the best LNER mileage in those days as 93,363 with an average mileage of 80,000. The total miles run by the 50 engines (including the five roller bearing engines) since new is 48 million, an average of 202 miles per calendar day; figures which I know cannot be approached by any steam locomotive class in this country."

Chapter 18
The end of Steam in Great Britain and France

Two great men were responsible for the design of the last steam locomotives in Great Britain and France: Robin (to his friends) Riddles and André Chapelon. I was fortunate in that both were my friends and I was privileged to write the biographies of both. Both were steam enthusiasts, but Riddles believed that steam must soon give way to electrification whilst Chapelon did not. Yet, paradoxically this is what happened in France but did not in Great Britain. In the latter country diesel power superseded steam, putting off main line electrification for many years (as Riddles had foreseen that it would). There was another difference: the steam engines that Riddles planned to run the railways until electrification came, were built; whereas the very advanced steam locomotives that Chapelon intended should carry steam into the indefinite future, were not.

The great 4-8-4 three-cylinder compound engine No. 242.A.1 was to have been the prototype of Chapelon's projected steam locomotive fleet. A single type of construction had been adopted to suit each of the principal locomotive types for passenger, mixed traffic and goods traffic respectively. There were four of the 'family' types: a 4-8-4 for heavy express trains, a streamlined 4-6-4 for high speed expresses over the principal main routes, a 2-8-4 for mixed traffic, and a 2-10-4 for heavy freight. All these would have the same boiler (though the with variations in length), a triple Kylchap exhaust, the same cylinder arrangement and mechanism, the same axles and axle boxes, and the same bissel trucks or bogies. The accessories would be identical – for example, feed-water heaters, air pumps, injectors, and cocks. The reason for the similarity of accessories was to make things easier for the enginemen, for on stepping onto the footplate of one of these engines there would be nothing to show which one of them the enginemen had mounted.

The new engines were to be three-cylinder compounds like No. A.1, but with HP cylinders 23.2in by 30in and LP 26in by 30in. New techniques had shown that a maximum cylinder horsepower was possible in a three-cylinder compound with a pressure of 320psi without too much loss of efficiency through insufficient volume in the LP cylinders. An additional advantage of using three cylinders was the ability to employ the same mechanism in all four types.

As a result of the decision to standardise parts and fittings, a number of construction practices, which had proved their worth in service and which would stand up to intensive work with the minimum of maintenance, could be incorporated in the designs of these four classes of large locomotives. The following are the principal ones which were selected:

(a) Roller bearing axle boxes for better lubrication and thus prevent the heating which had been the cause of so many locomotive failures.

(b) A monobloc chassis, instead of assemblies which could disrupt in service and have to be dismantled – a lengthy and expensive procedure.

(c) Axle boxes with controlled lateral displacement to provide easy riding over points and through sharp curves, so avoiding the tyre wear entailed in having thin flanges on coupled wheels.

(d) Automatic wedges to limit the longitudinal play of axle boxes in their guides, in order to avoid the shocks that shake an engine.

(e) Enlarged spokes to the wheels and thicker tyres, both of which ensure a better grip on the rim; and thick tyres also lengthen the distance run before they have to be renewed.

The recent increase of the permitted axle weight from 20 to 23 tons on the principal French main lines conferred the important advantage that the parts of a locomotive which have to stand up to higher power outputs, and consequent stresses, could be of greater dimensions than previously possible.

All the four engines would have a grate area of 65sq ft, a boiler pressure of 310psi, and 425°C of superheat. An interesting point arising from these designs, as Chapelon emphasised, was that having the same cylinders and mechanism and steam passages of suitable size, the tractive effort obtained at a given speed would be practically the same for all of them, irrespective as to whether an engine had large or small wheels. I found this a little difficult to grasp, but Chapelon explained that the greater haulage obtained with a small-wheeled engine is balanced by its greater resistance to movement; and therefore the main consideration in choosing the diameter of the coupled wheels for any particular engine is the number of revolutions per minute to which their mechanical strength makes it advisable to restrict them.

Taking the four types of locomotive in turn, Chapelon gave me the loads and speeds which each could have maintained up a 1 in 200 gradient. The 4-8-4 express locomotive with 7ft coupled wheels with 950 tons behind the tender could have managed a maximum speed of 87.5mph; the 4-6-4, which was to have had 7ft 3in coupled wheels was intended to surmount such a gradient with perhaps a load of 650 tons and, with its maximum speed of 125mph, climb it at a sustained 87.5mph; the 2-8-4 mixed traffic engine, which was to have 5ft 8in coupled wheels, could have pulled up to 1,200 tons at 56mph; and the 2-10-4 heavy freight locomotive, with its 5ft 5in wheels, could have managed a 2,000 ton train at 43mph up 1 in 200 and have run at 68.7mph on the level.

In 1946, alas, the whole project collapsed. The first engine, a 2-10-4, had been ordered and the first cylinders cast, when the Government directed the SNCF to reduce their demands for coal. The SNCF, in response, halted all plans for the construction of steam locomotives. Chapelon's protests were disregarded and plans for electrification were pushed ahead and speeded up. It is conceivable that this temporary shortage of coking coal, which the new engines did not want, was used as an excuse for electrification by advocates of this form of traction who wished to see steam disappear as soon as possible. For, if

Above: **The last Chapelon engine to run in France, SNCF 2-8-2
No.141.P.159 at St Brieve on August 1956 . . .**
(Philip J. Kelley).

Below: **. . . and, No.141.P.123 at St Malo in August 1956.**
(Philip J. Kelley).

Chapelon's plans had been completed it was well known that his genius would have given steam traction a fresh and lengthy lease of life and thrown doubts on the economic justification for main line electrification.

The decision was a great blow to André Chapelon, who, at the very moment when his great 4-8-4 express engine was making such a resounding entrance on the railway scene, saw the end of a dream, which had started all those long years ago, of a fleet of great steam locomotives, powerful and economical enough to challenge any other form of railway traction. That dream is illustrated by a photograph that hangs in the author's study, signed by André Chapelon, and showing him standing by his masterpiece – No. 242.A.1 and reproduced on page 2.

Riddles was faced with a problem which differed considerably from that the French railways. In spite of the disruption caused by the war, the SNCF was a going concern. In Great Britain, Nationalisation entailed the amalgamation of four great railway companies, each with entirely different locomotive practices and traditions. After the strains imposed by the years of war, and the necessary restrictions on the supply and maintenance of railway equipment, new locomotives were needed quickly and in large numbers. But before deciding on a programme for their construction, Riddles had to determine the best way of tackling the task. He could have elected to allow the CME's of the former companies to continue the same design policy in the Region approximating to the area of their old company, so that development and construction followed pre-Nationalisation practices, without any common standardisation.

Riddles said that there were some very vocal advocates for such a solution, but the result would have been that for each traffic purpose four different kinds of locomotive would have been produced; and there would have been differences in every component – differing in the materials of which they were made and with different specifications – even though designed for the same purpose. In addition, many of the locomotives would be unable to run freely outside the region of their origin, owing to weight and loading gauge limitations. If this solution was excluded, there were three possible choices: to select the designs of one of the four companies as the standard for British Railways; to nominate for each traffic category the best of an existing type for all future construction; or to develop a completely new range of standard designs. The first of these options was ruled out because the products of each of the former companies had reached a high standard of development and no one company was indisputably pre-eminent. The other two needed careful consideration, and Riddles set up a policy committee on 8th January 1948 for that purpose. They were to make recommendations as to the possibility of selecting in each traffic category the best regional type for all future construction in that category.

In conjuction with this investigation, Riddles arranged to have trials of different locomotives from the four former companies in three traffic categories on trains and under conditions as nearly identical as possible, running on various lines of the different Regions. He stressed that all

reports should be prepared in the same way and supported by dynamometer records, and that all the results should be made available, not only to the Regions, but also to the general public – for there was considerable partisan feeling, as between the former companies and their locomotives, by the large body of railway enthusiasts.

The interchange trials which followed took place between April and September 1948, and the three categories of locomotive that took part were express passenger, mixed traffic, and heavy freight. This book is only concerned with express passenger engines, and those which ran during these trials were the Stanier 'Duchess' class Pacific and the rebuilt 'Royal Scot' class 4-6-0, both from the former London Midland & Scottish Railway; the Gresley A4 class Pacific from the London & North Eastern Railway; the Collett 'King' class 4-6-0 from the Great Western Railway; and the Bulleid 'Merchant Navy' class Pacific from the Southern Railway. (The Great Western 'King' could only run on the Great Western and London & North Eastern routes because the width over its outside cylinders put it outside the loading gauge limits of the other two companies.)

Riddles' insistence on a wide publicity was well justified, because the trials showed that no one regional type was so superior to the others as to be an obvious selection for standard production. There were indeed marginal differences but many of these were caused either by driving methods or by the weather. In general, all the enginees did the work competently for which they had been designed.

In their studies, the Locomotive Standards Committee found that the margin between practices in design was as close as that displayed in the interchange trials, and they were therefore unable to recommend the adoption of any one type. However, some classes were clearly excluded on account of either loading gauge or weight restrictions. Thus, as we have noted, Great Western engines could not run over the erstwhile LMS and Southern lines, and LNER engines generally carried heavier axle loads than locomotives of other regions in the same traffic category. Another factor arose from the innate conservatism (with a small 'c'!) of enginemen regarding 'foreign' engines. This had been manifest after the 'Grouping' of the old companies in 1923. Great Northern Railway 4-4-0s, for instance, though popular enough on their parent line, were heartily disliked when moved to North Eastern and North British engine sheds, and after Nationaliation I was informed by an indignant Southern driver, on the footplate of a Great Western pannier tank at Waterloo, that it was a very poor engine compared to his LSWR M7 class 0-4-4 tank.

However, after the advent of a new CME on a railway his engines had been normally acceptable, even though quite different from those the footplatemen had been used to. Riddles, through his own experience as a young man on the London & North Western Railway, was well aware of this attitude, and he came to the conclusion that he would have to produce an entirely new series engines with a distinctive 'family' likeness. Furthermore post-war circumstances demanded engines which, though incorporating all that was best in modern practice, should be simple to drive, easy to maintain, and able to run with indifferent fuel.

Standard fittings would be used for all engines, and, in accordance with Riddles' maxim of 'get-at-ability', only two cylinders would be used where these would suffice for the job, and these and their valve gear would be outside. Wide fireboxes would be incorporated when practicable in order to obtain good steaming with poor coal, so as to raise the maximum steam production and lower the rate of combustion.

The immediate locomotive need was for a passenger engine with 30,000 to 35,000lb tractive effort. The top passenger range was covered adequately by Pacifics of three of the old companies and by the 4-6-0 'Kings' of the GWR. To build these standard locomotives, and the others, new sets of drawings had to be made and a good many new tools were necessary. Policy committees were set up to establish the new components.

One of Riddles' difficulties was that, unlike the CMEs of the old companies, he had no chief draughtsman. He had, indeed, not one drawing office but four. Chief draughtsmen were men of long and varied experience, who translated their CME's instructions into fact and even, on occasions, told CMEs why their ideas were impracticable. Riddles got over this difficulty in a most ingenious way by establishing a sort of corporate chief draughtsman. He formed the chief draughtsmen of Derby, Doncaster, Swindon, and Brighton into a body under the chairmanship of E.S. Cox as Executive Officer Design.

For express passenger work there were to be two Pacifics. Both were classified as mixed traffic, for, with coupled wheels of 6ft 2in diameter, it was intended that they should undertake such a range of duties as had been entrusted to Gresley's 'Green Arrow' class 2-6-2s. In fact, the larger of the two was regarded as able to undertake the work, not only of the 'Green Arrows', but also of the 'Castle' class 4-6-0s of the Great Western, the LMS rebuilt 'Royal Scots', and the 'West Country' Pacifics of the Southern. The smaller of the new Pacifics was intended for routes on which a powerful passenger locomotive was required but where axle load restrictions would prohibit the use of the larger engine. The two Pacifics were designated Class 7 and Class 6 respectively; their chassis were the same but the Class 6 had smaller cylinders and boiler. The larger boiler was 6ft 5$\frac{1}{2}$in in diameter, with 250psi pressure and 42sq ft grate area; whereas the smaller had a diameter of 6ft 1in, a pressure of 225psi and 36sq ft of grate area.

Draughting had been the subject of tests at Rugby and Swindon, and the results of these tests had been extremely interesting. It had been confirmed, said Riddles, that double and other special blast pipe arrangements could give improved results at maximum outputs, but at lower outputs their superiority was not so marked. Through the whole range of output the single blast pipe appeared the more satisfactory. Because, therefore, the majority of locomotive work demands less than the maximum output, the single blast pipe and chimney were retained on the two Pacifics and most of the other new locomotives.

The first of the Class 7 Pacifics, No. 70000, was turned out from Crewe on 2nd January 1951, and on 14th January the engine ran to Carlisle on test with the dynamometer car and empty carriages. Cox was on the footplate for the northbound run. For the return to Crewe on the following day Riddles and R.C. Bond (Chief Officer for Locomotive Construction and Maintenance) were on the engine; Riddles driving it from Carlisle to Penrith and Bond from Penrith to Crewe. (How those two steam locomotive enthusiasts must have enjoyed themselves!) The round trip was extremely successful.

The engine was as yet unnamed, but on 30th January 1951 it was named *Britannia* at Marylebone by the Right Honourable Alfred Barnes, Minister for Transport. The name *Britannia* had been selected by Riddles to commemorate his old company, the London & North Western Railway, the badge of which had been the figure of Britannia with her trident and shield; and he had a small table made for the Minister as a memento of the occasion on which was an enamelled representation of the badge and the engine. On my desk in front of me, as I write, is a beautiful cast metal model, made at Crewe in 1952, of No. 70000 *Britannia,* which was presented to me by Robin Riddles on the occasion of the publication of my book, *The Last Steam Locomotive Engineer: R.A. Riddles CBE.*

There were 55 'Britannias', of which 25 were completed in 1951, 20 more in 1952, and the final 10 in 1954. It had been intended to fit roller bearings on all the coupled wheels, but Riddles was not convinced as to the superiority of roller bearings over the much cheaper LMS plain bearings. He therefore had five engines equipped with roller bearings on the driving axle only, and another ten with plain bearings throughout. It does not appear that the roller bearings showed any advantage over the plain type.

Initial reception of the 'Britannias' was, as expected, mixed, owing to the customary suspicion of the footplatemen to the introduction of any departure from the designs and layout to which they were accustomed. But that, given a chance, the new engines were outstandingly good, was shown by the results obtained in the area of the old Great Eastern Railway. Here their arrival enabled the whole express timetable to be reconstructed and show the fastest runs ever performed over Great Eastern tracks, and the third fastest average speeds over any section of British Railways. The drivers loved them and seemed to delight in making the most phenomenal runs. At the other end of the scale, reception by the Great Western was distinctly chilly, and results, accordingly, were somewhat patchy. They were not Swindon engines and therefore little could be expected of them! But when a Riddles 9F class heavy goods engine, the last steam locomotive to be built for British Railways, and built at Swindon at that, was turned out in Great Western green and polished brass with a copper capped chimney (due to Reggie Hanks), it was remarkable how

Riddles 7MT class Pacific No.70035 *Rudyard Kipling* entering Norwich with the 'down' "Broadsman" on 19th July 1954.
(Philip J. Kelley).

Riddles 7MT class Pacific No.70033 *Charles Dickens* climbing Camden Bank on 18th August 1962 and passing the diesel hauled train of the future.
(T.E. Williams Collection, Courtesy National Railway Museum, York).

Great Western footplatemen could run it into Paddington on time at the head of the normally 'Castle'-hauled heavy South Wales expresses!

Not many new express locomotives have gone into service with so little trouble on the most exacting services as the 'Britannias'. Gresley's first Pacifics needed considerable modification before they were really good, Stanier's first Pacifics suffered initially from steaming and riding troubles before they become the excellent machines they soon were, and Bulleid's Pacifics had toubles that were never overcome until they were rebuilt. The only major defect experienced with the 'Britannias' lay in their driving wheels moving on the axles and this was easily cured by plugging the ends of the axles.

The names given to the engines constituted a delightfully mixed bag – many of them honouring famous locomotives of the past. It is worth mentioning the following as examples:

Coeur-de-Lion, Black Prince, Alfred the Great, Iron Duke, Morning Star, Charles Dickens, Sir John Moore, William Shakespeare, Solway Firth, John Milton, Boadicea, Hereward the Wake and *Hotspur.* In comparison one only has to think of the truly appalling names that are inflicted on some modern electric and diesel locomotives. They remind me of an occasion when, during the war, I was approaching by rail, a ghastly little seaport on the Persian Gulf called Bandar Shahpur. On the outskirts of the town some of the unfortunate British soldiers who were stationed there had hung a rusty old chamber pot on the railway fence, with a notice underneath which read 'Bandar Shahpur Chamber of Commerce'.

On 25th May 1951 that admirable journal *Engineering* wrote: "The most rationally minded railway officer, straight from reading the report on electrification, may be forgiven if, as he stands beside *John Milton* on the test bed, he rejoices that the country's economy at the present time will not allow heavy capital expenditure on the electrification of railways". Unfortunately, whether it could be afforded or not, a later administration decided that heavy and immediate capital expenditure on replacing steam by diesel haulage was the key to railway prosperity.

Riddles told me that his object in building the Class 6 Pacifics, or 'Clans', was to provide engines able to handle heavy passenger trains over routes in Scotland for which the axle loads of the 'Britannias' would be too heavy. But whereas they were very satisfactory engines, they lacked sufficient adhesion to meet his objective. he said that he had made a mistake in not going for a 4-8-0, which he believed would have solved the Scottish traffic problems – problems with which he had become well acquainted during his time as Mechanical and Electrical Engineer in Scotland.

In October 1952 there was a bad smash at Harrow, in which LMS Pacific No. 46202 *Princess Anne* was completely wrecked. This engine had only recently been rebuilt from Stanier's turbine Pacific and its destruction left a gap in the number of Class 8 Pacifics in the London Midland Region. Riddles took the opportunity to get authority to build a new Class 8 Pacific with which

running experience might be gained for any future Class 8 express engines; and so came No. 71000 *Duke of Gloucester.* As it was not practicable to provide two cylinders large enough for the power required, Riddles chose three, rather than four on account of the more even turning moment. A double chimney was fitted to improve the maximum output. Riddles decided on Caprotti valves, which he had always liked and believed that, if the theory of smooth and straight passages for steam was right, then one could hardly improve on a poppet valve, with full exhaust openings at all positions of the reversing gear. Having got his proposals approved by the Executive, Riddles instructed the Derby Drawing Office to develop the engine in conjunction with the Caprotti manufacturers. When completed the engine ran freely, but it was apparent that the front end draughting arrangements needed considerable improvement. Riddles was satisfied, however, that he had a Class 8 Pacific that was potentially better than any other in the country, and had he remained in his appointment and had steam been given the future that it should have had, he was certain that this trouble would have been cured. Unfortunately it was not to be and the necessary development never took place.

Some little time after he had departed from British Railways, Riddles arrived at Euston to ride north on the footplate of this last of his engines, which had been completed after his retirement. It was, he said, a nostalgic day, his last association with steam and the railway: a trip to Crewe with a stop at Rugby. There was an inspector he knew, but the driver and fireman were strangers to him. The driver was unaccustomed to the engine and, though they ran fairly well, they dropped time steadily and arrived at Rugby six minutes late. Whilst in the station, the inspector turned to Riddles and said, "Would you like the corner, Sir?" The driver, not knowing Riddles, looked a little concerned, but the inspector assured him that he had no need to worry.

Riddles took over the regulator for his last run to Crewe. He later said to me, "and so we started with me at the throttle. I loved the feel of the engine and the power that I was controlling; and as we picked up speed the engine sang to me". Under his expert handling the lost minutes were gradually regained; and the *Duke of Gloucester* was racing along the track over which he had ridden on the footplate of so many engines, with clear signals, over the well-known gradients, and observing the familiar speed restrictions . . . All too soon he was slowing his great engine round the curve at Crewe station; and his mind went back to the days so many years ago when, as a youth, he had watched train after train come into view round this same curve, dead on time, after leaving Euston so many hours before; and he wondered whether any steam man could wish for a finer finish. The engine rolled to a stop at just the right place and right on time; for he had picked up all the six minutes that had been lost, and the hands of Crewe station clock signalled mute approval, as they had done for generations of 'Precuresors', 'Experiments', 'Geogres', 'Princes',

'Claughtons', 'Royal Scots', 'Princesses', 'Duchesses' and 'Britannias', during the years that a Crewe apprentice had risen to the greatest pinnacle of steam engineering in British railway history. And so Robin Riddles passes from the railway service.

It was a great joy to him that the *Duke of Gloucester* was to be preserved, and not long before he died, at the age of 91, he was able to visit and see the engine when restoration was well on the way to completion. He told me what a wonderful job the restoration team was doing.

No. 72007 *Clan Mackintosh*, one of the BR Standard Class 6 Pacifics, of which only ten were built. Photographed passing Lancaster Old Goods Yard, 23rd May 1964 with an RCTS special. *(Gavin Morrison)*

Chapter
Epilogue

It will have become apparent to readers of this book that, even amongst the most eminent locomotive engineers, there were many different, and frequently contradictory, opinions about various aspects of locomotive design. They include, for instance: the advantages and disadvantages of simple expansion and compounding; the relative merits of Belpaire, round top, and trapezoidal fireboxes; different types of exhaust, single and double chimneys, etc.; whether grates should be wide or narrow; whether streamlining is worth the cost and loss of 'get-at-ability'; roller or plain bearings for coupled wheels; divided drive as compared with driving on a single axle; the importance or otherwise of short live steam pipes connecting the superheater header to the cylinders; the importance of a steam dome; and whether thermic syphons were worthwhile. There are, of course, many others. Whereas, about many of these, engineers have decided views, others depend to a certain extend on such factors as the mechanical knowledge included in driver training on the railway concerned, the quality of available fuel, the skill of mechanics in maintenance, contemporary conditions, and previous custom.

But all these considerations are, alas, behind us; for we seem to have come to the end of the steam age, with little likelihood of its return, except, perhaps, in areas where lack of appropriate equipment and of mechanical skill militates against the introduction of the more complex motive power.

Looking back over the years of steam locomotive development, it is remarkable, as André Chapelon once said to me, that there has been no successful departure from the basic principles embodied in George Stephenson's *Rocket* of 1829. For instance, water tube boilers, turbine drive, and other unorthodox diversions have all failed. Future advance, therefore, would probably have followed the well-tried principles; but we shall never know.

We are left with some interesting questions. Would Chapelon's new range of steam locomotive prove, as he had hoped, that steam can do all that electricity can, and more cheaply? With the advice of all the Chief Draughtsmen of the former companies, under the chairmanship of E.S. Cox, at his disposal, the 'Britannias' provided Riddles' response to the need for a simple rugged and easy to maintain locomotive to run all but the heaviest express trains for the next twenty years. They proved excellent engines, but could Chapelon have met British needs any better? Finally, in a letter to the author, J.F. Harrison wrote that, taking into account that they were found to be the cheapest of all the large express locomotives in shop and shed maintenance costs, "I think it is right to claim that the Peppercorn A1s were the best express passenger locomotives ever to run in this country". Fortunately an A2 (virtually identical with an A1 except for the wheel diameter) has been preserved: this is No.60532 *Blue Peter*. Is this then the finest of all our existing express locomotives and representative of the pinnacle of British express steam?

We may not be able to answer these questions, but all that has been written in this Epilogue justifies Riddles' statement that designing a steam locomotive is an art and not a science.

The "best" express passenger steam locomotive in Great Britain today? Peppercorn A2 class Pacific *Blue Peter* as restored in LNER apple green livery with the number 532, on a visit to Didcot Railway Centre in 1985.
(Peter Nicholson)

Index

COMPOUND EXPRESS ENGIN

M. DE GLEHN, A

"THE ENGINEER"